~~~~~

Also by John Krich

BUMP CITY

CHICAGO IS

A TOTALLY FREE MAN

MUSIC IN EVERY ROOM

ONE BIG BED

EL BEISBOL

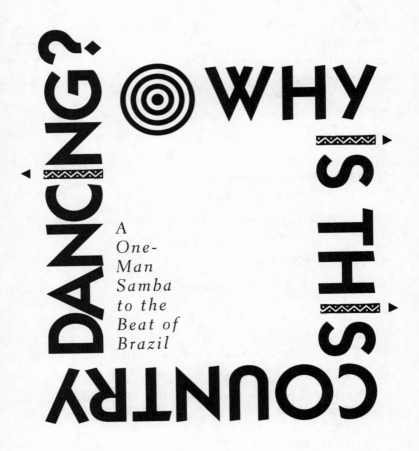

WHY IS THIS COUNTRY DANCING?

A One-Man Samba to the Beat of Brazil

John Krich

Simon & Schuster
New York London Toronto Sydney Tokyo Singapore

SIMON & SCHUSTER
SIMON & SCHUSTER BUILDING
ROCKEFELLER CENTER
1230 AVENUE OF THE AMERICAS
NEW YORK, NEW YORK 10020

DESIGNED BY SONGHEE KIM

MANUFACTURED IN THE UNITED STATES OF AMERICA

10   9   8   7   6   5   4   3   2   1

LIBRARY OF CONGRESS CATALOGING-IN-PUBLICATION DATA

KRICH, JOHN, DATE.
    WHY IS THIS COUNTRY DANCING?: A ONE-MAN SAMBA TO THE BEAT OF
    BRAZIL / JOHN KRICH.
      P.   CM.
    INCLUDES INDEX.
      1. BRAZIL—DESCRIPTION AND TRAVEL—1981–   2. POPULAR MUSIC—
    BRAZIL—HISTORY AND CRITICISM. 3. BRAZIL—SOCIAL LIFE AND CUSTOMS.
    4. BRAZIL—POPULAR CULTURE.   I. TITLE.
    F2517.K75   1993
    918.104'63—DC20   92-34927
                                                                              CIP

ISBN 0-671-76814-X

PORTIONS OF THIS BOOK APPEARED PREVIOUSLY IN *THE NEW YORK TIMES
SOPHISTICATED TRAVELER, EUROPEAN TRAVEL & LIFE, THE SAN FRANCISCO
EXAMINER, THE AMERICAN VOICE, ZYZZYVA,* AND *EAST BAY EXPRESS.*

▲▲▲
ACKNOWLEDGMENTS

A full obligato *obrigado* to all the musicians kind enough to concertize for me, especially those who offered more than an interview: Alceu, Sinval, Carlinhos, Luis Fidelis, Djavan. And to the supporting players in my Brazilian band, including backup singer Roselene Pinto Machado, the Machado family, Maria Luisa and Suely Mendonça, Eliane Arnold, Mike Kepp, Wolfgang Krust, Maria Ines Salgado, Irene Collaço, Don Klein, Micha Shnookie Peled, Liza Redding, Eduardo Cabrera, João Pombo Lopes, Steve Chapple, Itamara Koorax, Paulinho Pedro Azul, Dmitiri Ganzalevitch, Majela Vaz, Reuben de Oliveira, Nilson Barbosa, Lucio Alves, Luis Fernando Sarmento, Sergio Cabral, Bill and Maruska Hinchberger, Davia Nelson, Janet Carlson, Grace Cohen, Gladys, Silva, Sandra and those generous road managers, Yaddo and the National Endowment for the Arts.

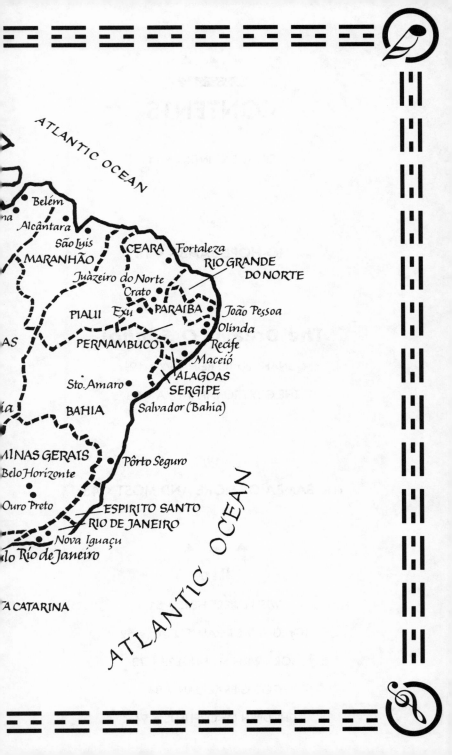

CONTENTS

THE SAMBA OF EXTERNAL DEBT ◆ 107

▲ ▲ ▲

South

HIGH-CRIME SAMBA ◆ 145

▲ ▲ ▲

Bahia

RISE AND FALL SAMBA ◆ 201

▲ ▲ ▲

North

▲ ▲ ▲

The World (*O Mundo*)

▲▲▲

EIGHT-BAR INTRO

If any country has a siren song, it's Brazil. Whatever associations you may have with our largest hemispheric neighbor, I am willing to bet they will have reached you through music or can be done to music. The book that follows takes a nation at its word—or in this case, its melody—and uses its wealth of musical emanations as the entree to a complex society. But that makes my approach sound too clinical. And Brazilian music is the opposite of clinical. The work you are about to read is the fruition of a passion for Brazilian pop that began when I was old enough to distinguish the Beatles from *bossa nova*. In this long-distance enthusiasm, I know that I am hardly alone. Today, Brazilian recordings are available in remarkable profusion, Brazilian influence is rife in much of the evolving "world beat," and, thanks to fiendishly patriotic expatriates who figure that just being from Brazil qualifies them to take up a musical trade, Brazilian rhythms infuse the music scene in such disparate locales as Florence, Tokyo, and New Orleans. On the night the Berlin Wall fell, the first image on the worldwide television coverage was a group of Germans, most likely from a workshop in advanced *samba*, celebrating with well-synchronized Brazilian percussion.

Given that Brazil is continental in size and universal in sound, a book in its honor must be a trifle intimidating. Hence, an eight-bar intro to set the pattern for my literary notion, an explanatory note before we strike up the band. For starters, I am not a musicologist. You will have to consult more technical texts to determine the difference in beats per measure between the *frevo* found in the Northeastern city of Recife and the *baião* found in the backcountry some hundred miles away—though some of the motivation for my journey was the dearth of materials in English which recognize so varied an art form. To most Americans, Brazilian music is *samba*. But that is the regional expression solely of

Rio de Janeiro. Brazil's many rhythms, practically one to a town, evolve with a dynamism that far outstrips the plodding efforts of researchers. So I have dwelled only lightly on the complex chronology of Brazil's musical development.

One poetic homage, penned in 1926 and renowned throughout the country, calls the sources of Brazilian music "Barbaric Indian dance, African nostalgia/ And the cries of the Portuguese song./ Lustful grief, kiss of three longings/ Amorous flower of three sad races." Large numbers of Native Americans still live and dance under the protection of Brazil's wilderness areas. The Portuguese who claimed title to this massive space, thanks to Cabral's landing in 1500 and a subsequent papal bull, were far less formal than their Spanish compatriots and far more prone to attacks of a seafaring people's *saudade*, a form of homesickness raised to a way of life. African slaves were brought here in greater number and came to dominate the cultural life as they have done in no other place, making all three races far less than sad. These must be starting points of any exploration of Brazil's music. What interests me is not how this "amorous flower" came to bloom but how it functions to beautify, distract, console, or entrance a modern melting-pot nation of 150 million—and what the scent of that flower offers to all who get near it.

A few handy tips then, on how to travel through a book that travels mostly by sound. My tripping to, and over, the beat of Brazil actually transpired over three Brazilian "summers," which in the Southern Hemisphere run from December through February. I have condensed and rearranged events for dramatic effect or when absolutely warranted. For example, I begin the book with my first claustrophobic experience of Carnival in Salvador, Bahia, then return later to the Carnival in another Northeastern city, Recife. As Carnival happens but once a year, on the weekend before Lent, which usually falls in late February, I needed this device to take readers to both of these events. The third of Brazil's major Carnivals, in Rio, has been so exhaustively covered by others that I decided to treat it largely via the prism of Brazil's bizarre television coverage. Aside from spending Christmas with a Brazilian family in a chapter that follows a New Year's in Rio, my account is otherwise chronological.

As there can be no music without people, and the vast majority of Brazilians live "like crabs" drawn to the sea, my journey generally follows the world's longest coastline. Except for forays into the mountain province of Minas Gerais and the backcountry known as the *sertão*, I move up the Atlantic from Rio and São Paulo in the industrialized South to São Luis and Belém in the blighted Northeast. For other geographic orientation, a map has been provided—on which to project a rough approximation of the range of Brazil's musical forms.

Brazilian music, freewheeling and eclectic, grabbing influences and inspiration as it rolls along, inspires one to transcend categories. Having long sought to expand the constricted "then-I-went-here'" form of common travelogue, I have indulged my doggerel muse with a number of riffs I call *sambas*. Placed as intermezzos or bridges between regional sections, they can be read as playful tributes to various Brazilian states of mind—and to the spirit of Brazilian songwriters. Another feature never attempted in a travel book is the discography that appears at the back of each chapter. Would I could also provide a tape, CD, or live singalong! I don't want the music to drown out my prose entirely, but any experience of this book would be greatly enhanced through getting your ears around some of the sounds described. The selections I have made are entirely subjective, with no payola involved. Wherever possible, I have tried to limit my recommendations to recordings currently distributed in the United States.

Finally, I hope my readers will suffer some very approximate translations of song lyrics as well as the large number of foreign words in the text. The Portuguese language, and especially the singsong lilt of Brazilian Portuguese—like American English, more adaptive and fluid than its mother tongue—fairly begs to burst into song. Without this mellifluous, slushing flow, this

Spanish spoken with marbles in one's mouth, Brazilian music as we know it could not exist. So I have tried to strike a balance between the comprehension of foreign readers and retaining the original meter that inspires Brazilians. A few handy phonetic hints: in Brazilian Portuguese, the written "r" is pronounced like an "h" and the "o" is more like our "u," making Rio into "Hee-oo"; the frequent "ão" ending is sounded with a slight "n," while "l" at the end of a word like "carnaval" is more like an "ow"; the "ç" is "s"; a "t" comes out more like "ch," as in the name of the singer Martinho da Vila, pronounced "Mar-cheen-you"; while "de," the common word for "of" or "by," is softened into "jee."

No book can be "about" music any more than it can be about the wind. And no single volume can encapsulate the mysteries and folk traditions of Brazil. I make no claims to expertise beyond being an expert on my experience of the country. My view is necessarily idiosyncratic, culture based, from the outside. The perceptions, judgments, drumbeats, are my own. The only claim to certainty I make is that, at every turn, I found confirmation of my starting hunch. No place on earth asserts the primacy of music like Brazil.

One image endures from my travels. On a bleak causeway outside Recife, surrounded by abandoned lots, I waited at a bus stop beside two too small children. A brother and sister, perhaps eight and ten, brown-skinned and blond-curled, dressed in hand-me-downs, come to the big city for Carnival. And each held in one hand a set of branches torn off some bush as scrawny as they were. It took me a while to realize that the dry pods hanging from the thin limbs weren't good for eating or for offering to some god but for making a scratching sound when they shook. In Brazil, the instruments literally grow on trees. And even if these children had nothing, they had a rhythm in their heads. I hope you can hear it on every page of this book.

NO-HOPE SAMBA

For a number of years, you have been going to Brazil in your car. Seat belt fastened for takeoff, you need only to fire up a stereo cassette. At once, the rolling ambience turns tropical. America defrosts. And it no longer matters that it's rush hour, with nowhere to park on the planet. Windows rolled up to shut out the freeway's Amazonian flow of rubber, you are singing in the shower of a rain forest cascade. A brace of yellow-billed toucans peeks at you in the rearview mirror. Macaws and monkeys twitter from the trunk. Swapping ambulance screeches for the call of the mild, you linger over the air-cushioned vowels of a language you can't speak but hum with fluency. You don't need to know the lyrics, don't want to know, so long as they transport you somewhere more lyrical than where you are going.

You are tired of the fog and the apartness, tired of staring at black-and-white documentaries on lushness. So one evening you head for the airport without consulting schedules or changing underwear. Using a wish list for a charge card, you board the next flight for Rio. Nobody knows you are going away: a secret between you and a demicontinent. It's only for a weekend, after all. Maybe for the rest of your life. Complimentary eyeshades and a guitar to cradle ease the shock and help you snooze until there is nothing but green below. The sun comes up over an earth so chlorophyll cloaked that even before you've sipped your first passion-fruit cocktail, you feel you've gone somewhere. The singing captain comes on the intercom, whispering a soft samba in which he apologizes for having to land. Hips and haunches are the only Brazilian carriers that can fly without fuel. And the plane is guided down by jaguar claws painted on a runway laid with glitter.

When you show your passport, the customs man rears back with hyena laughter and tears visas into confetti, stamps your forehead with lipstick and chicken blood. And you wish you had remembered to bring luggage because the porters are all dancing girls who shimmy so quickly to the curb that you cannot even see their sequined tap shoes. The taxi driver wears a rubber clown nose, lives his life off the meter, and knows where you are going without having to ask. Your hotel suite is stocked with pineapples and party favors; instead of a Bible beside the bed there's a feathered talisman, a carafe of tap water that is already lime flavored. The closet is hung with all the poses you'll ever need to get through life, harlequin or mandarin or inner-space astronaut. You don't need a closet. For the first time, you go to the party undisguised.

You float down the mosaic waves laid in the Copacabana Tropicana promenade, a sidewalk that's one seductive how-to intertwining of black and white, a taboo for all to step over. Every time you land on the buckled sidewalks, you feel moist earth springing back. The state buildings are mere hollow tusk carvings and champagne waterfalls course down edificio facades. You work on your impersonation of undulation all the way to the beach, giddy with the recognition that simple granular sand ought not to get this notorious. And this kind does not stick between your toes and the sun does not smart against your nonpigmented neck and you bronze evenly on the blanket of coconut husks with your name on it, a name lengthened with eight middle names, a dozen intimate diminutives. And the unclothed plainclothesmen don't have to warn you about carrying a camera and turds of schoolchildren do not drift on the surf and instead of perilous breakwaters, loudspeakers dot the shoreline. The whole harbor is wired for sound. Eternally hoarse from refraining to shout, sultry divas whisper in time with the tides.

Sugar Loaf is melting—two lumps, please—and the whole of Guanabara Bay is one foamy espresso, and now you are bathing in the extracted juice of the forest. When you emerge, three

G-stringed muses towel you off and grab you by the elastic on your flowered boxer trunks to entice you into their lair. A forty-story five-star hut, all bedding and parakeets. One of these she-cats is the Yoruba goddess Yêmenjá and another is the goddess Iracema and the third is a domestic with a remarkable resemblance to the Virgin Mary after reconstructive surgery. They are dressed solely in orchids harvested from the sea and they all have elongated navels that could give birth by themselves and toenails painted the color of the great tortoise. Their resplendence is the rub-off kind. These women love you for just what you want them to love you for, your wit not your expense account, your narrow wrists and your compassion, telling you that they know you are a different variety of stranger, which is no stranger at all. They're amazed at how quickly you get expert at the sniffed inhaling of essential perfumes known as the Carioca kiss.

Not only do they hand you a drum but the inexhaustible spontaneity to play it, nimble fingers to celebrate a religion on taut clitoral skins. Evening twinkles beyond the balcony and the muses whisk you away to the fancy undress ball which is always in progress. You know all the words to all the traditional songs. Without a twitch of study you graduate summa cum laude from the samba school. Everyone recognizes you as a long lost dancing partner, gang member, bastard son. You join in the daisychain that wreathes the city until dawn and never miss a step and never curse a soul and never wish you were anywhere else. No aching feet and no barefoot beggars, just the extras from Black Orpheus grown up into expressionist painters, diplomats, and medicine men. A hundred-year-old nursemaid puffing on a cigar cures you of the cancer you did not even know you had.

You sleep only in order to dance again, for you have coupled permanently with the waves. Now you understand how it feels for music to be as effortless as breathing. The notes, after all, are only gossip, and that's never hard, a story you must pass on about someone you'll never meet. And you aren't even disappointed when you at last grasp the words in their glorious banality. The world is divided into people for whom everything sounds better in a foreign language and the people for whom everything becomes terrifying in a foreign language. For the first time, you know why you are the former.

You are borne to your flight home on a palanquin in an uproarious processional of beaded priestesses. On the tarmac, you mutter their magic incantations but no vow about having to come back someday. You are not really leaving. Besides, there's only one journey that's one-way and you don't mind postponing that booking. Returning to find that nobody knows you had gone, you feel no need to convince them with slide shows or souvenirs or to convince yourself with seashells on the mantel. After all, the best travel agent is an eye that is closed. And you find that your longings to be elsewhere are neither less poignant nor more relieved and the fog in which you have always lived is neither thicker nor dissipated.

▲ ▲ ▲

The Dream (*O Sonho*)

Brazil is not a serious country.
—Charles de Gaulle

‹‹‹‹‹‹‹‹‹‹

UNAFRAID TO BE HAPPY

Now there is no escaping the music. It's too late for finking out on the bacchanal. Looking up, every stacked balcony, colonial and peeling or concrete and flimsy, has been turned into a vertical danceathon. The heat of bodies has replaced the day's tropical furnace and the cobblestoned boulevards have turned to trampolines for an aerobic populace. Bouncing on the balls of my sneakered feet, I periscope above the bobbing heads crowned in Indian feathers and Portuguese admirals' caps, the arms upraised in an exultant vanquishing of inhibition, the hands clapping like metronomes for copulation. *Pulando* is the term locals use for what everyone's doing, but it means far more than jumping up and down—it implies a leap to heaven, or, at least, the irrational. Grab hold of that slinky waist up ahead if you can, grip a passing set of female haunches if you dare. Sweat is the natural lubricant for our grinding parts. The sole way to make progress through this orange-and-yellow tinsel-draped orgy is to join the boa-length *conga* line snaking and shoving its way to nowhere. In this human gridlock, there are no handy exits from a slow surging pack whose only destination is dawn. Nothing can move and everybody is moving. On all sides, I'm pinned down by pleasure, hopelessly enmeshed in unleashed mirth.

"There is a law of physics which says that two bodies cannot occupy the same space," goes one of the oft-repeated homilies by which this multitude defines its particular brand of frenzy, "but that law does not operate in Brazil." Only *carne vale!* Just flesh counts, though the derivation of "carnival" is translated to mean a farewell to meat, which Catholics can't eat once the wild weekend gives way to next Wednesday's Lent. "Alegria!"—roughly, "Oh rapture!"—shout the newspaper headlines each February, by fortunate coincidence the height of the Southern Hemisphere's summer holidays. "Rei Momo"—a rotating and rotund Dionysian figure appointed to reign over the madness—"Commands His Subjects to Joy!" This good news is hardly news at all, merely the summons to dust off old costumes. "Folia Animates the Streets!"—and just because it's folly, that doesn't mean you shouldn't join in! "Brincar!" goes the command, that most Brazilian of verbs which takes "play" into multiple innuendos, all of them saucy! The press and TV make it sound like this outburst isn't planned or scheduled, orchestrated down to its last toot. With annual mock astonishment, they trumpet the return of the party.

What is the world's biggest party-pooper doing in the midst of the world's rowdiest, lengthiest, bring-your-own-bottle affair? Crashing the gates of Brazilian Carnival, I can hardly send an RSVP with polite regrets to 150 million hosts. At this most social of engagements, there is no room for small talk. Stripped down for action in sneakers and shorts, a whole country's "in crowd" is out in the streets, along with the outs. But what made me think I could saunter in without an invite? Or expect that an abject beginner would qualify for this advanced seminar on pelvic polyrhythms, this five-day workshop in overcoming claustrophobia?

Why, on my very first trip to Brazil, have I plunged straight into the action at Salvador da Bahia? Blame it on the *bossa nova*. Blame it on all the staccato guitar pluckers who whispered their onomatopoeic call to "Bye-eee-aaah!" Oh, Bahia, sounding like a sigh at pleasures sated! Unwittingly, I succumbed to the call contained in the most sophisticated *sambas* as well as the ceremonial dirges of transplanted African cults. Bahia, destination disguised as exhalation! Its proper name, Saint Salvador of the Bay of All Saints, was bestowed in 1512 by Cabral, Brazil's first Portuguese conqueror, making this the second oldest continuous settlement in the New World. Abbreviated as Salvador, never to be confused with unhappy El Salvador, Bahia is also known as A Velha Mulata—that ancient octaroon gal. Historic center of the trade in sugar and cocoa, requiring ten times the number of slaves ever brought to Virginia, Bahia is the axis of the Afro-to-anyfro fulcrum, fount of all things Brazilian!

It make sense that the country's founding capital should also be the number-one venue for participatory merrymaking. Ground zero for all Brazil's annual emotional detonation is the Praça Castro Alves, Salvador's catchall square. Hell's ballroom on an ocean bluff. The Campo Grande, a sedate square full of palms and tiled mosaics, has been commandeered as the lifting pad for this town of a million's collective leap. A seedy shopping street called the Sete do Setembro—like our Fourth of July, the date of Brazilian independence—has become one long flume of half-naked dervishes flowing toward the Bay of All Saints. From the opposite direction, up the cobblestone slopes of the crumbling Pelourinho, once the cruel heart of colonial Brazil and now the pacemaker of the culture brought here by the colony's African slaves, come the Afro-blocos, black nationalist dancing groups modeling the portable upholstery of splashy tribal wraps. Black and white merge in a combustible mix where everyone turns colorful, anything but gray.

Were I able to beat a retreat to my hotel room, I'd just have to put up with a loudspeaker rigged up outside my window that pours out bouncy tunes twenty-four hours a day. Even if I could part the waves of people, I'd remain trapped by sound. Fore and aft in the rocking processional are huge wheeled ships, their black prows all amplifiers, sending out heart-speeding sounds at a volume that curdles eardrums. An entire citizenry yields up its nervous system to the fervent command of the Bahian institution known as the *trio elétrico*—once three mandolin strummers but now full bands with rock drummers and beauteous backup singers. As their motorized stages lumber down the street as slow as they can go, the bands outrace each other by jacking up the volume and speeding up the frenetic rhythm of *marcha*. Locals claim the electric guitar itself was invented here in the mid-forties by a part-time musician and full-time electrician. The town has certainly perfected the art of turning a flatbed truck into a rolling bandstand built from balanced stacks of loudspeakers. Never has so little horsepower hauled so much amplification.

With a splash of neon on the side of its truck, this year's most popular *trio* advertises itself as Cheiro de Amor, the "smell of love." I think I'm picking up a whiff of that, along with the more cloying scent of *lança perfume*, an etherlike inhalant sprayed onto handkerchiefs dangling from many carousers' mouths. Organized *blocos* shake pom-poms and hippity-hop through the night in matching sleeveless togas which identify whimsical Carnival groups like Ecologia or Sympathy Is Almost Love, Habeas Copos, as in cups of Brahma beer, and Hypertensão, which refers to libidinal tensions. "Next Year Will Be Better" is the pledge made by one habitually disorganized bunch of street prancers. Another playful contingent offers ideological debate by calling itself "Next Year Will Be Worse"!

To my right, a distinguished and decidedly muscular black gentleman is dressed up as an outsized all-American high school drum majorette in blond wig, miniskirt, and go-go boots. In fact, if you can call anything in this town a fact, on a designated day of the festivities, there are thousands such transsexualized cheerleaders. The girl to my left is Batman, or Batlady. Charming mermaids slither past, rubbing their fins against eager fishermen. Some of these sirens flash gold-toothed smiles. Others make their interest known by suggestively lifting a corner of my shirt tail, as if they're trying to x-ray my pants. In the local argot, free-lance fantasists like these are known as the *pipoca* (popcorn). Around me, the action's getting hot enough to burst all kernels of logic.

I've fallen in line behind the Apaches, a typically mirthful and mixed-up Bahian mélange of blacks dressed as Indians out of Hollywood's West. In a wild, wild send-up of their Amazonian brethren, they strut their feathers and string their arrows in time. What animates them is a tribal beat emanating from the wrong continent. Ranting into a raspy microphone, their single singing chief pays tribute to ancestral African gods. The drumming corps is a marching band out of its straitjacket. Their martial rhythm is internationalist in inspiration, too—something they call *samba-reggae*. The beat that makes the old churches quake is repetitive to the point of inducing the infinite. But one kind of Indian is soon overtaken by another. I'm lost in the turbaned waves of the Filhos de Gandhi (Sons of Gandhi), the oldest and largest of the black associations, who appropriated the pacifist saint as a symbol of both peaceful coexistence and racial rebellion. Thousands get civilly disobedient in matching white turbans, sandals, and shocking blue socks, their holy headdresses looking like bowling towels.

I doubt if the Mahatma would approve of all this surplus carnality. The face of this *festa* is sometimes leering, unshaven, and, more often, clownlike, painted, and giddy. Through four nonstop nights that are just another snoozy weekend to the rest of the world, moods are getting meaner. It's already past the time when all of these folks should be safely in bed. In quieter spots, the roads turn to rocky mattresses for entwined couples, cushioned with an accumulating down of confetti and discarded beer cups. The better side streets are pissoirs. With streetlights shattered or burned out, I end up in dark alleys surrounded by more than a few types I'd never want to meet there. In this return to childhood, there are lots of problem kids with raging hormones, taking their innocence to the point where it becomes indistinguishable from mayhem. There are many guests who've overstayed their welcome.

I haven't been properly introduced to the grinning lady who finds enjoyment in rubbing her hands against my hamstrings, the drunk gent who has planted an elbow in my lower back, the groping stranger who is using the opportunity of our enforced coziness to dig his claws deep inside my front pockets. With an extra set of hands down my pants, it feels for a moment that I've grown tentacles, Vishnu-like, or that the khaki shorts I'm wearing are no longer my own. But I've taken the precaution of storing my spare change in the sole of one smelly sneaker. There's no space for me to bend over and claim my wad, only a couple of thousand *cruzeiros*, not to be confused with last year's *cruzados* or next year's *cruzados novos*, all of the above currencies getting more worthless by the hour in this land where the only currency that gets you anywhere is a steadfast allegiance to unreality. The pick-pocket soon discovers that my pockets are as empty as the national treasury.

My best protection is to merge with the mob and accept that I'm no better or worse than any other biped succumbing to the stimuli of snare-drum cadences, group hysteria, and unlimited cheap beer. Before I know it, I, too, am pulling an all-nighter so I can sing the sacred and profane praises of this wondrously poly-glot place. "Bahia, my eyes are shining/ My heart is palpitating/ From so much happiness!" goes one time-honored *samba* trib-ute. "You're the queen of universal beauty/ My dear Bahia/ Long before the Empire/ She was the first capital/ Her history, her glory/ Her name is tradition!" After five hundred years, this town hasn't begun to exhaust the possibilities inherent in its potent mix of peoples and beliefs. On its privileged perch between ocean and desert, this little Lisbon and compact Luanda grinds its cultural engines to make a mighty noise. We dance in discovery of Bahia's bright shortcut to the dark continent! Strut to savor Salvador's unhinged, nonpuritan version of America! All hail Oxum and Jesus, Mary and Yêmanjá! Blessings to Mother Africa, Father Portugal, and especially their bastard child, Brazil!

Now I raise both hands skyward in pagan hosannahs. There's no longer any room for two arms at my side. I can't tell whose legs are carrying my rump along. My one moment of glory comes when I tire of bouncing up and down like some stork attempting a takeoff. Throwing all caution and complexes aside, I break into "the jerk," a dance I've been perfecting ever since I began imitating James Brown in junior high. Within moments, I'm surrounded by a circle of brown Bahian teens doing their best to imitate my too-cool *Americano* moves. "'Ta legal!" they all cry, adding the thumbs-up sign which means not only that something is legal but that everything is okay, totally permissible. Their appreciative grins remind me that Carnival has no stylebook, dress code, or etiquette. "Otimo!" a few murmur, "ultimate" being the most common compliment in a land that tends toward the heights of every experience. Perhaps the surest way to escape assault and battery is by yielding to one's *fantasia*, that doubly rich word for a costume.

What sort of masquerade am I using anyway, not so much the accidental tourist as an inadvertent dancer? Personally, I'm no fan of excessive unsolicited body contact. I've rarely seen the point in contorting various anatomical parts before others in a manner that I wouldn't attempt while alone. I can do without intoxicated strangers seeking a grip on my attention span or a shortcut to my soul. Just when polite conversation turns to a din, when the carpet gets rolled up and everyone kicks up his heels, that's usually the time you'll see me sneaking out. That I've been moved to come here—to the veritable belly button of body-land—shows just how far some of us will go to find our own body. In my case, I've added around eight thousand frequent-flier miles when all I have to do is travel a few inches, migrate to that steamy realm just down south of my neck!

"Below the equator," goes another of those tired homilies that Brazilians trot out before newcomers, "there is no sin." Though I see more innocence on display than anything else—flesh displayed is flesh divested—my resistant Northern mind recoils with a set of judgmental questions: Don't these people ever seek out silence? Shimmy their way toward an inner life? To what purpose have I cast my lot with these sweaty unshod? This giving in to primal forces must indeed be quite an achievement, since I'm having such trouble doing it. There must be some lesson I've got to learn by taking my place amid the profusion of anonymous torsos, through applying for citizenship in this dictatorship of the beautiful.

Nobody seems to care that last year's Carnival of Democracy has inevitably given way to the Carnival of Hyperinflation. This *festa*—the key word in a country disguised as a party—is a collective triumph over *brutalidade*, that Portuguese term spoken in the Brazilian singsong that softens everything hellish, makes even quotidian misery sound dulcet. And I, too, am attempting to become *Sem medo de ser feliz*. Unafraid to be happy—that's the fearless slogan which animates this city, this country, this night. A Carnival group has appropriated the phrase from the recent electoral jingle of Lula, a burly factory worker nearly elected president in Brazil's first direct voting in twenty-nine years. With the return of some semblance of popular rule, even the Leftist candidates must compete to put the best song on voters' lips. This is one country where one of the politicians' campaign pledges has to be joy.

But is there only this one raucous, riotous route to bliss? Must there be but one authorized version of pleasure? Can this be the way happiness has to smell, reeking of stale beer? The way happiness has to taste, charred meat and pepper sauce lingering on the tongue? The way happiness has to sound, earsplitting in four-four time which has lost all subtlety or syncopation? The way happiness has to look, a numbing profusion of rear ends, armpit hairs, and broken teeth? The way happiness ought to feel to the touch, slippery and hot? And how come I have so many volunteer instructors when by all accounts they have so much reason to feel otherwise?

Hasn't anyone told this bunch about last year's 4,000 percent rise in prices or the mounting external debt? Maps show that Bahia is perilously close to a drought-stricken, oligarchic back-country where millions live with perpetual scarcity. This must be the same place where drug gangs murder hundreds daily and the police are no better, knocking off homeless children for a fee of five hundred dollars per head. It's a statistical certainty that many of these folks live in *favelas*, squatter towns without proper sanitation, on the brink of despair. Has everybody forgotten the destruction of the rain forest, the rape of the Indians, the long rule of the military, the flight of capital and brains, the interference of the multinationals, the alienation of postindustrial man, the atom bomb? Why is this country dancing?

The fifth largest nation on earth—a society that has tamed vast frontiers and constructed miraculous cities—hardly deserves to be dismissed as one vast paragon of urges unbridled. Brazilians are still galled by General de Gaulle's sneer about Brazil's lack of seriousness. Yet it remains obvious that no social order anywhere gets so serious about its frivolity. Ever since Carmen Miranda first worked a fruit salad into her hairdo, hip-shaking showgirls have been this nation's leading ambassadors. A culture exists here, not just for five days but all year, which is unique for its emphasis on sensuality, mysticism, tenderness, play, and especially rhythm. And that culture's apex, Brazilian popular music, this partying music in all its varied manifestations, is as much a contribution to world civilization as Gothic cathedrals or Persian miniatures.

Which means that what Brazil has to teach isn't in its stately halls or museums but in the dance halls, the bars, and especially the streets. A *gente nas ruas!* The people in the street, that's the Brazilian call to prayer. A pilgrimage here, then, can be viewed as the geographic antonym of a trek to India. Both aim at some eventual entrée to enlightenment. Except that one journey gets there through renouncing flesh, the other through shaking it. A quest for carnival knowledge by carnal means.

But how does one play tourist in the realm of the body? How to grab hold of a nation where the major monuments are ephemeral, the souvenirs are audio as much as visual, the most telling snapshots may be rimshots? What approach to make where the top landmarks require not so much sightseeing as "soundhearing?" Since melody and lyrics are what lured me, let the lyrical set my itinerary. Instead of airline schedules, I'll go by album covers. Instead of a guidebook, a drumbeat—so the nation I discover may resemble that imaginary emerald terrain to which I'm carried by Brazilian rhythms. Hitting all the high and low notes, I want to be transported to the land that produces the sounds that have already transported me—to compare the music of the country with the country of music.

Such a premise is surely ingenuous, as purposely childlike as the costumed action around me. But if we weren't all just a little naïve, we would never go anywhere. Without illusions, there are no journeys. And mine is to follow the music. Follow the music and it will set you free. Follow the music and hope that it takes me all the way to Brazil.

Music to Read By

TEMPO DE BAHIA—Compilation (Blue Moon)
SOUNDS OF BAHIA, VOL. 2—Compilation (World Pacific)
JAMBO—Chiclete Com Banana (Trio Gel)
O CARNAVAL DE GAL—Gal Costa (Philips)

THE GUY FROM IPANEMA

Getting to know a country is not that different from courting a member of the opposite sex. First impressions often count far too much. And, like so many North American men, my interest in this country began with a woman. No package tours ever tempted more tourists to book their vacations in Brazil than that unattainable beach bunny who was "tall and tan and young and lovely"—a twangy rendition of the Portuguese epithet *cheia de graça*, "full of grace." The difference is that I met her when I was just a boy. Which is all right, because she was only a girl.

Back in 1964, when I had reached that crucial threshold of thirteen, "The Girl from Ipanema" took the U.S. by storm— peddling the hot romance of cool *samba* to the tune of two million albums. My initial association with the bulk of South America was gawking at my customarily brainy parents, stripped down to beach towels on the deck of our vacation house, swaying along with this "new beat." They had no more idea of the proper dance steps than they did why this *bossa* happened to be *nova*. Or that these lightly plucked *sambas* were middle-class versions of the clattering, shattering originals created by Brazil's poor blacks. North Americans caught up in the craze knew only that this sound conjured up a nation at once savage and knowing, whose seat of government had to be on the beach. Before my generation was wooed away by rock rebellion, Sergio Mendes and Lalo Schifrin, Stan Getz and Charlie Byrd whisked me off to a land I rarely heard about in junior high. Record-liner notes, not history books, first informed me and many others that there was such a place as Brazil.

Looking back, it is clear that far more was being reflected by this cross-equatorial invasion than a mere sharing of international bonhomie. In each American colossus, the early sixties provided a shining moment when it looked like democratic values might win out over barbarism. A generational change in political leadership led to a burst of sophistication in high places, symbolized by two dynamic presidents with the same initials: J.K. for John Kennedy, "Jota Ka," as it's pronounced in Portuguese, for Juscelino Kubitschek, still widely honored as the only honest civilian leader between two grueling stretches of dictatorship. There was idealism in the streets: the ferment of the civil rights movement in the U.S., the resurgence of industrial unions and peasant organizing in Brazil. There was a revitalized national purpose and confidence, symbolized by Kennedy's pledge to land a man on the moon and by Kubitschek's earthbound miracle, the long-dreamed-of construction of a futuristic new "capital of hope" in Brazil's lunar interior. It was no accident that the man asked to compose an orchestral work for the inauguration of Brasília was Antonio Carlos Jobim, the composer of "The Girl from Ipanema."

Soon enough, the duel Camelots would be snuffed out: in one case, through an assassination and the Vietnam War, in the other, through the 1964 CIA-sponsored military putsch which deposed left-leaning João Goulart and ushered in nearly two decades of the *ditadura*. Yet the period's musical movement, aimed at self-consciously paring down and melding the best of both Americas' traditions, continues to echo in our ears to this day. Brazil's "Americanized" *bossa nova* would come to embody a greater truth—that no two nations on the planet could be more alike than the continent size, frontier-driven, slavery-haunted, immigrant catchalls known as the United States of America and Os Estados Unidos do Brasil.

The tunes that briefly united two hemispheres could only encourage my long-distance flirtation. Never mind that I was baffled that there could be a Brazilian with the Nordic name Astrud, the wife of singer João Gilberto, who won notoriety through her single English chorus of "Girl." Astrud Gilberto's voice certainly handed me my earliest definition of the adjective "sexy." Turned to song titles, places like Corcovado and Ipanema became idealized teenage images of problemless playboy playgrounds. The very word "Rio" took on an erogenous resonance. Poor Rio! The most common forms of deception on the planet are travel posters and girlie pictures—to which might be added album covers. And since the city's image has been formed by all three, it cannot help but be thrice disappointing.

My first ride into Rio de Janeiro would be enough to show me that most of what's man-made to this vaunted harbor has been a botch job. Grimy causeways lead from the airport along the lapping shallows of Guanabara Bay, toward tin-roofed clumps of poverty growing like hair under boulevard armpits. To get to the postcard sights, you've got to pass through neighborhoods you wouldn't want to stall in: the unrelieved bleakness of the Zona Norte, a sort of South American New Jersey, where it's hard to tell the difference between the warehouses and the clubhouses of the Carnival organizations which give these untouristed parts of town their only claim to distinction.

The Avenida Brasil's eight-lane approach to downtown is lined with tire dealers and labia-pink "love motels"—during the '92 Earth Summit, the U.S. Secret Service was put up in a particularly ostentatious assignation site—designed for maximum security, maximum infidelity. The docks and hoists of Rio's port haven't been shipshape since slavery was abolished. Highway underpinnings are covered with spray-painted calls to revolution. Buses ramble along with windows shattered. Downtown's glass-cube modernity is a bad mix with colonial cupolas. An initial ground-level glimpse turns Sugar Loaf—that oddly compelling hunk of urban rock which I first glimpsed on the sleeve of a Cannonball Adderley LP—into a worn, brown eraser stub. Lines of wire airbrushed out of the photos, the funicular tracks up to the peak, reflect in Botafogo's round sweep of harbor, waters as placid as they are abandoned to pollution. A trip to the swanker sections is accomplished through lengthy, exhaust-clogged tunnels, accompanied by every driver's sarcastic warning: "Please don't breathe unless you want thirty seconds taken of your life."

Am I let down because I've been led on for twenty-five years by a musical pinup, a bikini-clad tease I can never meet? Of course, I head straight for Ipanema Beach—at least, the place really exists. After a few hours of sodden jet-lag sleep, I am thrilled to get the perfect Brazilian greeting. Above an air conditioner's creaking last gasp, through the drapes which work fine against a full-bore tropical morn, my modest hotel room is invaded by music. In floods an onslaught of timpani, the binary clatter of bells, snares, and shakers. A wake-up call for the universe! But when I open the window to chart the progress of this renegade marching band, I see nothing but a storefront directly across the street featuring *Discos em Promoção*. Recorded *sambas* for sale! A loudspeaker is giving the neighborhood a free sample: the authentic sounds I crave turn out to be canned. In the ethnographically quarantined tourist zone where I've landed, the same rule applies to the authentic life of the city as it does to the newest generation of Ipanema girls in their skimpy swimwear. Look but don't touch.

In a ritual reenacted by many a *gringo*, I stagger out onto Rio's hedonist sands. As I've been warned, I carry nothing that can be stripped from me but my swim trunks and my solitude. A pale cartoon ghoul, I feel utterly out of synch with the zillion frisky Cariocas in the midst of another weekend's orgy of bodily display, beach volleyball and beer. Along the promenade, numbered posts divide the sands into the varied subgroupings of Brazilian society. On one hot slice, the poets; on another, the high priests; at a third, the near-naked bureaucrats, the former political prisoners tanning at their customary waterfront turf. Brazil's Times Square-by-the-sea comes at me in all its predictable elements: the local beauties in their razor-thin loincloth *tangas* rightfully nicknamed "dental floss"; the equally undulating *calçadas*, black-and-white waves of sidewalk mosaic transplanted by the seafaring Portuguese; the incessant hawkers offering oversized towels and souvenir soccer shirts; the distant humps of coastal jungle sloping seaward, sole hints of an end to the mighty boomerang arc of bathers, this two-mile curve offering a whole city cooling consolation.

Why is it we're comforted to discover certain spots are exactly as promoted? Somehow, dipping my tootsies into this renowned sandbox brings the same Pavlovian response of wonder as stepping into the postcard views of the Taj Mahal or Tiananmen Square. In mankind's symbolic language, there can only be one church called Notre Dame, one skyscraper called the Empire State Building, and one beach, Ipanema's contiguous Copacabana. But what really makes this beach-blanket Babylon different from all the others? As soon as my virgin feet begin to burn, I make for the shady oasis of a makeshift seaside tent, or *pagode* (from the Chinese *pagoda*, pronounced "pa-go-jee")—the name given to a stripped-down style of *samba* which has reappeared in recent years as a response to the overpromoted and overelectrified Carnival themes. A back-to-the-basics jam is already in session, grouped around enough empty bottles of Antarctica lager to make a bonfire in brown glass. The refreshment I'm offered is all musical.

In the cool center of the shade, a half dozen boys are fiendishly extracting all they can from the percussive building blocks of Brazilian music: perky, insistent *agogô* double-bell; squeaky, optimistic *cavaquinho*, a Portuguese mandolin we've come to know as the ukulele; impudent *caixa* snare drum and pompous *surdo* bass; moaning orgasmic *cuíca*, or African tension drum, as academics are wont to call this skin with a talking umbilical; attacking *atabaqués*, tom-tom, versatile *pandeiro*, our tambourine, preferably tapped with an elbow, a hip, the tip of the nose; their *tamborim*, a miniature struck with machine-gun force; *reco-reco* scratcher and *xique-xique* shaker, sometimes just dry beans inside a soda can, always sounding just like their names. The overlays of staccato rhythm get everyone moving, a forced march deliciously stalled. A circle of middle-aged mammas, shaking it in their G-strings, never runs out of traditional melodies to accompany the drumming din. Where few people carry beachside reading, every sun worshiper shows high literacy in the oral tradition, a photographic memory for the lyrical. From the start, I hear ample evidence of the average Brazilian's encyclopedic capacity for song.

To begin my investigations into the music, I must find the creator of the lifelong infatuation that has led me here. In a nation where flowery four-part Portuguese surnames are always reduced to familiar diminutives, Antonio Carlos Jobim is known to all Brazilians by the boyish "Tom"—though the grand old man of *bossa nova* is now in his mid-sixties. Five of the ten most-recorded Brazilian songs of all time bear his credit line—and how about most hummed?—including "One-Note Samba," and "A Felicidade." But Jobim is more than a prolific tunesmith, a Latin Cole Porter. Nearly every aspiring Rio musician I meet, at whatever level of seriousness along the pop spectrum, credits him with being the most innovative and imitated. Moacyr Luz, a singer of *musica popular Brasileira* (MPB), the term used to group everything in the wake of *bossa nova*, echoes the popular sentiment: "Jobim is our great genius because he dared to be simple."

Daring to phone him at home, I'm astonished to reach the composer after less than a dozen busy signals. "I'm sure you've noticed that our telephones are very whimsical," Jobim greets me with the whimsy found in his finest lyrics. Amazingly, I haven't had to fight my way past the jealous guard of some *empregada* (maid), a law unto themselves in a country where even the maids have maids. (One tells me her musician boss can't come to the phone because he is resting in anticipation of Carnival. Later, others will tell me their employers are resting in Carnival's aftermath.) Knowing that he splits his residence between Rio and New York, I'm not expecting Tom Jobim to have time for me. "My friend," he declaims, "we'll *invent* the time!"

It must have taken a genius to have invented so luscious a tribute to a locale as grubby as Ipanema. Strolling this narrow neighborhood squeezed between an inland lagoon and one of Rio's outer beaches, I find the air hazy, the condos heavily guarded, the avenues full of cut-rate juice joints and underpatronized malls. A block inland, we could be a million miles from the sea—except that Ipanema's bag ladies also tote folding beach chairs. But when Antonio Carlos Jobim's family transported him here, the trolley lines had just been extended from downtown. From the stretch of white sand praised by Isadora Duncan, branded by developers as the Praia Maravilhosa (Wondrous Beach), you could spy whales and great herons.

According to Jobim, real estate speculation ruined the whole town. Yet this nostalgic son of the neighborhood has said that real social justice will only come to Brazil once everyone can live in

Ipanema. One afternoon, I follow the crowd to the very spot from which this locale became forever popularized. A block from the beach, a swarm of perfectly tanned types are striking tambourines and blasting trumpets in an attempt to squeeze every ounce of pleasure out of the waning day. The point of this promenade seems mainly to keep hopping about in spandex fig leaves for as long as possible. T-shirts proclaim this group as Furiosa—a pun formed by the root of "furious" spelling "Rio." They have paused to serenade beer swillers on the packed covered porch of a cramped corner bar whose sign reads "Garota de Ipanema." *Garota* means girl, of course, but a very special sort of girl. At a table here, Vinícius de Morāes, the populist poet who lent respectability to Brazilian pop music by becoming *bossa nova*'s prime lyricist, was moved to scribble down his tribute to one Heloisa Pinheiro, the lithesome, long-haired daughter of a Brazilian general. Riding her fame as the original "Girl from Ipanema," Pinheiro has gone on to become a roving gossipmonger during the television coverage of Carnival balls. She also posed nude alongside her daughter in the Brazilian *Playboy*. If you can elbow your way inside, the original draft of lyrics and music are enshrined in a frame over the bar—formerly called the Veloso. But I don't find Tom Jobim there. He has boycotted the place ever since it cashed in on his song's notoriety.

Waiting to catch up with him, I find nothing but an energetic facsimile of North American jazz fusion at People, Jazzmania, and the other fashionable boîtes. In similar elite enclaves, the *bossa nova* was born through the fusion of the fifties' North American import—the "cool" sound pioneered by Miles Davis and Chet Baker—with native Afro-Brazilian rhythms. But the greater influence these days is rock, which Brazilians pronounce just like the sport hockey. MTV-style videos are used to teach English to teenagers on a popular nationwide show. The tabloids are full of Brazilian rock stars like the maniacal "Lobāo" ("Big Wolf") and the irreverent Paralamas do Sucesso (the Fenders of Success). At most public Rio events, rock, not *samba*, blares from civic loudspeakers. The Eagles and U-2 drown out the chants of *macumba* cult priestesses during New Year's celebrations on Copacabana Beach.

Fortunately, I'm tipped off that many veterans of *bossa nova*, Tom Jobim among them, are gathering for a rare reunion to benefit a terminally ill musician. Unfortunately, the show is being staged amid chandeliers and white linen at a ritzy nightclub usually reserved for *mulata* show girls to shake their sculptural *boom-booms* at Argentine tour groups. The setting, and concert, point up how much the "new beat" has aged. At this benefit, both audience and performers have lost much hair and zeal. Johnny Alf, an ebullient black scat singer, reminds me of Johnny Mathis. Os Cariocas, once a breathtaking harmonizing quartet, sounds just like the Kingston Trio. I'm at a high school reunion of finger-snapping, jive-talking "hep cats." The classiest class of '59.

I'm hoping to find João Gilberto, more than the first interpreter of "The Girl from Ipanema," the pure quavering soul of *bossa nova*. As hard to track as his singing-by-speaking Zen vocals and his teasingly off-tempo guitar style, Gilberto has become that oddest of anomalies: the antisocial Brazilian. One of the many apocryphal tales surrounding this legendary recluse describes how the singer Elba Ramalho purposely moved into Gilberto's apartment building to befriend him. When shy João called her to borrow a pack of playing cards, he made her shove them under the door, one at a time. Gilberto has been the object of lawsuits for canceling shows at the last minute—and tonight he's a no-show. "The artist struggles all his life to become known and accepted," is how Antonio Carlos Jobim will explain his former partner's predicament. "Then when it happens, all he wants to do is crawl inside a cave."

The groundbreaking songs that Gilberto and Jobim helped establish in the sixties are today's standards, the sliest of elevator music. At the time of my arrival, a gossipy new book about the formative moment of *bossa nova* tops Brazil's best-seller list. Not only does interest in the music remain high but the passage of time has hardly alleviated the noisy controversy engendered by such softly flowing music. It's hard to believe that academics and columnists once hurtled every epithet at this gentle sound's pioneers: reactionary, escapist, sanitized, above all, Americanized. But I have only to look briefly around the invaded Brazilian social landscape to see why such a howl went up among the self-appointed protectors of cultural purity when Jobim's stream-of-consciousness classic "Waters of March" turned up as the basis for a Coca-Cola jingle. Now I know why envious critics still snipe at this leading ambassador of Brazil for acknowledging that one of his major inspirations has been George Gershwin.

That there should be such hypersensitivity to the question of "foreign influences" in Brazilian culture is, of course, a backhanded admission of susceptibility. Over and again, I will hear musicians boast of their ability to "metabolize" North American and European sounds into something distinctively their own. Brazilian music, like Brazilian art, poetry, or religion, grows through synthesis. Brazilian musicians are plagued by their tolerance, a fresh-eared approach to every incoming sound from hip-hop to the honking of cars.

What goes along with the receptivity is a latent colonial mentality—hardly surprising, considering that Brazil was the last country in South America to be freed from the domination of a motherland. Among the common folk, especially, you hear the attitude, "What's foreign is best." And, given a long-term closed-market strategy that restricts many imports and has forced companies like Volkswagen and Ford to build plants in Brazil, most of what is foreign is from the United States. The symbols of cultural hegemony are all here: from MTV videos on the tube to a plethora of McDonald's—where fast food, Brazilian-style, is predictably slow. It takes far more than the promised *momentinho* to get your stale *Quarterão*.

I am here just in time for Rock in Rio II, billed as the biggest rock festival on earth, two weeks of frenzy held at Maracaña, the world's largest stadium. "I'm Going," say the T-shirts I see worn by almost everyone under forty, including Brazil's youthful President Collor. Only a few black nationalists in Rio's *samba* community protest the twenty million dollars donated by Coca-Cola to be lavished on foreign musicians. Prince will get more than a million for his appearance—covered by the Brazilian newspapers with a blow-by-blow account of the night he spent with some Carioca groupie. In the meantime, most Brazilian musicians continue to live from gig to gig. Top acts like Gal Costa and Gilberto Gil drop out of Rock in Rio in protest over underpayment and disrespectful treatment.

"We know that as Brazil goes," Richard Nixon once observed, "so will go the rest of the Latin American continent." The saturation of American culture is only partly due to the State Department's meddling and is caused mainly by Brazil's historic isolation from its Spanish-speaking neighbors. Brazil considers itself a continent apart from the rest of the continent—and who can blame it? Why look at the mirror of others with difficulties much like your own? For the same airfare, often for less, those who can afford travel and cultural interchange choose Disney World over Lima, New York—Nova Iorque—instead of Santiago. Unlike the Argentines and other neighbors, few Brazilians maintain a pretentious show of Eurocentrism. Style and economics both dictate direct links to the other America.

Music serves as a perfect reflection of Brazil's self-imposed quarantine. Few of the musicians I meet have ever heard the terms *salsa*, *merengue*, and *cumbia*. Yet nearly everyone can keep me appraised of the latest trends in funk, rap, and soul. You don't have to keep your ears open in Brazil for more than a few days to realize that the greatest influence on Brazilian music is no longer Portuguese *fado* or African *lundu*, not Jamaican *reggae* or Argentine *tango*. It is, and has been for longer than we might like to acknowledge, the hand of Hollywood and the U.S. recording industry. I'm shocked to find that many of the cabbies trapped in Rio's tunnels soothe their nerves with Frank Sinatra.

Now Jobim, who recorded with Sinatra, has taken a seat at the piano as a finale to the stodgy fund-raiser. And suddenly, the music sounds fresh. After just a few bars, I can't help agreeing with the assessment voiced by Caetano Veloso, one of *bossa nova*'s leading heirs: "The relationship between Brazilian and American music was wonderfully well settled by *bossa nova*. It was a moment of self-consciousness, a sophisticated moment when Brazilian popular music became aware of its own strength and significance, a moment of getting mature. That's what Jobim did. Anything less than that, it's old now. It's gone, gone in history."

"Desafinado" ("Out of Tune"), the historic song that lent its name to the movement some thirty years back, has not lost its bite. Equally contemporaneous are the lyrics by which Jobim answered Brazil's musical traditionalists. With characteristic insouciance, the composer couched his pitch for acceptance in the language of a wounded suitor. His song pleads for an answer to why the composer and his cohorts must be "put down" by those with "perfect pitch" and "privileged ears." After all, his ear is from God above, his love is sincere, and if his work must be classified as antimusical, his answer is that this *bossa nova* is "very natural."

Tom appears quite natural to me—affecting the traditional all-white outfit of the Carioca gentlemen. Though he possesses a youthful sweep of hair, which he keeps brushing back from his eyes, Jobim's cheeks are pale and puffy, his smile clenched. With bifocals, he looks even older than his age. "My life is such a mess, let's have a Brahma!" goes the confession in one of his recent tunes, referring to Brazil's most popular brand of beer. Hard living has taken its toll on this formerly lanky wisp whose songs make the best case I've ever heard for taking life easy. He's made a comeback in recent years as a singer, backed by a band that includes his son, a daughter, and various in-laws. His voice always sounds as if it could use a good throat-clearing, but even the groping to hit proper notes adds to its charm. "Where have you been, Mr. Bim?" he strains in English, imitating the inquiries of a New York customs officer. "Where have you been, Joe?"

I'm hoping to plumb Joe Bim's secrets on a lazy afternoon in some tropical backyard gazebo. Instead, I get a frantic lunch in a setting at least as characteristically Carioca: an old-fashioned boiler-plate *churrascaria* (barbecue house) called Plataforma. Doting old waiters replenish heapings of fresh-sliced steak and sausage, silver platters of onion rings and *petit pois*, the best french fries outside France along with obligatory beans and rice and *farofa*, the manioc flour that's a gustatory sawdust Brazilians sprinkle over everything.

Jobim always has a table set here. A couple of longtime pals, along with a visiting German bigwig from BMI, the international music publishers, have shown up for today's "Joe Carioca" show.

"I'm composing every morning these days. I'm working much better than I deserve. The way I've been living, all I deserve is to sit on the beach and watch the pretty girls go by."

Jobim's evident cheer, his nonstop quips, are fueled with beer, Brahma or any other brand, and frequent chasers of the firewater distilled from sugarcane that is to Brazil as vodka is to Russia. "Have a *cachaça* with me, won't you?" The word, like so many in Brazilian Portuguese, is of African origin—Mozambique's *kachasu*. Though this son of Ipanema is not what's known quaintly as a *Carioca da gema*—"of the yolk," meaning born in the more authentic *centro*—he seems the very embodiment of the stereotypical Rio man: always testing out an angle, trying gambits in a world that's both evil and delectable.

"Yes, I'm a Carioca. How can you tell? I'm a son of the Atlantic forest. I love all her animals. I listen to the birds. When I was growing up, Rio was still 90 percent forest. The water of the lagoon here was crystal clear and we had all kinds of conches and mullets. No air pollution, no real estate speculation. Brazil was so bucolic. We had only thirty million people then. Teddy Roosevelt used to hunt for jaguar in the Mato Grosso."

Compared to most of the world's major metropolises, Rio really is a frisky little girl. The sources of Rio's self-made myths are all quite recent: Copa's setting for seaside strolls, the Avenida Atlântica, wasn't laid until 1904; mass outbreaks of yellow fever came as late as 1906, the same year streetlights came to town; the first university didn't open until 1920, the same year as the city's mascot outspread Christ statue, erected from donations taken at Rio's churches.

In his music, and in his persona, Jobim revels in being a throwback to an earlier civility. He is the model of naïveté and the proof that tropical man can attain erudition. He delights in living with one foot in the jungle and one eye on the roulette wheel.

"In today's music, the chest vibrates with the electric bass. One is transported to paradise. In rock 'n' roll, there is strong reverence to the country of the downbeat. One-two, one-two, I know, I can count to a thousand! I don't come out of the fox-trot, the *lambada*, the *lambooda*, or the *lamboogie*! I come from the boogie-woogie, from the polyrhythmic and the unequal! I have this Jewish doctor in New York who said to me, 'Mister Jobim, I have a wife who works like a clock.' I never understood what he meant, but I like that! If something swings, everyone feels compelled to call it jazz. Jazz is the name for anything that swings, and because of the African element, there are three places in the world that swing: the States, Cuba, and Brazil. Rodgers and Hart, Duke Ellington . . . Jimmy Dorsey, Glenn Miller. I was exposed to all of them growing up, through the movies. And of course, I love classical music, too."

When it comes to politics, Jobim readily classifies himself as an idealist turned cynic. "Fellow musicians have asked me to go with them to Cuba. But I told them, 'When I choose to go to an island, I prefer Manhattan!' As Villa-Lobos once said, 'Naturally, the future of the world is socialism, but at the moment, I cannot afford to lose a market like the USA!' " Asking Tom how he stood in the recent presidential campaign between the rightist scion

Collor and the visionary leftist Lula, he gladly volunteers, "I'm very proud. My whole family voted for Lula. And then we were all very relieved when he lost!"

Everyone at the table roars with approval. Yet Jobim's acceptance by a corrupt world is a bitter pill he washes down with plenty of booze.

"For the purists, even Pixinguinha"—the prolific king of the *chôrinho*, Brazil's lilting instrumental music derived from the Portuguese court—"is not pure enough. But the pure *samba* doesn't exist anymore. With big stadiums and electronic instruments, it had to change. They even say that my nickname 'Tom' is American. But my darling sister named me that. It was from Antonio, because in Portuguese the 'm' is pronounced like an 'n'. She was trying to call me a 'Ton-Ton.' Like those murdering fellows in Haiti! Yet everyone thinks it's American! Once, a gentleman in a bar accosted me, suggesting that my music was too American. As they say, 'I sold my soul to the company store!' I love Tennessee Ernie Ford! And country music, of course! My father came from the south of Brazil, from the land of the *gauchos*. So I told that gentleman, 'Yes, I'm an American! A South American!'"

Jobim's swagger rings as hollow as his defensiveness. He clings to the pose of the offended party in order to have some way to participate in the native dialogue, to break out of his isolation. For no matter how many drinking buddies you gather at your table, it really is lonely at the top—especially in Brazil, where the top is such a minuscule point of such a wide pyramid. Doing something as well as Jobim has done leaves him imitated, extolled, excoriated—but never with enough proper company.

"Even here they discriminate against me!" Jobim roars, entirely aware of the irony, since the waiters keep heaping his plate with steak and *batatas fritas*, keep refilling both his glasses. "But my music is so Brazilian! Can't you feel it?" Jobim asks everybody and nobody at his long table. "If you listen to the music of Antonio Carlos Jobim, you will be saved! My music says, 'Live and let live.' Let the birds live, save the forest. I'm the original ecologist." Years ago, his sarcastic advice to the Indians was to get a striped shirt and a job in São Paulo. "My music isn't profane, it's profound."

Tom has undoubtedly used these same lines to charm dozens of audiences, but I don't mind that he's off and getting ever more incoherent.

"We're at three thousand feet here. The evening air is fresh, the oxygen is thinner. And that's important, because at my age, you have an inadequate profusion of cavernous bodies!" He offers a wink to one and all, but I don't quite get what he's driving at. "In New York, you don't get enough blood to get the real Mc-Coy. You know what the real McCoy is, don't you?" This Americanized Joe Bim, who lingers lovingly over American lingo like "real McCoy," is Brazilian enough to share the common preoccupation with male virility. "That's why I'm in Rio, where the blood gets thinner, runs faster. Being here affects the whole system."

Tom Jobim is one Brazilian whose garrulousness has gotten the best of him. He plays the court jester before crowds he knows perfectly well are not worth pleasing.

"Come on, my friend! Don't you want another *cachaça*?" I leave the greatest living Brazilian composer with a drink in each hand. "Just keep this in mind when you do your research! People think they are very intelligent when they can name things. Villa-Lobos used to say, 'I'm a neoprimitive concrete abstractionist.' Because all the labels are meaningless. When he was dying, you know, he was the one who told the press, 'I'm not composing, I'm decomposing!' He also told me, when he was working on scores for movies, 'The outside ear has nothing to do with the inside ear.' In other words, the way you dress the music isn't what makes it erudite or not. If you use orchestra, flute, or guitar. Villa-Lobos and Gershwin, what's the difference what you call it so long as it swings? You can say the same thing about the woman you love."

Is Jobim finally getting around to the Girl from Ipanema? Or referring to Rio, his lifelong passion? Or cautioning me before I plunge further into the music?

"You call the woman you love Maria, so you can go around thinking that you know Maria. But remember, my friend! That woman remains a mystery. Maria is only a name. . . ."

Music to Read By

PASSARIM—Antonio Carlos Jobim and His New Band
(Warner Bros.)
WAVE—Antonio Carlos Jobim (CTI)
THE LEGENDARY JOÃO GILBERTO—João Gilberto (World Pacific)
THE GIRL FROM IPANEMA/THE BOSSA NOVA YEARS—Stan Getz (Verve)
BOSSA NOVA: TWENTY YEARS AFTER—Assorted (Polygram)
VINÍCIUS, TOQUINHO, MARIA CREUZA EN LA FUSA—Vinícius de Moraes
(Trova)
A VONTADE—Baden Powell (Polygram)

THE SAMBA OF MORE AND MOST

Sing a song of Brazil, so much more than a nut! A good Carnival carol needs plenty of ironia, so don't spare our sensibilities or sense of the comic! Give us a litany of the gargantuan, the largest and the loathsomest, a catalog of boasts for a nation disguised as the Guinness Book of World Records! Compose a statistical samba, pull out all the stunning numbers. This is the place where there's always more and most, even of less.

Brazil is a biggie, not so easy for mapmakers to ignore, more than 8.5 million square kilometers, just a tad smaller than China or the United States. With fewer mountains or deserts, and more usable, arable, potentially productive earth than any other country on earth, Russia and Canada included. Such a land never runs out of land, or time, space or hope, never makes so many mistakes that they can't be corrected! First Brazil wood, then sugar, then coffee, rubber, gold! Some new treasure always comes along to trigger a new stampede, sweeping away all memory of past booms and busts.

With 7,000 kilometers of beaches, a record for sunbathing and surfing and waves and species of wavy palms, too. With the longest highways and the most unendurably long rides on them. Man's emptiest stretches—the Mato Grosso (the name means Big Forest) and Amazonia are emptier than the Sahara—are out in the perennially boundless frontier Brazilians crow about but rarely bother to see. Brazil's got bragging rights to the longest river, of course, beating the Nile by a mile, so the mad measurers report, but definitely the greatest in volume of muddy output, a third of our tearful planet's fresh water and a higher percent of its beleaguered turtles, rare diseases, plant varieties, medicinal products, oxygen. Most photosynthesis. Brazilians can even boast that their terrain does most of the world's breathing! Does it not follow that they must do the most living?

At the same time, with all but 4 percent of its populace crammed along its coast, this is one of the most thickly settled places! Seventy percent in big cities! With one of the fastest-growing and youngest citizenry, 70 percent under thirty. And what about the most fertile women? According to one study, 30 percent of fifty-year-olds had between ten and fifteen offspring. Brazil, you see, excels in the production of Brasileiros, the sixth most huge, walloping, and impenetrable population in the world. How do we invent a scale for determining if they're the most genetically mixed and mixed up?

This is a world between First and Third Worlds, comfortable only within its own relativity. Forty-seven percent of the land-mass of South America that hardly considers itself part of South America at all! Yet it's South America taken to extremes: the best and worst in its cordiality and cruelty, penchant for the absurd! The largest Catholic country, oh yes! Which means it's got the greatest number of illegal abortions, too. Five million in one recent year! The most saints, the most cults! The largest numbers who worship the Virgin Mary, Oxum and Oxalá, too! The most slaves came here, some three million forcibly removed from Africa, which at some points in Brazil is less than two thousand miles from the Americas, another record in proximity.

Where do they perpetuate the most unequal distribution of wealth, land, and public responsibility? Same refrain. The answer is Brazil, where the richest 4 percent control 43 percent of the country's resources, one-fourth live in abject poverty, one-third are malnourished, almost one-fifth live in unpaved slums. It's where the top 1 percent own 40 percent of the farms, and in some states 2 percent receive 40 percent of the income. With plantations as big as Belgium! With areas where the infant-mortality rate challenges the worst on the planet, regions where the average income is still under $140 a year, life expectancy is as low as thirty-five for 80 percent of the people. And what about the longevity of rare jaguars, endangered dolphins, union activists, or peasant rebels? Of course, Brazil's government spends among the least in public health.

Brazil, be proud of being the more and mostest! You lead the world in deaths on the job—once an hour, a Brazilian worker succumbs to some fatal accident! Brazil claims to have con-structed the tenth-largest economy in the world, decidedly the most expansive in the "developing" world. So why should it also have developed the most massive external debt, ever mounting? Compete for records in inflation count, the misery index? The world's greatest producer of coffee and oranges, sugar and gaso-hol, second in cocoa and third in timber, with great reserves of mineral and ore. So why is more seemingly so little? Leading to the record when it comes to abandoned children. Latest estimate: fifteen million living and dying on the street.

In the history field, too, this country piles on the contradic-tions. Christened the Island of the True Cross, it wasn't an island at all, and the nickname that stuck came from a red dye wood which would become its first commercial product. A colony for longer than any of its yoked neighbors—over three centuries—it was larger than the country that ruled it by the largest ratio. Fact: only country to have its foreign emperor permanently move his court there. Brazil, the only country that could be said to have colonized itself! The last country to abolish slavery, though it may be the country where the descendants of slaves have man-aged to exert the greatest influence. Where no people could be more casual, no government more hierarchical! Since 1889, when Brazil supposedly gained independence, there's hardly been a year when the government wasn't run by the military's chosen son. Its most recent president, elected at forty, is but another Brazilian extreme, one of the world's most juvenile heads of state.

What's the story, big B.? Fess up! The long-term chronology bespeaks the gentlest of nations, where the great changes come about with a minimum of violence. Yet the local ledger confirms this is a murder machine, a loss leader in lynchings, kidnappings, gangs. A full 40 percent of the adult work force can't get through a newspaper, but who needs to read signs? The greatest number of laws on the books, the greatest number of violations and violators. The highest per capita rate of traffic deaths. Do you get the idea that people here live to the fullest, which means dying at a dizzying clip? Another record to be proud of: world's most crowded prisons. Most doomed attempts at breakout, Brazil. Most cries muffled, Brazil. Most chants screamed out most loudly, Brazil. Rants, most melodious.

Why not the most musicians, with inspiration drawn from the most numerous species of birds, the widest selection of warblers? Twenty thousand strummers alone in São Paulo state, by the musicians' union's estimate. The biggest Carnival, of course, the greatest sheer tonnage of fun, the highest thrust of sublimation and mass violence and displaced energy, the largest drumming corps—over a thousand in some Rio organizations—the loudest shows, the curviest dancers, the quickest-moving and highest-heeled frenetic feet. The biggest sports stadium in the world is here, too. Capacity: 250,000, plus banners, bared breasts, and bells. More guitarists per square-inch, more composers per neighborhood. Not most instruments, but never mind! Brazilians play Coca-Cola coolers, they play the air. Play the lottery. Play the Encyclopedia Britannica. Play the facts.

More and most. Sing it, don't seek it. And don't ask for too many results or too much verification. No matter if it's scandal, disaster, lasciviousness, lies: this place has the numbers! Continent within a continent, Brazil is too big to be so uncharted! Too near to seem so far. Too rich to be so poor, too poor to be so rich. So chant our anthem to Brazil, the refrain of more and most! Where most isn't necessarily best. Just whistle another bouncy paean to a wonderland where the rich are richest, the poor poor-

est, the happy happiest, the most abject abjectest, the craven cravenest, the kind kindlier, cruel undoubtedly crueler, tough guys toughest, dream girls dreamiest. It's a truth that's not necessarily tape-measurable! The most sophistication, the most illiteracy. The biggest at the smallest gestures, the best at the worst vices! Repeat chorus. The most answers, the fewest solutions.

▲▲▲

Rio

Rio de Janeiro,
My joy and delight!
By day, there's no water.
By night, there's no light!
—Traditional samba, translated by
Elizabeth Bishop

〰〰〰〰〰

WISH I WERE HERE

It doesn't take long to start turning Brazilian. My internal clock, still set to Stateside rhythms, gives me a head start in adapting to a land where jet lag is a way of life. The surest sign of my sudden assimilation is that my sleep schedule is becoming skewed in favor of late and later. If you're punctual here, people say that you're going by *tempo británico*. Brazilian Standard means that everybody is living in their own time zone.

Fortunately, I no longer have to check out at noon. Determined to escape the unnatural world of the tourist, I've rented a fully furnished fifth-floor flat on the Rua Paissandu, that rare Rio street which is perfectly straight and bisects a desirable middle ground between downtown and the beaches. Once, this was a palm-lined way for royal processions that led from the promenade along the bay to the wedding-cake Palace of Guanabara. Just around the corner, there's a mustard-colored mansion turned clinic, a seat of power for modern Rio's princes, the plastic surgeons. On that rare day when there's neither smog nor storms, I can follow the highest fronds upward and notice the looming bluish hulk of Corcovado peak topped with the arms-open silhouette of Christ the Redeemer. The statue that symbolizes this city to the world embraces pox-ridden Rio at a safe remove.

Now I am finally living among the people—though I can't actually say that I've spoken to any of them as yet. Liberated from the beady surveillance of desk clerks, all the letting in and out is done by two uniformed gnomes, both perpetually grumpy from twelve-hour eating and sleeping lobby shifts. Forget bellhop sycophants fawning for a tip. Neither of these live-in doormen ever offers me so much as a "Boa dia." With each passing day, there seems less reason to bother having a day. I soon give up on reaching anybody in the recording industry before lunch. Just at sunset, a half dozen stereos ring out their internationalist alarms. Rod Stewart and Phil Collins waft down the regal arcade of palms toward the asphalt painted with a slogan urging on Brazil's World Cup soccer team. "Brazil—Eu Acrediteu!" it says "Brazil, I believe!" I believe I'll go back to bed.

Does going native in this town mean staying indoors until the coast is clear? Or is this just my hesitance at finally making the leap from traveler to resident, onlooker to participant? A less than subtle shift in consciousness occurs when Sugar Loaf becomes just another setting for an afternoon jog. I never realized what happens to your sense of place once you've got to do the same things in that place which you've been doing back home! Instead of four-star restaurants, you start looking for the best grocery. Instead of a minibar in your room, the nearest place to fetch bottled water. Not the housekeeping extension but the nearest laundromat (a relatively new innovation in Brazil, where the staff will run your machines for a few extra *cruzeiros*). In place of room service, you come to treasure the most fragrant neighborhood bakery, the quickest and cleanest *lanchonetes*, as in lunch, and *sorveterias*, as in sherbert, the most mind-stirring *cafezinho*, that essential swallow of Brazilian coffee.

A classic Carioca afternoon finds me wandering the town in the company of a case of mistaken identity. I've been recommended by mutual friends to somebody known only by the first name Zeca. Somehow, I convince myself that he's a matinee idol singer named Zeca Pagodinha. But this Zeca isn't musical at all. He's come from the provinces to make his mark as a theater director. While searching for a lunch spot, this stocky, curly-haired Zeca voices many of the stereotypical complaints about Cariocas. They're all two-faced hustlers who talk big but "when the crunch comes, or even a first rehearsal, they're off to the beach!" Cariocas, he claims, all are latent surfer boys, shallow and faddist. "Here people have no commitment to work, no compunction about honoring a schedule," Zeca complains for an inordinate amount of unscheduled time.

"Don't think we get used to the inefficiency, to the difficulty involved in even the smallest acts," Zeca tells me. "The Third World is just as hard for us to live in as it is for you." At the Third World's best ice cream spot, he spends another half hour introducing me to the juiciest bits of Carioca slang. My lexicon of survival in the sexual arena must include *avião* (airplane, i.e., a fine woman). Then there's *perseguida*, the "pursued," meaning the female organs. The sex act itself is *bimbada* not *lambada*, or better yet, *molhar o biscoito*. To wet the biscuit.

While we wet ours with melting scoops of double coconut, Zeca confesses why he's got to get going soon. He has recently met *um grande amor* (his great love), and tonight is her birthday. In a bookshop downtown, he has found the perfect gift, the rare biography of a black poet they both admire. He has only been carrying on with this assistant at the theater company for a week. But Zeca is in heaven. "She's only twenty-two and a real black one!" This obsession with the unattainable African goddess is yet another common Carioca trait that Zeca appears to have absorbed. I'm reminded of the common refrain paraphrased in a Jorge Ben tune: "Why complain? I drive a VW bug, live in a tropical country, have a black girlfriend—and once a year, there's Carnival!"

Still, Zeca is in no hurry to purchase his birthday tribute. I have to copy the one key I'm allowed to my apartment, and he helps me comb the neighborhood until we see a sidewalk sign-board advertising a second-floor *chaveiro*. However, this lock-smith's office shares space with a driving school. The one resident driver is taking a siesta face down on his desk. Where he should have a typewriter, there's a white Siberian husky pup balled up on the blotter. When the jovial instructor comes out of his coma, he and Zeca leisurely discuss the care and feeding of this rare, fur-ridden breed in an equatorial land. All I want is a spare key and I've entered a Borges story: the lost auto school, floating on an Alaskan ice floe toward Rio and points south. We're as wilted as the poor dog from waiting in the heat, so Zeca postpones his farewell once more with another drink. When he looks at his watch, he pretends to be shocked that it's nearly five o'clock. "Too late for the bookstore," he says with relief. "It's too hot to go to *centro* anyway." When it comes to Cariocas, it takes one to know one. Rather than attempt a fifteen-minute subway ride, he'll greet the love of his life empty-handed.

Am I merely taking my place among a vampire race, who retreat into workaday coffins to rest up for nightly flights? Apparently, I, too, must eschew the sun, lest the stake of underdevel-opment be driven into my heart!

Though I've learned to use Rio's surprisingly clean subway—Cariocas, of all people, should never be condemned to a moment under the ground—I find that I go there mostly to scan the record stores next to the turnstiles. Like all true urban wonders, Rio possesses neighborhoods whose names exude poetry. Paris has Montparnasse, San Francisco has Russian Hill, this town has efflorescent Laranjeiras, cloistered Cosme Velho, nautical Urca, seedy Lapa, trendy Botafogo. But after extended perambulations,

I discover that the mansion which serves as the archives for composer Villa-Lobos wasn't his real house at all. What point in viewing stodgy colonial art when I'm just a stroll from the hat collection at the Carmen Miranda Museum? Is Rio really Paris with jungle or Calcutta with beaches? Buenos Aires stripped to its skivvies? Hong Kong after the crash or Miami after a janitor's strike? How can a half-undressed city call itself world class?

Off Paissandu, I have only to choose any side street before the essential Rio asserts itself: the Rio with a fearsome will toward casualness that some call egalitarian, some find persistently grubby. There's the *pipoqueira*, an old man who cooks up batches of popcorn on his cart in the tropical heat. There's the hole-in-the-wall steak house, complete with blue Portuguese tiles and ceiling fans. I consider myself to have gone native when I learn to seek out juice stands run by Arabs. Only in blended-up Brazil would people line up for *quibe*, a deep-fried meat cake, to munch along with *vitaminas*, milk shakes made with the fruit of the *caju* (cashew) or the pulp of *abacate* (avocado). Marked only by its steady patronage, I come to recognize the neighborhood storefront that takes daily bets on the *jogo do bicho*, a supposedly illegal numbers game played with animal symbols. But how much greatness can emerge solely from bookie joints and corner *botequims*?

Rio is running a slick ad campaign against dengue fever—whose presence in the city is a testament to just how much certain parts of town resemble jungle encampments. But mosquitoes swarm inside the supermarkets. In this bad parody of the American kind, the shelves are full but brands are few. Brazil's laws are highly protectionist, which means there are Brazilian biscuits only—their Lorna Doones are, of course, called Marias—and even Brazilian wines passably produced by Italian immigrants. Instead of resulting in a strengthened economy for all, the consumer gets decreasing quality at ever rising cost. Freezers shudder under the continual task of keeping food cold in the tropics. Their unwiped silver sides reek of old cheese, rotting mangoes, sour yogurt. Why, in countries not your own, does everything taste better but smell worse?

Bad as it is to be a Brazilian housewife, it's worse still to have a checking account. Thanks to an anti-inflation austerity plan instituted by President Collor, freezing assets in accounts of more than $1,200 and allowing withdrawals of under $600, there's a bank run every day. Stupendous lines snake around every branch office or spill down the block before the automatic tellers. "For the love of God," wrote one saver to the government, "please liberate my miserable money!" Though such dictatorship over personal savings would be an unpardonable, impeachable sin in North America, Brazilian patience has still not found its limits. If time equals money, both are losing value here.

It's a most curious time to have arrived in Brazil. When wasn't? At least, this is one of the few moments in the last century when I don't have to suffer the guilt of spending my dollars in a country under military rule. Visions of *samba* dancers blind outsiders to the truth that Brazil belongs to an entrenched elite of landowning families, corporate bosses, and generals. Getúlio Vargas, a populist-minded, mild-mannered demagogue, ran the show from the thirties through the fifties—and might have made another comeback but for an impulsive suicide. Like every human personality, each country offers one persistent irony, a self-defeating behavioral tic that just doesn't make sense. Brazil's is that no people so freewheeling has ever been ruled so unfreely. In terms of repression, this seemingly unrepressed society is Latin America's trendsetter and repeat offender—just emerging from its latest twenty-five-year bout of dictatorship that began with a 1964 CIA-encouraged coup. Financed by massive borrowing, the military regime achieved the short-lived "economic miracle" of the 1970s—which left behind the destruction of the Amazon rain forest, the largest foreign debt in the Third World, and an ever widening gap between rich and poor.

Despite decades of torture, censorship, and the banning of opposition parties, millions of Brazilians, and Brazilian musicians, participated in the 1984 *Diretas Já!* campaign to restore direct presidential elections. But Tancredo Neves, the beneficiary of the *abertura*, or opening to democracy, died mysteriously on the eve of his inauguration. After more years of corruption, the first true popular vote came in 1990, resulting in a final-round face-off between Fernando Collor de Mello, the dashing and largely unknown scion of a wealthy provincial family, and Luis Inácio da Silva, known to all as Lula (meaning "squid"), a bearded, swarthy, and self-educated Northeast migrant who had been the leader of São Paulo's militant metalworkers' strikes. (At the time, these privileged among Brazil's proletariat earned the equivalent of sixty cents an hour.) Each of these representatives of the younger generation had been unexpectedly thrust forward to represent Brazil's polar extremes: Collor a polo-playing white knight who charged out of nowhere on an anticorruption platform to rescue the right-wing's exhausted forces; Lula a professed Marxist rising to challenge the rich on a tide of long-suppressed populism and the grass-roots organizing of the Catholic Church's many "liberation-theology" activists.

Brazilian politics, like our own, have become increasingly personality-driven. At one point, polls showed that most voters actually favored a popular TV game-show host. Others called for a draft of the soccer star Pele. And it was largely on his good looks that Collor took center stage. Branded a "son of the military," he had made token progress as the governor of Alagoas, a poor state with infant-mortality rates matching those in the worst parts of Africa. His father once shot a fellow deputy in the Brazilian Senate—and got off scot-free. On the other hand, Lula wore a tie for the first time in his life on the occasion of the election's final televised debate. "My mother cried when I got a job as a metal-worker," he said on the eve of the vote. "Imagine if she could see me now!" In endorsing him for the presidency, rival leftist Leonel Brizola, longtime governor of Rio, had exclaimed, "I want to see the Brazilian elite try to swallow this bearded little toad!"

Of course, little was reported of the elections in the United

States. On a day when headlines hailed a "return to democracy" in Romania and Bulgaria, the first democratic elections in our largest American neighbor for over a quarter century got reported in the back pages of international miscellany. While Poland's Lech Walesa was built up as a genuine rank-and-file hero, few North Americans have heard of the equally authentic and charismatic Lula. In the end, his Workers' Party captured every big city, except in rich São Paulo. During the campaign, Collor's motorcade was stoned in Rio. His victory margin of 35 to 31 million was attained only through the usual dirty methods: a mysterious voting day breakdown of public transportation in the poor sections of several major cities; an election-eve scandal in which a former girlfriend of Lula's was paid to reveal that he had once pressured her into an abortion. Blatant appeals were made to the black poor's traditional predilection to be protected by a benevolent "white prince." Playing upon the ignorance of the rural indigent, local pro-Collor officials spread rumors that Lula's "Communist program" included the compulsory confiscation of their land, their automobiles, and their wives! With the support of numerous intellectuals and musicians, Lula nearly pulled off the most stunning victory of progressive forces in Latin America since the ascendance of Fidel Castro.

In the first months of his administration, Collor took some bold, if symbolic, steps. He appointed a well-known ecologist as his minister of the interior and personally pushed the button to dynamite the illegal landing strips of miners interloping into designated Amazon Indian refuges. He also arrested numerous bureaucratic fat cats, known in Brazil as maharajahs. But his economic plan brought the economy to a standstill without addressing the underlying causes of Brazil's rampant inflation. Upon my arrival in Rio, I find the gossip mills running full steam with the scurrilous gossip Brazilians call *fofoca*: Collor is a closet transvestite; Collor plans to make himself king for life. These private rumors would surface in dramatic accusations by the president's own brother of corruption and cocaine use. Eventually, evidence of influence-peddling in the millions and personal extravagance with government funds would trigger an unprecedented nation-wide revulsion leading to Collor's impeachment. No wonder the beleaguered Collor resorted to an American-style government by "photo opportunity"—or, more accurately, government by T-shirt. The president's daily jog afforded him a great opportunity to emblazon good causes on his manly chest. Brazilian cartoonists had a ball caricaturing this perspiring patrician Marathon Man elegantly running in place.

I feel like I'm doing the same. Considering a change from my sterile Paissandu perch, I'm intrigued when a budding young singer offers me a chance to house-sit in a hillside apartment that I figure to be a true Carioca roost. In this vertical city, the lower-income residents claim the moral, as well as the actual, high ground. The seaviews improve with poverty. But my spirits crash when I get inside a third-floor barrack overlooking a slather of concrete sludge, which keeps this slope from sliding into the sea. Dishes have been stacked in the sink for months, the bare mattresses on the floor are motheaten and strewn with porn magazines featuring the exploits of hermaphrodites.

For the first of many times, I'm given vociferous apologies for the *bagunça*. In a country where drivers regularly toss their trash out of cars bearing "Save the Amazon" bumper stickers, this one term covers all variations of slobbery and disorganization. Sorry, someone usually gets around to saying, but I can't invite you home because of the *bagunça*. Sorry for being three hours late, but as you can see, my life is a *bagunça*. Once acknowledged, there is no need for any attempt at cleanup. The *bagunça* is the bane of Brazilian existence, what you get when you shove things aside and take shortcuts. But it is also a perverse source of pride: irrefutable proof that you are throwing yourself into life's disorderly mix.

One meeting with a musician leads me into a typical Brazilian mess. Paulinho da Viola, the sweetest and most cerebral of the *samba*'s conservators, has escaped to a suburban enclave in Barra da Tijuca. In a development guarded by high brick walls and armed security men, this fawnlike, insouciant son of an inner-city music teacher has constructed his oasis of gentility. But a single glimpse of the water-stained furniture, a flea market's worth of lamps, books, and memorabilia set on the front lawn, indicates something has gone terribly wrong. Brazil has even intruded upon this split-level retreat.

"The house was built over an underground spring. The roof was designed at the wrong angle for drainage. And all because the architect was our friend." He leads me on a tour of a household in tumult, sunken playrooms and dens filled with hastily packed boxes and antiques damaged by a basement flood. "This is the problem with my country. The poor in the *favelas*, they know how to make things work. You think their shacks are going to come down every time it rains, but they've learned to build what lasts." It's the first of many theories I'll hear about the trouble with Paradise. "It's our educated class that doesn't know anything. They're all decadent, thoughtless imitators."

Paulinho turns out to be far more than an untutored troubadour. He talks at length about new research which claims that the *fado*, the Portuguese national musical lament, actually began in Brazil and was brought to the mother country by sailors. He tries to describe how he once wrote a *samba* which attempted to incorporate dissonant elements he heard in Miles Davis's "Bitches' Brew." In his study, the shelves are bulging with the favorite reading matter of a Sorbonne radical: Althusser, Guevara, Isaac Deutscher's biography of Trotsky. At first chagrined that I've noticed these signs of a militant past, the *sambista* is soon showing me treasured artifacts of the militant peasant movements that offered hope for change in the early sixties. It's a shock to see photos of Brazilians bearing placards and banners, going into the streets for something other than drunken revelry. In this far-removed study, I begin to sense the collective trauma imposed by thirty years of military clampdown. After such an interruption, with a new generation suited for little but mindless consumerism, the country's political life has to begin from scratch.

All Paulinho da Viola can do is shake his head and continue the reconstruction of his extravagant refuge, his mini-Brasília. On the way out, I'm shown the worst tragedy caused by the flooding. Soaked through are thousands of rare albums, 78s, and early LPs, mostly North American, running the gamut from Johnny Dodds to Carmen Miranda, Django Reinhardt to Xavier Cugat, Louis Armstrong and Jimmy Lunceford to bandleader Severino Araujo, the Brazilian Glenn Miller. In the house's green inner courtyard, a team of housekeepers is laying them out, one by one—making the spoiled collectibles look like stepping stones to some other world. Paulinho da Viola is clearly heartbroken. All he has to repair the damage, all Brazil has, is the aid of a burning sun that bakes the covers crisp in no time. But the maids are giggling and tossing the shellacked 78s haphazardly to the ground. They've already broken vintage bits of brittle vinyl. They just don't know the value of what they're handling. This Brazilian dream house has awfully shaky foundations.

So why not hole up in mine, stay in my boxer shorts, and stage a countdown to evening? In Rio, I realize that I'm not cut out to be an expatriate. Suffering a crowded bus ride while scanning for pickpockets, I get the cultural version of an out-of-body experience. Call it an out-of-body-politic experience. It's hard enough to surmount the difficulties one is born into. I don't have the need to take on a whole new set. When Copacabana Beach becomes a site to visit only for the best rates of exchange, it doesn't matter if you can impress friends back home with postcards featuring rows of double-barreled beach beauties' buttocks—imprinted with those three little letters almost as spine-tingling as the three little words. RIO—WISH YOU WERE HERE! The trouble is that I wish I were here.

I've heard that the last bathers on Ipanema Beach are in the habit of giving the sunset a standing ovation. The applause is probably not so much a homage to the last exposition of color as it is an appreciative welcome for the balm and forgiveness to come. A farewell to the heat and frustration, the workaday world that doesn't work very well! Once the banks are closed, there can be no bank lines. Bring on the *conga* line! In the glare, you get too clear a glimpse of too much mess that only darkness can sweep away, too many places that the night's beneficent rhythms can't cleanse. Without its music, Rio is just another harried hellhole. Anytown, Third World.

Music to Read By

EU CANTO SAMBA—Paulinho da Viola (RCA)
SAUDADES DE GUANABARA—Beth Carvalho (Philips)
M—Marisa Monte (EMI)
PERSONALIDADE—Jorge Ben (Polygram)
OPERA DO MALANDRO—Chico Buarque (EMI)

TONIGHT WE'RE ALL EQUAL

A noite e uma criança," declare the Brazilians, explaining why nothing is more all-American in their America than the all-nighter. In this country of extremes, the night isn't just young, it's a child, an infant, a toddler. When it comes to the limitless possibilities of the dark, there's never a "last call." Night is a constant beginning.

Before long, the favorite stop on my daily rounds becomes the newsstands from whence I can plot my fresh start. My neighborhood's kiosks are clogged with magazines as slickly designed and printed as any in the world. In the area of the media, more than any other, Brazil lives up to the image of a country between First and Third Worlds. There is no starvation of information. So I can always consult one of Rio's daily papers for complete listings of concerts, ongoing shows, cabaret singers, *samba* rehearsals under the listing "Carnavalesco." I skip right past the sections filled with gory photos of gang-related murders out in the Fluminese, Rio's suburban, subhuman ring of terror. It's enough economic news for me to know that the newspaper costs more today than it did yesterday. The only schedule I need has to do with my plans for a musical night.

Tropical in feeling, Rio's dusks-to-dawns are positively arctic in span. Every sundown makes for an expandable folder in which to drop every sort of diversion or vice. Shall we dine at midnight, take in a concert, a party—and then? Sample a disco or *gafieira* dance hall? I've been told that the latter is a sedate sort of ballroom, transported to the big city by God-fearing folk. In Brazil, however, sedate is a relative term. From a loft bar of the downtown *gafieira* called Estudentina, I look down on a floor crammed with stylish aficionados of every dip and spin since the fox-trot. This might be a setting for one of those World War II flicks where homesick GIs look for trouble and assorted tropical *señoritas* before closing the place with a blood-stirring, steamy brawl. The house band wears Hawaiian shirts and does energetic *bolero* send-ups of "I Left My Heart in San Francisco" and "Chattanooga Choo-Choo." If only such innocently tinny sounds, such overflowing raucousness, still existed up north! The USA could use a couple hundred *gafieiras*, the way it could use a good ten-cent cigar. Left over from more genteel times is a huge placard enumerating interdictions against certain forms of dress, conduct, and alcohol. Hand-scripted at the very bottom is the only house maxim this current crowd lives by: "Where there is dancing, there is a hope."

In a city that flouts rules like no other, I find myself barred from my very first concert. So long as I'm in sandals, I can't get into the country's premiere pop showcase, Canecão. This cavernous dinner club, dwarfed by its own billboards and stuck ungraciously at the last speedway turn leading into the tunnel to Copacabana, still clings to airs of elegance. A hasty retreat to the nearby home of a sympathetic foreign correspondent lands me sneakers three sizes too small. We get back just in time for the performance of Elba Ramalho, a leggy film actress valiantly and forever staving off middle age. Perform she does, with three hours of nonstop crooning and prancing. Audiences here expect no less. The Brazilian "show"—they've adopted the Hollywood word—is highly ritualized and illustrates much about the social role of music in this society. No musician dares appear in public here without offering a highly choreographed showcase for his or her entire new album plus an assortment of trademark tunes. A full song list is provided so the audience can follow along as they would with a hymnal in church. Only this congregation already knows all the words and doesn't mind drowning out the pastor.

It could be any Brazilian up on stage leading the choir, anyone with sculptural bone structure and a suntan. The Brazilian crowd is a tribe, Brazilian society strikingly tribal, at once highly hierarchical and democratic. Everybody can take turns in the spotlight or on the throne, nobody is so regal that he or she has not been touched, kissed, and fondled by all the rest. "So-and-so is a lesbian, such-and-such has a gay lover," the most far-removed fans repeat with absolute confidence, in a country where the odds are that many will be bisexual. And Elba is a bit of an exhibitionist in a culture where you have to go a long way to exhibit much that hasn't already been seen. At one point, she does a quick change of see-through outfits without bothering to go offstage. In semidarkness, behind a half screen, she offers a prolonged view of her cellolike backside. Every musical idol, female or male, is expected to show the flesh. It's not some crude business of selling sex. It's more that they won't be accepted unless they reveal all. The connection between Brazilian musicians and their listeners is unflaggingly intimate.

Yet it is perfectly acceptable for Northeastern native Elba to interrupt the show with a political diatribe. While her rhythm section chugs lightly in the background, consciously breaking into a countrified oom-pah-pah lilt, she appeals for an end to the wanton exploitation of her fellow Nordestinos, driven from their barren fields by droughts and inequities of land distribution. This seems an odd setting for her to proselytize on behalf of the cause of complete secession for her home region. But Elba's separatist cries bring just as many cheers as her hip shaking. "Por quê paro? Paro por quê?" the inexhaustible crowd shouts for an encore, as they always do. Why are you stopping? You're stopping why? In this oral-based culture, musicians are expected to double as leaders, even prophets. Songs preserve the group memory, catalog the health of the community, point the way along the collective trail.

But why do Brazilians find that trail so much easier to see at night? It's hard enough for me to tell boy from girl, hooker from high-fashion model. On the Avenida Atlântica, that oceanside esplanade freak show, lost Andean bands toot their pan pipes, and the pros get so pushy they pin single men against walls to make a hard sell. Under floodlights, the beach is a crime-ridden no-man's-land. The glitter along the Copacabana strip is gone forever.

Until recently, American Express handbooks recommended a high-toned nightspot called the "Help!" Discotheque. As in "Help, I need somebody!" My first clue that something may be amiss is that nearly everybody else going inside is a miss. Their clothes are all skintight, slitted, and cleaved, but again, that's nothing unusual. They could be wholesome college girls, a tutti-frutti of Brazilian complexions, tanned and cheery—though it turns out they are here to work their way through school. Upstairs, this looks like one of too many such shrines to U.S. pop culture which I've visited throughout the world: the same synthesized pulse pounding, the same top ten screechy libidinal hits that I've heard in Saigon and Santo Domingo. Sometimes, to paraphrase Siggy Baby, a disco is just a disco. But this is Rio's largest and flashiest supermarket of flesh. There must be a thousand females to a hundred leering, bush-jacketed, foreign guys. The women here take their full evening's worth of generalized Brazilian friskiness before deciding who to bring home at what price. How I want to convince myself that one co-ed's leap into my lap is a sincere sample of the natives' vaunted sexual libertinism. She soon begins dropping hints about new shoes for her illegitimate baby, the new stockings she covets. I get out of her clutches by mumbling a word learned from the title of another Jobim tune. "Triste, triste!" Sad, sad. It's too sad to have to pay for the girl from Ipanema.

The most lurid sight of all turns out to be the images on a giant projection screen mounted as a backdrop to all the rotating mirrors and timed spotlights, behind the stage full of barefoot, volunteer go-go dancers. In place of the usual MTV loops, the metallica bands writhing in banks of fake fog, there are effects of smoke and fire unlike any dreamed up in Hollywood. The disco wants its patrons to be appraised of the latest developments on CNN, with running commentary in Portuguese. Not-so-innocent bystanders, these Brazilians go on dancing to the beat of a world in conflict: Serbs slaying Croats, Israelis chasing Palestinians, "Georgey Bushy," as he's pronounced, threatening Saddam Hussein. "Let Bush and Saddam arm-wrestle one-on-one in the desert!" was the solution to the Gulf War proposed by Rio's populist governor Leonel Brizola. "Give Bush half of Saddam's mustache!" a leading musician will tell me. For the Brazilians, the answer is always to mate with your opposite, to embrace the devil. In fact, the war prompts zillions to masquerade as the oil-toting, uppity Saddam during Carnival. In Rio, the disco beat pounds while the rockets explode. The machinery of destruction is perfectly in synch with the machinery of pleasure. The world's bloody mayhem makes the Brazilian version look pretty harmless.

Before my first trip, I heard the following boasts from expatriate Brazilian men: that they had slept with man, boy, and goat; that I would get a hard-on the moment I stepped onto Copacabana Beach and never lose it; that eager women were waiting on every park bench to be summoned into action; that a hundred rubbers weren't enough supplies for one Don Juan's month's vacation back home, a point he proved by bringing back a series of explicit Polaroids. Brazil's rate of AIDS infection, highest in the world outside the United States and portions of Africa, is spurred on by a tradition of promiscuity that dates back to slavery days. Codes of *machismo* dictate that Brazilian women are forced to "trust in God" rather than condoms—known by the descriptive term *camisinhas de Venus* (little shirts of Venus). They also allow men to deny their homosexual acts so long as they remain the aggressors. In Rio, whole blocks are lined with transsexual prostitutes, nearly nude in the tropical night, the better to show off all that black-market hormones have wrought. A confused clientele murders these creatures at such a rate that, in Carioca slang, they've become known as "Gillettes" because of the razor blades they conceal in their mouths for self-defense.

In terms of time invested and passion spent, Rio's number-one nocturnal preoccupation isn't sex but *samba*. That's most obvious at the *ensaios* (rehearsals) staged by Rio's *samba* schools on weekends in the months leading up to February's Carnival. Nobody knows exactly why the Carnival organizations that represent the neighborhoods of Rio during the annual pageant got named schools, in Portuguese, *escolas de samba*. It's said that the first such group, "Deixa Falar!"—the wanton "Let Them Talk!," soon to be followed by the equally playful "Come Moscas" ("Fly Eaters")—was founded in 1928 near an actual elementary school. It's also said that "pupil" was a slang term for the young volunteer dancers. A more likely explanation is that when the *samba* was evolving from the first jam sessions of master drummers, the people of the slums were heard to say, "That's where the professors are!" To enroll, all you needed was a spoon to bang against a frying pan.

Today, the *samba* schools are highly institutionalized—probably more visible and durable than the institutions of Rio's government. Since the twenties, these organizations have brought notoriety to the depressingly grimy areas of Rio's Zona Norte. All over Brazil, you can find loyalists who act like they've been raised in Mangueira or Vila Isabela when they've never even been to

Rio. Certainly, nothing is more serious in this town than the competition to win first place in creativity at the annual four-night Carnival parade of the twelve so-called grand schools— gargantuan, actually, each with up to three thousand dancers and five hundred drummers.

Each year, the schools' *sambas de enredo* (songs chosen to accompany a single "theme" illustrated through the floats and costumes) are released and evaluated by all Rio long before the big show. As a result, the schools function as song factories. At least two thousand new *sambas* are composed to vie for the honor of becoming the Carnival theme (with the winner determined less by originality than through connections and politics). The schools use their *ensaios* not so much to coordinate their parading as to keep their music on the neighborhood's lips, to raise money, and whip up "school spirit." These are mostly misnamed excuses for another party—where the proper attire ranges from tank tops to strapless gowns, suede go-go boots to rubber sandals with Day-Glo straps. A dozen or so drummers, just a sampling of each school's full compliment, is enough to energize the crowds that gather in *quadras* (grubby, open-air gyms lit with bare bulbs and serviced by numerous built-in bars). The only requirement for entry to this wildest of classrooms is, as it has always been, "Who can *samba*, stays. Who cannot, out!"

Still, I'm offered escort to a rehearsal of Salgueiro, one of Rio's oldest schools, by Reginaldo, a leading *puxador*—so named because the lead voices that rise over the drumming are said to "push" the Carnival parade along. I'm not surprised when this singer tells me that he's an admirer of the wide-bodied, deep-voiced American love-crooner Barry White. Reginaldo could be Barry's cousin. He is a huge presence, enlarged further by a white linen suit, complete with white vest and matching white fedora, who barely fits into his vintage Chevy Corvette. "It's the *samba* that's brought me all this!" he exclaims as we careen through abandoned side streets, running red lights all the way. "I never had to look it up in a dictionary. It's in the blood. Our music is the only way for our race to become known through the whole world. That's why, with each passing day, I try to hug the music closer!"

Asked to imagine Brazil without music, Reginaldo answers without missing a beat, "Can you imagine if I wasn't black and you weren't white?" It doesn't bother him that I have what he calls "the smell of dollars." He can't wait to show me the great Salgueiro's headquarters. "We have Germans and French dancing with us now, though we are trying to keep out the Japanese!" Outside the clubhouse that's painted a bright red, Salgueiro's team color, everyone recognizes the star singer and deferentially gives us space. "What a panorama!" he boasts about the gymnasium barely made festive with plastic flags strung all around.

It's a big night here because this year's costumes have just arrived. Being unloaded off the back end of trucks' trailers are hundreds of hoop dresses, thousands of colonial servants' outfits with sewn-on wings in the symbolic form of explorer ships' sails. In the old days, people sewed their own costumes. Now everyone contributes piecework and the costumes are assembled elsewhere. "Each costs up to three thousand dollars," says Reginaldo, "which is all the year's savings for someone from the slums." Their investment pays off by bringing to life a daydream appropriate to the ancestors of slaves, "Sou amigo do rei"—"I'm a friend of the king!"

At other rehearsals, a variety of sample *fantasias*—in a country where a costume is more than a fantasy and vice versa—are available for order, displayed on dummies or in photographs. For twenty thousand *cruzeiros*, plenty of bucks at any going rate, there's a hat that can put an entire Swiss chalet on your head. A more traditional choice is the human parrot, made from thousands of emerald feathers. Or there's the *guerreiro Americano* outfit: skintight camouflage pants sprayed high-tech silver, with grenades on each hip, a helmet studded with silver bullets big as phalli, a cape made of the U.S. and Soviet flags. This is all to match one school's theme of "The Final Judgment"—emphasized by a *samba* whose refrain suggests "It's a crazy world, nobody notices how near the end we are!" Carnival is Rio's big school play. Only here there are no tryouts. Everybody gets to dress up and take center stage.

Seated before a microphone at a fold-out table set at center court, Salgueiro's Caucasian president is giving a pep talk—from the tone of it, more like a coach's scolding harangue. Though he is wearing African beads, a tank top and a single hoop earring, his slicked-back hair reveals a face hardened on the streets. Beside him is a son whose pork-chop sideburns and black locks overflowing his collar make him look like some character straight out of Jersey City. Supposedly, he was arraigned, but acquitted, for the jealousy-driven murder of a well-known actress. When I ask Reginaldo for confirmation, this is one time he pretends not to hear me. He doesn't want to cross the school president, a gangster godfather whose syndicate makes most of its profits from the illegal gambling game *jogo do bicho.*

But even this new class of patrons—who back the schools as others of their ilk might invest in a racehorse—stand aside before the power of the music. All talk adjourned, the *porta-bandeiras,* a comely young couple sporting the school's flag, step forward to practice their sexy parody of a colonial minuet. Groups of Baianas, sprightly seniors in triple-thick glasses who will wear wide gowns of African origin, whirl and spin to their geriatric content. Then the festivities break down into a generalized *conga* line which gets into high gear only after three in the morning. This year's theme *samba* has been memorized in half an hour. Echoing in these concrete seat boxes, the drumming corps' layers of contrapuntal pounding are perfectly synchronized. Everybody in this place already has the *ginga* ("jing-a"), a ready control of the lightning-quick shuffling which constitutes the *samba*'s basic step, an ease of swaying the hips that can't be taught. Who needs a dress rehearsal mainly to undress?

If the rich have their swank clubs in Leblon, the poor know that they are having more fun and that their music is better. In

Brazil, the national anthem should be the bouncy Ivan Lins ditty entitled "Tonight We're All Equal." During the witching hours—when everyone is open for business, emotional or otherwise—the most stable currencies to hold are raw nerve and raw flesh. Whatever's on the agenda tomorrow can wait. Pleasure, humor, people, can't. No self-respecting Carioca wants to be caught getting into bed before the sun signals the reassertion of the reality principle. Must each of my overextended, overbefriended Rio evenings end with some overloaded made-in Brazil Volkswagen bug making dawn rounds down boulevards empty but for orange-suited street sweepers? Setting out on another wild night, a drunken cabby cusses out my interpreter for being a prostitute, then insists on getting out with us at São Cristovão, the weekend fair of Northeastern immigrants. The driver gives up the rest of his night's fares to dance with us under a tent to accordion music. No matter where I go, none of my owlish company wants to be the first to throw in the towel.

Late, late one evening I'm tipped off to an informal *reunião* of Rio composers unveiling new songs. I arrive just past three—it would have been rude to come earlier! When the party talk stops, a single guitar gets passed around and each guest in turn shows a more plaintive voice and a greater manual dexterity. For the first of many times, I become aware of what it means when everybody in sight has grown out his fingernails. Apparently, I've stumbled upon the dozen or so most committed and original young composers of MPB, which means any sort of serious exploration of post–*bossa nova* pop idioms. Cross-legged on the floor of a living room with sofas and bric-a-brac shoved against the wall, I get to hear some of the finest sounds of my entire journey. As with the cuisine and other aspects of a nation's culture, music is better when it's homemade.

Among those test-marketing new melodies into the dawn are many who've come through censorship, exile, and even imprisonment during the worst years of Brazilian military dictatorship. "We are of the generation," one tells me, "that has nothing but hope." The poignancy in their laments stems from more than broken hearts or the profound longing so perfectly expressed by the Portuguese language. "A dictatorship still exists in music," says my host, a struggling songwriter with plaintive eyes and a black beard named Moacyr Luz. "Do you know what it's like to make music where a child dies of hunger every five minutes? We don't want to make music for intellectuals to drink by. We're lucky if any of us have money for our next months' rent. Three months is our whole future. But music is what our hearts are asking for."

In other lands, these furrowed fellows and bejeweled earth mothers might be found in more academic settings. In fact, one character with ghostly eye sockets and unkempt beard straight out of a Dostoevski novel turns out to be Aldir Blanc, a lyricist renowned for numerous satiric hits as well as the fact that he was trained as a psychiatrist. He looks like he's living in a garret and tells me as much. "I made two hundred dollars," he complains, "off a song played on television two thousand times." Others in the reunion are former teachers, lawyers, historians. In Brazil, the call of music is too strong. And it's at night that the country of music comes into its own.

"This is the time when our native Indians would eat and throw a party. For the black slaves, too, the night was the only opportunity for them to play their music." It's at four in the morning, of course, that one unknown composer offers me the best excuse for his countrymen's widespread nocturnalism. "At night, everything is beautiful. All defects and inequalities are hidden. There's that mystery. Anything is possible at night. Everyone is capable of seducing everyone else."

Until daybreak, this cream of Carioca intellectuals allow themselves to be seduced by the guitar, sharing their promiscuous lover. From the hillsides beyond comes a percussive backup, the civic rhythm section of the *samba* rehearsals. What a siege of sound laid before power's citadel! The drums pound forth like sporadic artillery fire from various bivouacked armies. The com-

posers always have one more tune to try out. What's the hurry?
We have all night.

Music to Read By

A INCRIVEL BATERIA—Mestre Marcal (Polydor)
PERSONALIDADE—Elba Ramalho (Philips)
AO VIVO, 100A APRESENTACÃO—João Bosco (RCA)
LES GRANDS SUCÉS—Chico Buarque (Vogue)
JUNTOS—Ivan Lins (Philips)
FLOR DA PELE—Ney Matogrosso and Rafael Rebello (Som Livre)

BORN WITH SIX FINGERS

One man beating a stick against a shoe box or coaxing a clang out of two bottles kissing—out of such simple elements are born the great glories. *Samba* is purported to be a direct relative of the *semba*, an Angolan fertility rite which involves the violent bouncing together of belly buttons. Others suggest the derivation is *kusamba*, an Ngangela word meaning to skip, to gambol, to express uninhibited joy. In terms of musical genealogy, the *samba*'s obvious forebear was the *umbigada*, a ritual performed in a circle where each new dancer's turn was designated with a thrust of the hips. A more technical definition would be a binary, percussive rhythm in which the first beat is never sounded—causing a continual, hesitant urgency. That holds true, more or less, for the *samba pagode*, *samba raiado*, *samba de partido alto*, *samba do morro*, *samba de terreiro*, *samba cançao*, *samba enredo*, *samba choro*, *samba do breque*, *sambalero*, *sambalanço*, *sambão*, and *samba jazzificado*, which is hardly a *samba* at all. A less technical definition can be found in a traditional Carnival tune, "Who would *samba* deny, cannot be a nice guy. Either he's sick in the head or has feet full of lead!"

Like the Afro-American forms that so forcefully underpin North American culture, the beat which means Brazil to the world is relatively new. As with gospel or soul in North America, the *samba*'s roots are in the work songs of the plantation. Though banned by generals and priests, the *lundu* and the *maxixe*, lamenting yet raucous rhythms identified with the African slaves, found their way into civil society as elegant Brazilian-style tangos. The *samba* blossomed once blacks gained sophistication in the big cities. The word was probably first used at dance parties attended by freed slaves in Bahia during the 1870s. Supposedly, a Baiana named Tia Amelia brought the rhythm south to the slums of Rio, from which it was carried forth by such luminaries as her son Donga—composer of the first recorded *samba*, the 1916 "Pelo Telefone" ("On the Telephone"), a ditty about "The chief of police/Over the telephone/Sent word to me/That at the Carioca/There is a roulette game/Where everyone can play."

In the roaring twenties, Rio was to the *samba* what Chicago was to jazz. But the *samba*'s closest cousin is our urban blues. The *samba* is nothing less than Rio's oral history and ongoing rap, one big rolling tune to which new verses can be added forever. Only in Brazil the blues come out of such sadness that there is no room for it to sound sad at all. Compared to our my-man-done-me-wrongs, the language is more satiric and biting. In Brazil, we get less of the moan and howl. Instead, we get the *grito de carnaval*. The cry of release! But the emotion is always a pain that hurts good, the evocation of that indefinable longing inherited from the Portuguese through their favorite catchword, *saudade*. Call it homesickness, nostalgia for happier days, suffering over love lost and dreams squandered, and, ultimately, a confrontation with every man's inherent state of solitude.

"It is the feeling one has when one's true friend, the only one who ever understands us, has gone away and will never return," waxes Grande Othelo, a luminary nightclub artist from the glorious forties, adding, "*Saudade* has no translation." My translation for this most frequently used word in Brazilian music would be the blues.

Listen to eighty-eight-year-old Carlos Cachaça and you might just as well be hearing Blind Lemon Jefferson or Mississippi Fred McDowell. "Without *samba*, there's an emptiness that could never be filled. It's the pill for our sickness, a medicine for the heart. There is no substitute. Whether you're happy or sad, you remember a big passion and that makes you suffer. Instead of fighting in the streets, or hitting one another, we make a song. Take away the *samba* and we're nobody."

The question is whether Brazil has ever treated its *sambistas* like somebodies. The great musicians of Rio still get their recognition largely from Carnival tributes and the ghetto grapevine. One swank nightclub books the Velha Guardia da Portela—old-timers from the Portela *samba* school, Rio's first, who function much like New Orleans' Preservation Hall Jazz Band—only because they are fronted by white singer Christina Buarque, younger sister of pop star Chico. "You want to know the future of my country?" asks this youngest of the remarkable Buarque de Holanda clan, which has produced Brazil's leading historian as well as the author of Brazil's standard dictionary. "It's *merda*." The shits. "These people, the best of our past, are treated worse than your jazz greats. When I wanted to perform with them on TV Globo, do you know what the producers told me? 'We can't put these people on camera. These old blacks, they are too ugly.' "

Paralleling the treatment of North American jazz men, Brazil's national treasures are prophets unknown, exploited, often left for dead. "I could go downtown to collect my royalties from the record companies," jokes Cachaça, lifelong collaborator of the prolific Cartola and composer of over five hundred *sambas* himself. "But the check they would give me wouldn't cover my busfare." To support his music, he worked thirty-eight years for the railroad, starting out in the yards. Besides, he says, "My wife was a very strong woman, the kind all *sambistas* need!"

To find this legend, a tall man with scour-brush mustache and deceptively somber countenance, I had to stoop through an opening in the Casbah-like warren of permanent shacks that forms the slum of Mangueira (mango tree). Like every old-timer I call on, he would not be moved from his home turf by all the world's record contracts. "They say I'm like a *carapato* (a tick). I stay attached to the neighborhood. And why not? Even my six great-grandchildren are here, though some don't know me." At least, Cachaça's shanty boasts a small kitchen and a loft bedroom up a trap door. His many awards and plaques sit in cabinets that haven't been dusted for decades. He leans his elbow on an antique wooden dining table. He has put on his best white shirt for me. In fact, he's been waiting anxiously all morning for my arrival. The last fellow to pay any attention to him was a roving Japanese ethnomusicologist.

"It's no fun since I had to give up drinking three years ago," confesses the octogenarian. "Now I have to get my fun watching others drink." He had been named after Brazil's main liquor because "I was one of three Carloses who used to hang around the Praça Onze, singing and running errands. But I was the only one, at fourteen, who liked to have a *cachaça*." Soon enough, he was writing themes for Carnival. "The first Carnival I remember was perhaps 1912. The blocks fought with confetti and sometimes with our fists. They played what we called *marcha rancho*—only brass instruments. And we would stay in our costumes for up to three months! A Pierrot, that was popular, or if not, your wife's dress."

But fame within the *samba* schools did not win him respectability. "Once, I composed a waltz, just to prove to my brother that I was a *musico*. The *sambistas* didn't need theory. As they say, you don't need to go to a *samba* university. But we were more creative. Back then, the *samba* had at least ten basic rhythms. Not anymore. Many things have been lost in Rio. The clean air, the *verde!*" The greenery, he means. From this hillside far from the sea, I see only power stations, service roads, gray viaducts. That does mean all is misery in what one Cartola classic called, "the world of zinc roofs." Besides, as Cachaça's partner once sang, "*Samba* grows from a seedling that exists only in Mangueira." He would prefer that I stay here with him until dawn, or forever. "Here, we believe everything is *boa*, it's all good. Even when the government censored our songs, we said that even the *censura* is *boa*." In faint voice, Carlos Cachaça sings me a favorite among his compositions, which goes roughly, "Nobody is suffering. Nobody is sad because the dawn over the *morro* is very beautiful."

On a prime location at the top of the bluff is the home of Dona Zica, Cartola's widow, the fabled "godmother of all *samba* schools." This dignified matron with blue-rinsed hair shows me the small garden laid around her front steps which inspired Cartola's greatest ballad, "As Rosas Não Falam" ("The Roses Don't Talk"). "The only thing my husband did wrong in sixty years," she says with a wink, "was to die before me." Half of the merry widow's rooms are taken up with trophies and placards earned by her husband's music. The other half is stuffed with half-sewn, satiny costumes for the Mangueira school. "Everyone in Mangueira was once a slave in Minas Gerais and we all root for the Flamengo soccer team." Each statement is made with equal jollity. If there is some boundary here between magic and real life, I can't trace it. Dona Zica even has a parrot that sings the *samba*.

Like a life in the blues, the *samba* breeds a *samba* culture, *samba* talk, *samba* dress. So many *sambistas* are found at the Petiscos de Vila—an outdoor café within striking distance of a statue of Noel Rosa, the *samba*'s Cole Porter and favorite son of the Vila Isabel district—that this must be the only restaurant in the world which has posted the sign "Proibido Cantar e Batucar"! Forbidden to sing and drum—like all such admonitions in Brazil, this is just another rule to be broken. One midnight over beer and deep-fried cod cakes, I meet Wanderson, a white *cavaquinho* player in such demand that he happily strums until cramping for three or four schools and Paulão, a bearded, glowering bear of a guitarist with an advanced degree in sociology. "I don't know why I do this, the way musicians are treated," he says. "Sometimes, the producers and the nightclub managers offer me so little that I just have to tell them, 'Please do me a favor and lose my telephone number!' " They're all expecting Martinho da Vila, Rio's gravel-voiced dean of *sambistas*, who, like many singers, has taken the name of the school for which he first sang. They joke that he may have been delayed by an amorous encounter with a *pequena*, approximately "young chick."

I follow these professionals to a midnight recording session in the worst section of Lapa, a neighborhood on the fringe of downtown that, since the 1970s, has been living up to its guidebook description as "a den of pimps, thieves, and inverts." Our destination is up a freight elevator—which closes so fast that, warns Wanderson, "it cuts off your balls"—on the top floor of the only building on the block that isn't a quaint, grillwork-laden rattrap where the rooms rent by the hour. Didn't jazz also begin in a brothel?

Safely ensconced in their paneled, state-of-the-art hideaway— typifying Brazil's sophistication amid inequity—these musicians help churn out compact-disc versions of the "theme *sambas*" that will be sung in all the smaller cities of the South. Defying No Smoking signs, they fill the two glassed-in booths with the scent of tobacco. "There's not a law in this country worth the paper on which it's written," Paulão the sociologist points out. "Not even the constitution!" The musicians do their work with little strain. Tonight they are providing the backup for a singer who comes from Vitória, a large provincial town. "He took the only plane, the one that makes so many stops that the bus arrives first," the musicians tease this hick who goes by the professional handle of Edson Papo Furado. His last name is taken from a slang term that means claptrap, idle chatter, b.s. In his *samba* composition, however, he is the king of Brazil who declares, "In this land, under my reign, there is no racism, sickness, or sadness." Wanderson insists that they keep recording alternate tracks until "the sound makes the hair stand up on your arms."

To glorify and exploit the music made here, Rio constructed the Passarela do Samba, or so-called Sambódromo—an obligatory stop for sightseers and soundhearers alike. It took 120 days of labor and 7,000 cubic meters of concrete to construct this hallowed, half-mile-long parade ground, lined on both sides with raked, concrete viewing galleries—another stark example of misplaced modernism by Oscar Niemeyer, a populist disciple of Le Corbusier and architect of Brasília. Set in the shadow of an elevated freeway in a poor warehouse district, the Sambódromo's covered grandstands and luxury boxes look like two elongated motor homes. They double during the rest of the year as an elementary school. Crowned with a freestanding arch at the parade route's end, this sterile promenade was inaugurated in 1984. Nothing could be more Orwellian than placing the tumult and color of Rio's poor neighborhoods within the prison-yard confines of this fake stretch of Rio street life—made safe for tourists and high-rolling Brazilians. The Sambódromo turned Rio's greatest indigenous expression into a paid-admission spectator sport—a largely made-for-TV competition held over four consecutive nights. The few foreigners who pay exorbitant prices to attend the Carnival here usually can't sit through more than a few of the spectacularly indulgent marches of the three-to-four-thousand-strong schools. Having worked all year on floats and footwork, each of these battalions of frenzy makes the most of its ninety minutes to strut its stuff before the nation. In that space of time, its "theme *samba*" for the year is sung at least thirty times. By four in the morning, hundreds of taxis wait outside the gate, waiting to take maximum advantage of wilting tourists.

But a good *samba* can break out anywhere, always sweeter as a spontaneous act. So it is fitting that my best moments at the Sambódromo come when I'm passing by accident only to find thousands pressing their way through the fences that surround the compound. Following the crowds, I stumble upon an outdoor practice of Kizomba, a nationalist African *bloco* attracting a crush of thousands to a side basketball court for a powerful chant-and-response session straight out of Soweto. Perola Negra, the "Black Pearl" who is the hefty Mahalia Jackson of *samba*, raises a mellifluous chant for hours over a beat laid down by an all-star band of *pagodistas*. A second time, I really hit the jackpot, cakewalking my way right into a final, pre-Carnival rehearsal of the Imperatriz school. All that is missing are the costumes, but I get to flit between every *ala* (wing) of the parade, driven by unending rows of snare-pounders and tambourine-twirlers.

After ten minutes' marching at the Sambódromo, I'm not only covered with sweat but I've also learned the group's annual song, with its refrain about the "worlds of pleasure" contributed to Brazil by the African. How can I argue with that, especially on a hot night in Rio when a sudden shower serves only momentarily to bring down the temperatures of three thousand steaming bodies? Whole *samba* parades are constructed upon a tribute to an obscure, bygone composer, a forgotten slave revolt, the history of rice cultivation, the glory of the banana. The entire Carnival is a celebration of the cultural victory of black over white, African over European—and the ranks of the dancers, I notice, are filled not only with stray Swedish tourists but with lily-white Brazilian professionals. Up in the northern version of America, one of the most persistent forms of racism is the lack of a public means for admitting just how much black and white have influenced one another: how many whites find comfort in the songs of Billie Holiday, for instance, or how many blacks love Billy Graham and pizza. What happens in Brazil is the equivalent of millions of white Americans eating chitterlings or volunteering to join gospel choirs. In the USA, black rhythms have had to conquer the white soul sneakily, through Motown or dinner jazz or blue-eyed rock 'n' roll. Here, black hegemony is unquestioned and undisguised. *Samba* is king.

No wonder every *sambista* I meet opens another chapter of Rio's textbook in dignity under fire, optimism without foundation. Close to the Sambódromo, in a notorious housing project overlooking the cemetery of Catumbi, I find eighty-eight-year-old Moreira da Silva still dancing the dance in his pajamas. This lecherous master of *samba do breque*—a singing "broken" with improvised conversational byplay—has just taken a new wife. "An old goat needs fresh meat," he says of the overabundant lass who lies supine in the bedroom, reading a comic. She doesn't move an inch during our entire visit, even when her husband breaks into a performance of an old hit about a Rio pimp who wins the lottery and takes a trip to America. A more recent success, "Sou Candidato," tells of a maid who runs for office to clean up corruption. "The only time I had trouble with the censors," says da Silva, "is when I used the words *sarcafógos*"—a colorful term for testicles—"and *fogandu o gansu*"—drowning the duck. This also refers to intercourse. "We are all mere bipeds," is the motto of this dirty old man, "all endowed with the same desires!" Excusing himself to watch a favorite soap opera, he marvels, "These days, any *mulata* who shakes her ass gets a contract in Japan. But I can't blame them. What's wrong with that?"

What's wrong is that the *samba*'s very power to sell records and promote tourism is endangering its creative future. While some preservation-minded younger musicians have attempted to regain a bygone simplicity through the promotion of their *samba pagode*, purist Paulinho da Viola sums up the problem: "In the old days, there were five or six ways to build a *samba*. Now everyone is simply imitating what they've heard. No one has the time to create in a relaxed manner. It's the pressure of modern life. It doesn't matter if you call it *pagode* or whatever. There are only two kinds of *samba*, good and bad. And the *samba* today is like an orange that's been squeezed too hard. The juice has run out and we're left with the pulp in our hands."

Don't tell that to Neguinho da Beija-Flor, a representative of *samba* future. Part of the rising *pagode* movement, he is among the first dark-skinned blacks to have built a thriving recording career out of his role as lead singer with a *samba* school. In the same way that North American black pop stars have finally been able to reap the rewards of their music in recent years, so a new generation of Brazilian blacks is finding the *samba* one of the handier means of advancement—almost as good as becoming a pro soccer player. I find Neguinho in a luxury apartment over-looking Copacabana, far from the Nilópolis slum where he was brought up. Coming to the door clutching a portable phone, wrapped in a half-open bathrobe, this taut, athletic young man says of his new beachfront address, "If you get up in the middle of the night, you can't help being inspired by this view."

With the characteristic humility of a *sambista*, Neguinho insists, "Success is just an accident which chooses you. *Samba* changed a lot in the eighties. It got more respectable and more organized. The record company only took me as an experiment, but they have done well. When Beija-Flor was first champion of the Carnival, I wrote a song about *futebol* that became a big hit even though it was my most stupid." Neguinho claims that his music is most influenced by his having grown up "in the slums, close to a *terreiro* where I heard all the religious ceremonies. All my best songs have to do with kids on the street, bad distribution of money between people, too many poor and too few rich. Like the Rocinha slum, where forty thousand people live on a hillside right next to mansions. I wrote about how the army and the church should take responsibility for our homeless children. A censor in Brasília wouldn't let me record it. In Brazil, you think everything is all right, because you see everyone having a good time. On this beach, you see them playing *futebol* together, but one boy has nice clothes, clear skin and clean hair, the other one not."

Such conditions are what forced Neguinho to leave the place he grew up. "Unfortunately, I had to move here for protection. Once you make a little money, everyone needs some. All my childhood friends wanted me to build them houses. Some threatened to kidnap my children." Neguinho's bushy-haired son and daughter dance around his feet. Climbing up into his lap as he sits at a breakfast table overlooking the beach, they play with the gold chains hanging on his bare chest. "See my daughter here, she's already singing." In fact, she is banging a spoon against a cassette case. "Being a musician is like being born with six fingers. My father played the trumpet, and my son, I'm sure he'll have six fingers, too."

Sometimes, it seems like this whole country has six fingers. "Nothing catches the attention of the people like music," Neguinho concludes, looking wistfully at another day's frivolity starting up just below his condo. "I'm not worried about the future of the music. I am worried about the future of my country. I don't want to see all my earnings stolen from me by some president. I tell you, living in Brazil is like walking a tightrope." And does that threaten the *samba*? "No, *samba* is like a gift. It's like this doll here." To illustrate, Neguinho reaches into his daughter's lap and grabs her blond-haired, blue-eyed Barbie. "You can give it new clothes. You can wrap it in a newspaper, or in fancy paper and a ribbon. But it is still the *samba* and the *samba* doesn't like to leave Brazil."

I'm glad that this new generation is carrying on a reverence for Rio's fragile art form. We can hear it now—a solace, a challenge, a power—starting up on the sands below. The drums tremble, the two-toned *agogô* bells ring faint yet crystalline. "The *samba* is always in its death agony," says Neguinho, "yet the *samba* never dies."

Music to Read By

BRAZIL—ROOTS—SAMBA—Compilation (Rounder)
CANTA, CANTA, MINHA GENTE—Martinho da Vila (BMG)

O CANTA DE GUERREIRA—Clara Nunes (EMI)
PERSONALIDADE—Alcione (Philips)
O MELHOR DE SAMBA—Compilation (RCA)
GRANDES SAMBISTAS—Velha Guardia da Portela (Ethnic)
O SAMBA—Compilation (Luaka Bop/Warner Bros.)
POETAS DE CALÇADA—Neguinho da Beija-Flor (Columbia)

GOD IS BRAZILIAN

In the days leading up to the New Year, strange sights are popping up all over Laranjeiras. In no discernible pattern, at selected corners of my resolutely staid Rio neighborhood, various household items have been left on or around the sidewalk. On closer inspection, these offerings look to have been carefully collected and aligned: unlit cigars crisscrossed atop matchbooks forming a circle; stubs of burning candles dotted between fans of assorted poultry feathers; bottle caps, open tins of aromatic oils, hearts of palm, crumpled cigarette packs, cosmetics, lottery tickets (presumably losers). So miniaturized is the scale of these anointed trash heaps that I nearly squash one or two before I realize that these are the gutter altars of *umbanda*—a bastardized mix of the basic elements of the African *candomblé* rites with a generalized pop animism. Every lovingly arranged curbside shrine attests to a flea market theology.

These are the first harbingers of Rio's Reveillon, as December 31 is called. The date has become linked with the worship of Yêmanjá, the Yoruba goddess of the sea. To bring good luck along with the change of calendar, untold *terreiros* (congregations) head for Copacabana. They dance and chant before the waves, then launch small boats laden with offerings. On my year's last morning jog around the underpopulated curve of

Botafogo beach, I run straight into a half dozen or so devotees, not just dressed in white but white-skinned as well, led by a bony, cigar-toking bead-laden black *mãe de santos* (sainted mother). She supervises her flock in christening—so to speak—one such tiny ship with chants and a generalized spewing of liquid from Coke bottles. No Diet Coke for the goddess. The few sunbathers out this early in the day line up to get their futures told, or better yet, work themselves into a trance. From suntan oil to holy water, it's astounding how quickly these bystanders make the transition from flesh to spirit worlds.

Brazilians, so the Brazilians will tell you, believe in everything: not just Catholicism and *candomblé* or the much-cataloged blending of the two. There's also a strong following for astrology, numerology, Hare Krishna, a spot of Islam, Rosicrucianism, Masonry, Mormonism, not to mention various occult rites involving mind-altering Amazonian herbs and plants. There's even a popular cult centered around one academic Freudian psychologist's faith in the curative powers of *tesão*, intense sexual attraction. From charms and superstition and phases of the moon to almost anything in a pamphlet or newspaper column, the unlucky throngs are susceptible to everything aimed at keeping calamities at bay. When all else fails, there's even the opportunity to put one's stock in the apocalypse—and the prophecies of Nostradamus are particularly popular among a populace that expresses relief at the prospect of the world's demise. It sounds downright comforting when phrased as *O fim do mundo*. Though numerous religions are constantly springing up and dying out, Brazilians don't necessarily do their spiritual business in an organized way that can be exploited by TV evangelists. Brazilians are more like congregations of one.

Take the university-educated member of the instrumental group Uakti who digresses to tell me how the hills of his native Minas Gerais are the world's leading landing pad for UFOs. Why, he and the band have spoken to spacemen supplied by mountain villagers! In the town of Arembepe, during the sixties a jet-set hangout graced by Mick Jagger and others, the fishermen painted their doors with representations of Martians who touched down to fuel up from a local sulfur plant (which has since polluted the beaches). According to this musician, the extraterrestrials always land in the triangle between Minas and Bahia, which he claimed as the earth's leading spot in terms of vibrational density. And take the tale, told with complete sincerity by a former Marxist revolutionary, about a vindictive raid by Bahian police on a *candomblé* house which resulted in such a curse being laid on the cops that they were seen a day later outside their headquarters dressed entirely in women's clothing. The gendarmes supposedly had no recollection of what had transpired during the interim. The anecdotes are endless, the genie is always just about to leap out of the bottle. Scratch a Brazilian and you find a mystic.

Prefeito Fortuna is Rio's hippest of the hip, a veteran actor in guerrilla theater and a new-age entrepreneur. One of his pet projects is an attempt to train homeless children to become circus performers. Another is the Circo Voador, a permanent outdoor tent which is the city's premier space for alternative music and theater. Catching up with him at a concert as he rushes about to embrace his thousand closest admirers, this ebullient imp doesn't want to talk avant-garde art or protest politics. With a Moonie's light in his eyes, Fortuna begins proselytizing for the cause that is his current salvation, the growing hallucinatory sect known as Santo Daime. Fortuna invites me to the next Sunday meeting, held in a sparse yet elegant outdoor tabernacle on a plot in the densely wooded Tijuca Forest. The setting makes me feel I'm deep in the rain forest, but the worshipers look as though they're straight out of a Baptist prayer meeting on the Kansas plains. Santo Daime is just such a combination. The cultists are dressed entirely in white, wear biblical sandals, and speak in a holy hush. The long central table that forms a nave is laden with a magnificent array of tropical flowers. Men and women must sit on separate sides of the open-air church. Strict group conformity—

like an interdiction against crossing one's legs—is enforced by male congregationalists with felt sheriff's stars sewn on their shirts. This is a surprisingly puritan religion for Brazil, but there is a Brazilian twist. As Fortuna tells me, this is an "Amazonian" Christianity.

Daime means "give me," and in this case, what the followers want to be given is a drug made from some obscure jungle plant. Flanked by Jesus and the Virgin Mary hanging from the tabernacle beams, there's a portrait of the cult's late founder, a bearded Gurdjieff-like priest who supposedly made contact in the forest with an Indian shaman. This Indian initiated the padre in his chemical means of finding God. At the ceremony I witness, there is no drug taking. Newcomers must get through the dogma before being invited back to taste the sacrament and go off on ten-hour trips. I hear a droning sermon about nature and peace, followed by a guitar-strumming hootenanny.

What's most striking is that none of these zealous converts has a darkly shaded face. Santo Daime is a primarily middle-class response to a black animism, a homegrown hippie affair doing battle with Africa in the war of the occult. Perhaps that explains why the ceremonial music here is so mundane. Hand-held shakers and cymbals accompany the chorus, but the melodies are as endless as Irish jigs. There is no kick to this pious dirge. I feel I've taken a drug myself, one that makes the world go in slow motion. Yet, when I depart, I get heartfelt hugs and deep gazes full of Christian love. Taking her place with the womenfolk in the opposite pews, my Brazilian translator has a grand time humming along with her eyes shut. Do these people carry a permanent hymnal in their heads, useful for any occasion, applicable to any deity?

To find true faith these days, you have to go a bit further than New Year's on Copacabana. Of course, I don't learn this until the famed celebrations are over. Isn't travel always like that? You go ten thousand miles only to find that what you're looking for has moved ten miles farther: over to the "red beach" on Urca, up the road a patch, past the reach of guidebooks. The Reveillon begins with the scattering of office calendars on the streets of *centro*. Time turns to confetti, and by nightfall a million souls have gathered on the sands of the big beach. Waterfalls of fireworks cascade off the facades of the big hotels. But the *candomblé* sects grow fewer each year, wisely retreating from the mob. The circles of touched priestesses in their white kerchiefs and men in droopy sailors' pants are far outnumbered by rowdy teens and tour packages.

Believe it or not, I can't even scratch up a good party on New Year's in Rio. Such an achievement has to be more than a matter of mere luck: It takes real planning, a special antisocial technique. The three last-second invitations I score lead me to drawing rooms where the haute bourgeoisie nibble canapes and occasionally acknowledge the coarse rabble beneath their balconies. One hostess proudly shows me a gilt-framed photo of one of Brazil's recent military dictators exhibiting his equestrian prowess by jumping his horse over a crouched subordinate. At the last place I knock, a man comes to the door in his pajamas. By 2 A.M., this party is over—since it was thrown by expats, not Brazilians.

My evening is saved only by some garrulous Spaniards who invite me to their table at a sidewalk café. Among their group is a rather haughty, fortyish woman who turns out to be one of Brazil's leading concert pianists and avant-garde composers. Music, music everywhere—and always more than a drop to drink. She invites us to her fin-de-siècle mansion back in Botafogo, an inheritance to which she's added a magnificent studio. I spend the first moments of the New Year, and well past dawn into the next day, listening in a hungover stupor to her tapes of verbatim jungle droning spliced together with computer-driven pings, squeaks, and wheezes. This is my big splurge of classical music, which in Brazil is known as *música erudite*. This composer's atonality is a bit erudite for me, but at least it invokes a sort of dull hypnosis. Call it electronic voodoo.

You have to get up early in the morning to find something as trance inducing. I have to get up at 4 A.M. to be exact, for a rendezvous with a wild-eyed, mangy-haired filmmaker who has been documenting a single manifestation of Afro-Brazilian religion for over two years. Tourist touts in Rio and Bahia will always take you to a staged ceremony where some cigar-toking witch pours chicken blood over fit-throwing initiates. *Candomblé* is not hocus-pocus but a sober, lifelong vigilance. Sometimes called *macumba*, sometimes appropriated as *umbanda*, Brazil's variant on Cuba's *santería* and Haiti's *voudon*, this custom of Nigeria's Yoruba tribe centers on the conjuring and placating of a host of protective spirits called *orixás*. Every believer performs specific rituals, wears certain colored bracelets and beads, prepares certain foods, and, of course, drums specific beats and sings specific chants to get in touch with gods as individualized in their habits and as fickle in their attentions as mere humans. Oxalá, Oxum, and Yêmanjá are really pesky forces of nature. These mother-fuckers do not sermonize or patronize or agonize. They don't strike holy poses. They ride lightning bolts.

Those who would keep such gods content must turn to the continual guidance provided by membership in a house, not a church, under the watchful eye of the flock patriarch (*pai de santos*) and/or matriarch (*mãe de santos*). The filmmaker guides me to such a house, some fifty miles north, by racing the dawn on the empty freeway through the Fluminese, the Bay of Guanabara's swampy ring of shame. In Brazil, the suburbs do not connote status; the farther one gets from the coastal beaches, the poorer. But just before we arrive at this sect's headquarters in the town of Nova Iguaçu, the devotees head off to the sea. I hoped to watch them observe the Catholic saint's day of Saint Sebastian by paying homage to his African equivalent, Oxum. Five minutes sooner and we would have caught them. When it comes to the otherworldly, Brazilians are faultlessly on time.

No matter, there will be no shortage of ceremonies later in the day. And I lose all track of day or night once I've passed through protective portals made of concrete blocks, past a front yard where fresh lilies have been placed before holy urns, then into a cleared, furnitureless space of yellow linoleum. Guarding this ceremonial living room is the embodiment of this house's reigning god, a life-size porcelain statue of a balding white Lazarus, his skin covered in sores beneath a tiger hide worn Tarzan-style over one shoulder. Before this curious figure is a doggy bowl heaped with freshly made popcorn. Enough to satisfy a whole matinee. In this religion, every divinity is associated with a specific form of fiber. The question for *candomblé* is: has your god had his Wheaties?

Supervised by Dona Neuza, a surprisingly young *mãe de santos* who carries herself with an elder's severity, a team of respectful teenage girls is busy in the kitchen preparing beans and rice. The KP crew has been working all night. During important periods in the calendar, followers sometimes forgo sleep for up to three days. When they can take it no longer, they sneak up onto the roof, where bedrolls have been laid out underneath the clotheslines continually sagging under a full load of drying white linens, dresses, sashes. What a visual delight, what sanctified laundry! This place truly functions as a communal household. Given the length of the proceedings, I wonder just how much the members can give to their other families. What a difference between the well-swept orderliness of this place and the rutted, mud streets of Nova Iguaçu! The average income in this sprawling settlement is less than 180 dollars a year.

By ten in the morning, just when I'm beginning to nod off, the congregation returns from the beach. Once more, I'm astounded by how integrated this Afro religion really is. Over half the *candomblé* faithful are young and white. The fairest among them look a bit ridiculous to me in their West African garb, all-white tunics and floppy pants, a burden of trade beads ringing their necks. But all of them are eager to give testimony to the positive effects of this practice on their lives. To a man and woman, and several men who are openly and obviously gay, they want me to know how much more luckless and useless their lives would be without the guidance of their chosen god. "Look at me," one Bahian devotee told a Brazilian sociologist, "I'm a black woman who can't read or write. But I'm living with a man from the Faculdade de Medicina. See what Oxalá did for me!"

I hope the celebrants will proceed immediately to the platform where three big tom-toms await a good pounding. As I'll discover over the next twelve or so hours, *candomblé* doesn't hold scheduled masses. The moment must be right for contacting the spirits. Sometimes the start of the rituals is triggered by one member's sudden distress. A fitfulness and moaning must be worked through, expunged with chants. Everyone has to have plenty of time to repair costumes, nibble, and gossip. Yielding to the diurnal by heading upstairs for a nap, I return to find that the interpreter I've brought along has had her face painted in white clay pawprints across her cheeks and forehead like some virgin about to be sacrificed. She tells me that the *pai de santos* had thrown the *buzios* (seashells) to foresee her future—and warned her of traveling on airplanes. She looks stunned and softened for conversion. In less than an hour, I've nearly lost my translator.

After an hour or two more in this house, all boundaries begin dissolving. I don't know if it's mere grogginess, but I lose track of the difference between a rite and a chore, the everyday and the extraordinary. The *pai de santos*, our father who art on earth, will explain everything. I trust this man at once because there is nothing holy about his bearing. He's a handsome, very dark man in his mid-thirties with a sturdy gait and a certain lassitude about the way he taps a feathery talisman against his hip. After observing with caustic gaze the proper return of oils and candles to his private sanctuary, he takes his customary place in a sort of director's chair *cum* throne beside the tom-toms. He reminds me at once of certain Buddhist holy men in the Orient. There are no tricks up his sleeve, no hocus-pocus to his manner. He speaks in a calm, even voice. He has a most perfect posture, less erect than forthright, at ease with himself. This *pai* occupies his space on the planet with great compact force.

Actually, Reuben de Oliveira reminds me in looks and concentration of another African-American wizard, baseball's Henry Aaron. Does he also share Hammerin' Hank's sure sense of timing? Suffering my simpleminded questions, de Oliveira explains that his duties often do boil down to sensing the right moment to begin an intervention. Learning specific liturgy is the easy part. A *pai de santos* must be a kind of vibrational tuning fork for the congregation. Aside from being a counselor, consoler, psychiatrist, and fortune-teller for two dozen or so wayward souls, he has to know which *orixás* may be working spells or casting down plagues, and which *trabalhão* (big work) should be done to bring down divine intervention.

I see this when a set of shakes descends from nowhere to send a young girl sobbing onto her knees in the center of the vast floor. Talk about group therapy! This group encircles, surrounds, strokes, and cajoles the sufferer out of her blues. A nod of the head from the *pai de santos*, a whip of his talisman, changes the pace of the three drummers' attack or summons a particular elder among the women to calm and stroke the kneeling girl. Reuben de Oliveira choreographs the dance like an intuitive Balanchine. Eventually, the result is transcendence, the appearance of a holy spirit inside one or another believer, signaled by strange coyote whoops or howls, a shaking of the extremities, and finally a collapse into full muscle spasm. The drums beat on, the ladies keep dipping and bowing in their flowered kerchiefs, their bare feet hardly visible beneath their long hems. The trance is nothing frightening, just good medicine. "In the whole world," goes one *candomblé* chant, "nothing is hidden from the Great One!" The human mind is simply working out its kinks.

In a break between exorcisms, Reuben de Oliveira appears relieved to talk about the days when he was just another Rio street scalawag who sat in cafés all day composing *sambas*. It's hard to believe, considering his earnest concentration on his flock, but this *pai de santos* once had aspirations to be a full-time *sambista*. He even goes to his office to fetch the typed lyrics of several original compositions. Scratch a priest and find a musician. But everything about this religion has to do with music. Each *orixá* is associated with a specific tempo meant to set the devotees off on their strutting at a particular pace. Some gods are *allegro*, some *andante*. Every *samba*, even the most sexy and banal, has as its subtext the call to one or another god. That's the great secret of all Brazilian popular music, which today's musicians are no more eager to give away than were the slaves who covered their African deities with images of Saint Jerome and Saint Bartholomew. As much a part of one vast canticle as Gregorian chants or Handel's *Messiah*, Brazilian music is sacred music.

What else did I expect in a nation susceptible to all creeds? In Brazil, the spirituality, like the sexuality, is polymorphous. I've got to get my interpreter out of this den before she becomes another of Oxalá's handmaidens. And the congregation has been urging us to set out before nightfall. It's just now, exposed on a bleak street corner while waiting for an infrequent bus back to Rio, that I'm told Nova Iguaçu is known as "the murder capital of Brazil." Suddenly, I'm wishing that bus would come faster.

The next afternoon, the city of São Sebastião de Rio de Janeiro stages its official homage to its patron saint. Saint Sebastian, assaulted and wounded all over by arrows, has been taken up by the Catholic Church as its poster boy in a campaign against urban violence. Amid the processional which winds along a bayside park in the neighborhood of Gloria, signs preach brotherly understanding. The only glory here belongs to the underdogs, the sufferers, the perpetually pierced. The mostly older women and their dutiful, dressed-up granddaughters are led by a shriveled bishop, barely strong enough to carry the weight of his preposterously huge red miter. These must be Brazil's true martyrs: the ones who never miss a day in church or at work. These are the saints who accept all, take it all, without making noise or kicking up their heels. So much for Catholicism, as religions go. Give me the boogying messengers of fate and the forest! Give me the drums any day. Not only do they parade without music, but these devotees of Saint Sebastian are without a doubt the unhappiest bunch I see in Brazil.

Music to Read By

AFRO-BRAZILIAN RELIGIOUS SONGS—Assorted (Lyrichord)

CHILDREN OF ORPHEUS

There's got to be more to Brazilian music than *samba*, far more to Brazil than the quarantined rich and the hyperactive remainder. About to end my sojourn in Rio, I've yet to find much resemblance between today's monster home to seven million survivalists and that bucolic roost depicted in the movie *Black Orpheus*. When that film was made in the fifties, the population was ten times less, the surrounding sea and sky quantifiably bluer. Especially in Technicolor! Not only did that ancient myth transposed to Brazil feed my imagination about a land where the poor always get the best views, but the soundtrack's main theme song, "Manhã de Carnaval," taught me my first Portuguese word. *Manha* was so succinct and poetic a way to say "Morning"! I could hardly know that, at the time of its release, this celluloid vision of Rio was attacked in the city it depicted as more colonial mythologizing of the "happy natives." After all, the director was a Frenchman named Marcel Camus. Worse still, the story line was Greek!

In *Black Orpheus*, Brazil's children were shown to be barefoot Apollos of the slums. Each morning, they made the sun rise from the sea with strums on their guitars. Today, such kids would be likely to end up as *meninos da rua* (boys and girls of the street).

"The homeless children of Brazil with their tits growing, their dicks growing," one Caetano Veloso song bluntly puts it. According to alarmist estimates, there may now be between eight and fifteen million outcast minors—up to 10 percent of all Brazilians. As many as two million roam the streets of Rio. A 1988 study showed that 54 percent of Brazil's children and adolescents were being raised by families earning less than $35 a year. Forty million out of Brazil's fifty-eight million kids grow up in poverty. Abandoned or forced to hustle by desperate parents, these children start out wiping windshields and shining shoes but end up as gang members, thieves, drug peddlers, and prostitutes, landing eventually in overcrowded orphanages and prisons.

Long before they are found shot, burned, or castrated in back alleys, children are the primary victims of Brazil's disarray. Three hundred fifty thousand die each year before age five. Diarrhea is the prime cause of death among those under two. Only 13 percent ever finish primary school—and many have no schools to attend. Many boys contract AIDS—68 percent of Rio's male prostitutes are infected. Teenage girls die from abortions induced by a method known as "the heavy one"—a good kick to the stomach, a habitual sport practiced by Brazilian police. Most of the street kids spend their days in glue-sniffing stupors. "I sniff glue so I won't feel anything when I'm beaten," one *menino da rua* told a Brazilian sociologist, "I dream all day of a school where I can learn reading and writing and the *capoeira* dance."

Though children are not always the perpetrators, they are the easiest to blame for Brazil's growing criminality. The 1989 Justice Department statistics show that a murder takes place every hour in Rio, along with sixty-one robberies. There are eight pickpocket thefts a minute—and these are merely the ones reported! Given a government that lines its own pockets while ignoring education and welfare programs, someone has to take care of this growing menace. Death squads, often recruited from the ranks of policemen already used to preying on children, began by avenging individual crimes. In neighborhoods unseen by foreigners they go on random murder sprees, wiping out as many as a dozen children at a time with machine guns.

"When you kill a *pivetezinho*," one prominent businessman was quoted as saying about these underage pests, "you are making a benefit for society." Such is the burgeoning ideology which inspires the so-called *justiceiros*. Sporting nicknames like "Lefty," some have become folk heroes who openly boast of killings the way they might speak of a deer hunt. One renowned *justiceiro*, who said he could not become a doctor because he "hated the sight of blood," was known to have committed at least seventy-two executions. The "final solution" is another Brazilian-style shortcut. A note placed atop one nine-year-old boy strangled on Copacabana Beach read, "I killed you because you had no future."

Where vigilantism has blossomed into a kind of euthanasia, 4,611 kids were murdered in Brazil between 1988 and 1990—according to one Federal University of Rio study. "Don't kill our kids!" is the slogan spray-painted on many walls in poor neighborhoods. However, some of the *samba* schools, functioning as unofficial welfare agencies in the slums of Rio, have begun to use their resources to combat this problem. Call it a sequined "safety net." A real school, the kind with teachers and books, has been started by Beija-Flor, a group named for the hummingbird and based in the working-class suburb of Nilópolis. Beija-Flor is the newest, most socially conscious and innovative of the *grande* or elite schools. That's largely because of their artistic director, Joãozinho Trinta. Among contemporary *carnavalescos*, he alone has achieved a notoriety surpassing his organization. Since taking charge in 1974, Trinta has won two championships by consciously reinvigorating the dissident tradition of the Carnival. One year, Beija-Flor caused a scandal by parading in beggars' rags. The reference here to *The Threepenny Opera*, with its conscious theatricalization of poverty, is more than coincidental. Viewing Carnival as a means to make the masses analyze while they shimmy, Trinta is the most Brechtian of Rio's playwrights of play.

In the frantic weeks leading up to Carnival, it's not easy to track down this mobile dramatist, this on-the-go designer of stage sets on wheels. Beija-Flor's main office in Nilópolis is a day's drive south and, judging from the other rehearsal headquarters I've seen, probably not listed in the local Yellow Pages under "Schools, Samba." Fortunately, I've run into an aspiring actress from Recife who earns her rent money pasting sequins on costumes at Beija-Flor's Rio workshop. I get a busy signal dozens of times before deciding to just get Brazilian and head down there without an appointment.

The production center for Carnival floats and props is only a few blocks from the parade grounds of the Sambódromo. Rio's official launching pad for gaiety is set in a grim neighborhood of body shops, bare-bones corner taverns, and public housing with windows barred by wrought-iron. Even when I've eliminated every other number on the block, I'm still not certain what lies behind the high wooden fence painted in diagonal stripes with the Brazilian national colors—ocean blue, jungle green, and sunburn yellow. There is no sign to indicate that this is the secret lab where Beija-Flor is hatching its latest experiment in extravagantly pushing the limits of popular consciousness.

Then I notice the wire outlines of a thirty-foot-high swan, partially filled in with papier-mâché, is craning its long neck over the fence. When I knock, a cutout opens in the gay striping, just big enough to show a professionally skeptical face. Security around each year's Carnival innovations is understandably tight. Any unusually breathtaking design, any new wrinkle on how to get a dozen or so gargantuan tableaux down the parade route, is guarded from the competition just like a new toothpaste formula or an industrial secret. But Brazilian tight is still pretty leaky. The mention of my friend's name wins me a clip-on day pass. To get to the enclosed office at one end of the work space, I have to navigate around the big swan, a fifty-foot-long platform bearing a half-finished house of mirrors, a cubistic pyramid of a cutout cardboard *favela*. Now I find out why the phone is always busy. Beija-Flor's one harried secretary is doing publicity, ordering food, tracking down errant workers or the exact point between here and Nilópolis where the press might find the peripatetic Senhor Trinta. A TV reporter and two documentary filmmakers, elbows on a mahogany conference table, have been waiting for interviews all morning. All I can do is join the seated *fila*, that bit of Brazilian vocabulary connoting a line which extends for insufferable lengths.

While waiting for this tropical Santa, I am offered a full tour of the elves' workshop. Or are these Brazil's cathedral makers, and Joãozinho the supervising Brunelleschi? I can't conceive of how everything I'm viewing is related to this year's topic, "Alice in Brazilian Wonderland." Under peaked metal roofs as high as those in any shipyard, in a heat unrivaled by the worst Victorian stoker's hole, the employees are constructing an annual *Titanic* that is launched but once before its sinking. Nobody seems to be in charge of the cutting rooms for costumes and float draping. Teams of young recruits, mostly boys in shorts, walk barefoot amid a minefield of stitchings and splinters and shavings. There are a few Singer sewing machines plied by long-suffering seamstresses, but most everything else is done by hand. This includes the task of manufacturing thousands of individualized mirrors, measured with square forms and cut with X-Acto knives, then applied to any surface that requires flash. Papier-mâché is being mixed in huge witches' vats. The smell of adhesive is uncut, close to combustion in the heat. This job is a glue-sniffers' heaven. To meet each year's deadline, everybody will work round-the-clock shifts from now until the very moment before the parade sets out.

I'm feeling groggy with fumes by the time Joãozinho Trinta flies past the *fila* and into a locked conference room, a stocky whirl of energy barking out instructions to an escort of assistants. Trinta is a tidy, nut-brown man with wavy hair in long gray locks, an Indian face as wide as a squashed breadfruit. He wears a floppy shirt in a loud pattern of brown coconuts and tan palm trees. His manner is theatrical, Wildeian. He is partway toward being what the Brazilians call, in affection and disdain, a *bicha loca*, crazy creature in the feminine. But there is nothing dizzy about Trinta, the chief executive officer of an enterprise as complex and crucial as any in Brazilian society. When he finally has time to pull up a chair beside me, he is all business.

But how does one become a great *carnavalesco?* Not from getting a graduate degree at the *Faculdade* of Fun, a Ph.D. in whoopee-making. "I have always been a person with a vision for the spectacular," he explains. "I came to Rio from my home state of Maranhão in 1951. I was going to study classical dance. Instead, I became involved with theater. I began designing and mounting productions at the opera. And slowly, I was drawn to the greatest spectacle of all. I came to realize that the *samba* school parade is an opera of the street. Each year, the show involves a libretto (the theme, or *enredo*), scene design, music, choreography, an orchestra (*bateria*), a corps de ballet (*passistas*), a chorus, principal characters (*estaques*), and so on. It is the greatest gift for me to try and create this audiovisual pageant out of the dynamism that is Brazil!"

As a *carnavalesco*, Trinta is one of a handful of creators handed the gift of near total freedom from censorship or persecution. Ranging from attacks on government corruption to glorification of slave uprisings to a recent crop of ecological alerts centered on the Amazon rainforest, the yearly topics of Rio's *samba* schools have remained immune to interference even through repressive times. "The themes have changed in recent years. There are a good deal less historical themes, or at least, they are treated in a more contemporary way—as when I told the story of the French invasion of Maranhão from the point of view of an eighty-year-old. Everything is done in a more surreal way, with an extensive use of folklore and legends. And I opened the way to use more of the ordinary references out of daily life like *futebol* or the *jogo de bicho*. I've got enough Carnival themes until past the year two thousand. Now everything is possible because we aren't afraid to see as children."

It's becoming clear why Trinta has become the first director of frivolity to take action on behalf of homeless kids. "I chose to work with Lewis Carroll's *Alice in Wonderland* because this is the first story in world literature that takes children seriously. And we must do that here, where children are being murdered on the streets. *Alice* represents a break with Victorianism, as does our culture. Also, it's nonsensical, illogical—so it wasn't very difficult to create a Brazilian version."

Looking around the vast warehouse, it certainly doesn't look easy. With Trinta's help, I can more or less follow the logical progression of the floats. That one over there, with the gigantic mushrooms, must be for the tea party. Now I get the satire of a hillside covered with *favela* shacks, each cramped household built with a huge television screen inside, the Brazilian equivalent of a "welfare Cadillac." The immense cornucopia in reverse, creating the optical illusion of an endless downward slope into which politicians and dancing girls alike are tumbling, must be the maelstrom into which Alice has fallen.

"Alice represents the collective conscience of Brazil. She lies down in the grass, a little sleepy like our whole country. Then she meets the rabbit. He's late, which makes him a very Brazilian rabbit. She falls into an abyss without traditions or culture. Politicians show her many doors, but none of them lead anywhere. There's no way out for Brazil, except through the very small door out to the garden. That's nature, our abundance. When Alice drinks, she gets smaller. That's like our underdevelopment. When she eats the pudding, our *pudim de leite*"—*flan* custard— "she becomes a giant, out of control! Like our vast resources! She cries and forms a lake, drowning in her own tears as we do with the laments of Carnival. Sitting under the mushroom, she's like our children on drugs, asking, 'Who am I?' She's lost her identity. She sees the people sipping at the tea party while others are starving. The elite munching on biscuits made from children. Then there's the house of cards, like our economy. And we end with the caterpillar who becomes a butterfly—well, you know what country that is."

Trinta smiles contentedly at the tidiness of his metaphors. "During Carnival, everyone is looking for these subtexts. It has nothing to do with the erotic. It's a time when the people on the bottom of society can show everyone that they really know what's happening. If I don't have the liberty to do exactly what I want, I wouldn't do this. The truth protects me, I have no fear. Sometimes, I have problems with complaints from the Church—like when I dressed Christ as a beggar. But we do have more freedom in Carnival because the Carnival is powerful."

With the added power of television, Rio's big-money *samba* schools—divided into first and second divisions, again just like sports clubs—become rolling editorial cartoons, satiric sketches on a stupendous scale, acts of guerrilla theater given the widest possible stage. This year, one of Trinta's competitors has chosen to illustrate the theme "Brasil e Brega"—roughly translated as "Brazil Is Kitsch." Their song lyrics complain about how the real money of the country is the dollar and how even Rio's gangsters speak English. Dancing hot dogs, surfers, and stereotyped send-ups of Carmen Miranda drive home the point. The Carnival show is a sacred ground upon which the country can purify itself. As Joãozinho says, "Art transmits things on an unconscious level, offers a truth with a powerful energy. A person with no stories to tell is an unhappy person."

But he is just warming up, waxing into the ozone. "We're better organized than the government. As you can see, we get everything done. And what's the power behind us? It is the power of joy. There are three great power sources in the world: electricity, from the industrial revolution; atomic power, from the nuclear revolution; and *alegria*, from the internal revolution! The last one—this joy—gives the *samba* school its life and its sense of responsibility. There's a lesson in each part of the parade. The

Baianas, they teach us to respect age: They can still dance, they're still alive. You know the Caetano song where he says that 'the only people who don't follow the beat of the *trios elétricos* have already died'? The beat of the *surdo*, the big bass drum, is the beat of the heart. These vibrations, these rhythms, are the blood of our ancestors, the form of our soul!"

I have a feeling that we're about to get into the nitty-gritty, the central cabala of Brazil's unfounded optimism. "In nine years, Brazil will have the consciousness of a new civilization. That's because three and seven are great numbers. My name is Trinta, which means thirty." And what about his first name, "Little John," as in Robin Hood's merry band?

"In the countries of the North, of the cold and the industrial revolution, you have a saying which sums up your civilization, your view of life. You say, 'Time is money.' But in the South, in the heart of every Latin, there's another phrase which defines everything. It began, I believe, as a *Carioca* phrase. And it sums up all that we are, our great Brazilian civilization." Now I'm hoping for the key that unlocks the puzzle. "You know what it is? Tudo bom? Tudo bom? . . ." He whispers this like a Tibetan *mantra*, though all he's repeating is the most common form of polite greeting, the Brazilian hello in the form of the question, "Is everything good?" He answers himself, "Everything good. We can say that with so many inflections, in so many ways that the *gringos* could never do! We can be sarcastic. But at the base of it, we do believe that everything *is* good. Everything about life turns out to be good, in some way or another."

No wonder Joãozinho has chosen to spend his time in this dream factory. "This is why the next great civilization will emerge, like a serpent, from the Amazon. Look at the geography. You see, Brazil is shaped like a big heart." In case we can't visualize, he draws a Valentine on the back of the number-filled napkin. "Brazil provides the heart for the world. But what happens when you turn a heart upside down? It becomes a big *bunda*." The ass again. We can't seem to get away from the rear perspective. "And at the bottom of the *bunda*, there is always lots of shit. There is plenty of filth for us to clean up!" But Joãozinho isn't laughing. "You've heard the saying that we're not a serious country? Well, I thank God that we're not. That while serious countries prepare for war, we prepare for *samba*. We organize for joy, we work hard for happiness. In the North, you have to fight battles so your pilots will have nice toys. Video games. I hear now that you are all searching for the child within—because you've killed it. But for us, we honor that child. That child always remains alive!"

The claim doesn't quite square with the current rate of killing specific, individual children. Have some Brazilians kept their infancy going to the point that they can't handle a little responsible, adult suppression of their destructive urges? Joãozinho Trinta has made Beija-Flor take responsibility by sponsoring the first *samba* school composed solely of homeless children. He calls it Flor da Manhã—that word from *Black Orpheus!*—the Morning Flower. "Everyone likes to dance, and getting these children to dance together teaches them to be less egoistic. In our hometown of Nilópolis, we are already running a school and orphanage for four hundred pupils and we will be expanding. In the future, we hope to work with drug addicts. We've established a shelter in central Rio and tomorrow we're having a rehearsal there. If you are leaving, postpone your flight! You must come to visit our Flor da Manhã. See how Brazil is turning from the caterpillar into the butterfly!"

I can hardly resist such an invitation—and make this my last stop on the way to the airport. Off a bare, oval *praça* in a section of central Rio bordering on the northern docks, I enter a half-block warehouse big enough to house an entire slum. Some export company has donated this great space, long as two football fields. Not much has as yet been put to use. A shelter has been made from the former bookkeeping office at the far back of the steel balcony which rings the concrete yard. Cots are crammed in barely a foot apart, laid with coarse army blankets. There is space for fifty kids, at most, but I only run into a few, playing a rough game of tag under the rafters.

Even had I not encountered them here, I would know them instantly as street children. What is the telltale tip-off that a human being has lost their center of gravity? Or been mauled and mangled into something at once less and more than what most of us are? The boys are dressed up in ill-matched hand-me-down shorts, sneakers, threadbare sport shirts. Some wear large crosses that flop on bony, prepubescent chests. Others have just been given fresh haircuts. But there's something about them that cannot be shampooed away, showered off, dressed up. It's a certain look in the eyes which they share with their older, hobo counterparts. You have to look a second time to see it sometimes, the way the age of a dog is not always apparent until you examine the eyes. Something in there has been beaten back, misdirected. The light from within has been tamped down.

The boys can always punch and bluster and bully their way past the awkward stages of development. For the girls, today's double exposure—not just to life on the street but to an inspection by reporters and do-gooders—is excruciating. They try to stay in a circle among themselves. A few have shot up with hormones, their gangling stork legs outgrowing cutoff jeans. A few need do no work to live up to the term "angelic." Around their foreheads, most have wrapped small pieces of white sheet, sprayed in glitter, Flor da Manhã. This is their only attempt at a uniform costume, but it makes the girls look like precocious 1920s flappers. What I don't get is how these residents, who get little more at this point than a bed, found their way here. When I ask a supervisor from Beija-Flor, he explains, "The children's word of mouth is faster than our post office. And they don't need stamps."

Dwarfed by all the exposed metal, a single bulletin board offers an organizational chart of the parade they are planning. Just like the big *samba* school, the children will dance in various *alas*. Inspired by the children themselves, the sections are a compendium of hustles, a microcosm of life on the street. They will dress up as *engraxantes* (shoeshine boys), *amendoins* (vendors of almonds), *baleiros* (candy sellers), *flanelinhas* (street-corner car washers), even officers of the PM (*police militar*), not to mention *gravidas* (pregnant girls). This may be another of Trinta's dialectical conceits: the children must build their fantasies from realism, their reality out of fantasy. Before they can strut as princes and princesses, Orpheus and Eurydice, they must act the larger-than-life role of themselves.

By this time, *paparazzi* and television crews are swarming into every corner of the warehouse. Even some officers of the Rio police have dropped by for the sake of good PR. But the show begins only with the arrival of Joãozinho Trinta and his entourage. He pats the children on the head, questions a few about their progress, seems genuinely to recognize some of his charges. But his attention this day is clearly directed toward the hovering press. He poses like a peacock for the flashbulbs, holds an impromptu press conference. Asked how we bleeding hearts can best toss some charitable donations his way, Trinta replies, Schweitzer-like, "Don't think in terms of your money. If you want, go out and buy us a piece of fabric. Choose something beautiful for a single costume." Like a proud parent, he beams from afar when the kids take up their workstations. The boys hammer together mock shoeshine boxes. The girls pose at sewing machines for the costumes. When pressed, they readily admit that no one has taught them as yet how to use the machines.

As with so much of the effort to remedy Brazil's social hemorrhaging, this one is pathetically underscaled. Eventually, the kids are grouped in a line and make a short show of a parade. The boys drum fiercely, the girls *samba*. A few are spectacularly good, most are a trifle offbeat and listless. Unlike in the movies, these urchins don't have natural rhythm. They can't just pick up guitars and start strumming. With much coaxing and the best intentions of all involved, they manage to get in a dancing mood for a conspicuously short time. They take their place in the tropical paradise for ten minutes or so. Life is not a French film and the children of Orpheus don't all grow up to sing like Luiz Bonfá.

"What a beautiful morning!" the old sound-track theme song had gone. "The morning of Carnival!" For the Morning Flower school, a new day is not a given. Though there's plenty of beating, a hyperventilated pounding of valves, I leave Rio still waiting for a clear cardiogram of Brazil's big heart.

Music to Read By

BLACK ORPHEUS SOUND TRACK—Luiz Bonfá (Verve)
BRAZIL: SONGS OF PROTEST—Zelia Barbosa (Monitor)

THE SAMBA OF EXTERNAL DEBT

Do you know the man who gives the best rate? Are you the man who gets the best rate? Can you find your way to a friendly neighborhood money changer, fate saver, last-resort redeemer? Don't you depend on dancing to the tune of a cambista *whose daily quotations sing sweeter than any* sambista? *Or don't you rate?*

Are you on a first-name basis with this fellow who follows your ups and downs through the national ups and downs printed in the newspaper? It's always front-page news in Brazil, these fluctuations in the dolar turismo, *the* dolar paralelo. *But parallel to what, if not graph charts where the indicators are forever plunging like necklines? And if there are two currencies for all to see, must there not also be two economies, two governments-in-hiding? Where to go when the situation is so bleak that the black market is outmoded? Where everyone trades in moral gray margins? What happens when a whole country is so hooked on changing and changing back that nothing ever changes?*

Are you aware that this inflação *is one great roller-coaster ride? Do you suffer steamy afternoons on the local bus crowded with pickpockets merely to save a few* cruzados? *Carrying only as little as you must of the dwindling greenback reserves which you've stashed under your sofa? Do you trudge weekly or biweekly through the door of the travel agencies, full of pretty posters, where nobody purchases tickets to anywhere anymore? Head up the back stairs protected by layers of plate glass and secretaries with knowing nods and buzzers hidden under their desks who let you into a second lobby, this one always crowded, where business* is brisk? What do the citizens start to feel about a city when every storefront is a front?

And how is it that the man inside always has piles of cash when everyone else is running low? Bills fresh from the mint when the banks are all out? Or that a Brink's truck brother-in-law is forever on his way over with reserves safety-pinned in his inside jacket pocket? And how does your man know the rates for traveler's checks drop in that hour after the banks close? Why does he cash your checks when no one else will? And what exactly does he make on the deal? After all the formalities, the friendly inquiries about the health of your family, is he merely the lesser evil beside back-alley sleight-of-hand artists? Are you aware that people with a license to steal rarely bother with the outdoors, rickety buses, and heat? That their vaults are always air-conditioned and they are always very cool?

Don't you wonder why you are one of those scribbling your life away, writing drafts instead of manifestos? Do you figure, like everyone else, that you are holding onto the value of your savings a little longer by using a check for everything from a pair of sandals to a piece of candy? Or do you do it merely because you can't figure out how much cash to carry when the outlay today may not have anything to do with the prices yesterday? When what you earned last month isn't worth spending this week? Or is it that your checks are more easily replaced if robbed, nabbed, temporarily borrowed? Can you imagine how it feels to be the citizen of nation where the president's picture on a piece of paper inspires less confidence than a Don Juan's whispers? What happened to the panoply of scholars and poets portrayed on bills that nobody would bother to counterfeit? Have you noticed that the latest thousand note is graced by the Yanomami Indians? Is it another denomination on the way to extinction? Can you hold Brazil to the light and see the genuine watermark?

Though you're no economist, don't you know full well that the cause of this monetary jungle fever can't be got at with half remedies, aspirin, and cold compresses? You weren't one of those from the grand families who scored some spare change from the World Bank for the huge dams, the road clearings through the jungle wilderness, the clear-cutting of plantations, the Paulista industrial parks? Were you? You didn't know that you would be the one to have to pay it back? Did you? Neither could you be one of the international funders with funds to spare at usurious rates, throwing good money after bad, earning interest until Armageddon.

Don't we all know, in Brazil, there is always a jeito? A way around all obstacles, a means to detour the ruling exigencies? Unbalance any budget? Unwrinkle those pressing demands? Part the clouds in that ever-threatening tropical sky? Feel your way toward the path of least resistance like you're feeling the curve of warm hips? But don't you wish, just sometimes, that there was no parallel paper in your nation without parallel? That your real money wasn't the dollar? That you weren't carrying the burden of external debt along with your shopping bags as you head home down the crowded Avenida Rio Branco? At least, the debt is invisible, which makes it safer to carry than a camera or even a money belt.

Do you fear the man behind all those locks will one day lock you out? That he may inform you that the price has dropped so low that you can no longer climb under? What happens when the currency loses currency? When even black is not black enough? Will you rate? Calculate? Don't you wish you didn't need the friendly cambista? That you didn't have to learn the moves to this tawdry tango, shuffle along to this money-changing samba? Are you among the quick handed who profit from the daily back and forth, this spare change sparse change no change on-the-margins shicky-boom-boom changing that makes for another seductive and distinctively Brazilian rhythm? Are you the man? Do you need the man?

▲▲▲
South

*The style of the Brazilian people
is antithetical to authoritarianism
and all forms of repression.*

—Vinícius de Morães

〰〰〰〰〰

MINING THE GOLD

"I have crossed a thousand bridges in my search for something real," sings Milton Nascimento, the leading troubadour of Minas Gerais—a vast inland province far more musical than its "General Mines." I have just crossed an aerial bridge, as Brazilians term their shuttle flights, in my search for the genuine sources of the so-called Minas sound.

Landing in the state capital of Belo Horizonte, it's immediately clear why Brazil's third-largest city has been blessed with so evocative a name. "Bay-lo-ree-zon-chee," as it's pronounced, is Portuguese for Big Sky Country. The airport is plunked down in the midst of a vast, undulating plateau full of heavings and fissures. In every direction, the view is at once barren and boundless. A calm cloudless expanse lies like a compressing weight upon one compacted, mineral lode. The dank hills are green in spots, but uncluttered by anarchic jungle. No palms, no slums; as far as I can see, no people. The horizon is indeed beautiful—and never mind what's at closer range.

Is this "breast of iron," as regional poets have dubbed it, really in the same country, on the same planet, as Rio? It's not beaches or boom-booms that count in Minas, but quick fortunes culled from the obliging Serra do Espinhaço. During the first half of the 1700s, more gold was unearthed here than in all previous or future prospecting in the New World. Repeat: more gold than the Incas possessed or California's rush was to yield. Few in the grimy midlands of England or Germany have heard of this place, yet the wealth produced in Minas is said to have powered the earliest stages of Europe's industrial revolution. The discovery of diamonds in 1728 further fueled the migration of engineers, middlemen, and slaves to this most isolated and independent of Brazil's regions. With the twentieth century, the yield turned to the more utilitarian iron, manganese, and bauxite. Even today, the crafty Mineiros (as Minas natives are called) wouldn't be caught dead peddling trade beads or dope but pull from their back pockets precious gems wrapped in tissue. The gift shops are crammed with karat scales and packed-to-go sparkly geode clumps, big as sofas. If there ever was an Eldorado, Minas Gerais is it.

Belo Horizonte, Belo for short, is one huge asphalt X marking the spot of buried treasure. In its architecture, its conservative mores, and its music, Minas bears a most un-Brazilian affinity to the rest of insular, Catholic Latin America. But there's not a glimmering of old Europe in Brazil's first planned city. Having increased in population thirtyfold since 1945, this thoroughly American town is meant not for strolling but for cruising in pickup trucks—which Brazilians effect at vicious speeds. Severely straight boulevards vector over miles of ridges and humps that one imagines to be mounds of mining effluent. Grimy shopping strips are sealed off from one another by ridges and crests. Only the crush of holiday shoppers animates *centro*'s wide boulevards. Vast suburban sections of plush condos sit beside artificial lakes, all flood-lit plastic ferns and flagstone retaining walls, more bank-vault quiet than anything I'd ever thought to see in Brazil. Everything looks new yet already in need of redoing.

Minas is hardly the haunt of hollow-eyed miners, a West

Virginia in the tropics. The more analogous spot is Texas. My first night explorations confirm the redneck saying, "There are only two kinds of music: country and western." In one dark, circular dance pit, I get a taste of *sertaneja*, the rural balladeering so close in its woof and wail to the Grand Ol' Opry. In Brazil, such stylings are performed by beefy, pompadour-coiffed *duplas* (duos of male singers). Invariably, these groups try to be marquee-catching with alliterative names like Mathias e Mato Grosso or the ever-popular Chitãozinho e Xororó. Just like their Nashville counterparts, the two crooning hulks I see in Minas wear tight jeans and embroidered cowboy shirts, but their sound is more plodding and electrified.

At the Cuia e Mala, a steakhouse named after the drinking gourd and leather pouch carried by Brazilian cowpokes, the band strums acoustic guitars. A well-heeled crowd gets back to their farmhand roots with whoops and hollers befitting the wildest hootenanny. Like the Confederacy, too, the only black in sight wears the wide skirt and kerchief of the faithful plantation hand. She is tending to a mesquite fire under the Texas-size cauldron of beans. Dressed in denim coveralls and stetson hats, the singing waiters are eternally cheerful folk who make a show of transporting hot plates from the grill like a fire brigade passing pails of water. The people, music, scene, and food—down to the sun-dried meats and jars of pickled mangoes—are what's known as *caipiras*. Meaning cowboy, it could just as well be Brazilian for "good ol' boy."

Judging from the number of *churrascarias*, or Texas-style barbecues, which dot the swank Savassi section, there's enough fat in this land for a ton of guitar pickers to live off. At the Cevejeria Brasil, a corner tavern with exposed brick walls, I ask one of the waiters to point me toward the nearest musical crowd. Before identifying a gaggle of off-duty troubadours, the waiter does better, inviting me to a practice of his own *samba* band. In what other country could it be so easy to be an amateur musicologist or a groupie or both? That stocky fellow who looks like a São Paulo lawyer in freshly ironed rugby shirt and aviator glasses turns out to be Fernando Brant, lyricist and collaborator on many of Milton Nascimento's formative anthems. The region's noted ethnographer and composer, Tavinho Moura, can be found over the exposed kitchen's charcoal pit, supervising a side of lamb. This is like driving into Austin and sauntering up to Willie Nelson and Waylon Jennings.

That waifish longhair at the head of the table happens to be Beto Guedes, a falsetto-voiced idol who helped launch the soaring "Minas sound" back in the seventies. Like many a honky-tonk type, he appears to have been crying over too many beers. Beto's head jerks with involuntary twitches, shaking blond locks in greasy clumps that look like they haven't been shampooed in months. An attempt to speak English sets him off on a drunken lesson in comparative measurement. Hunched over a napkin, he scrawls, "One meter, yes? How many foots in the meter? How much inches in one kilometer? A mile a smile, but how many smiles?"

Nobody really wants to expound on musical theory. "Mineiros have a saying that being excited is not the same as doing something," Fernando Brant explains. This emphasis on deeds over words explains why Minas has produced most of Brazil's leaders—beginning with the fiery Mineiro dentist known as Tiradentes, the "Teeth-Puller," who inspired the first armed rebellion against Portugal (which happened in 1789, the same year as the drafting of the U.S. Constitution). In recent years, Juscelino Kubitschek, mayor of Belo and builder of Brasília, and Minas governor Tancredo Neves, who died on the verge of completing Brazil's recent return to democracy, exemplify a tradition of mixing populism with pragmatism. "What matters in politics is not the facts but the versions," states one Mineiro homily. It's not part of the local disposition to make a big fuss or put on showbiz airs.

As an initiation, the musicians offer me a treat that's not on the café menu. Out of a paper bag, I am handed a fuzzy brown object that's a cross between a kiwi and an Idaho spud. It's called a *pequi*, and from what I am told, this is what the early settlers survived on before the mines delivered. "That taste of the *pequi* is the story of Minas," one musician declares. "This fruit is for us what the apple is for the Beatles," another jokes. "If we can try hamburgers," urges a third, "you can get used to the *pequi*." I do my best, taking polite pecks that leave teeth marks in a bright orange core with the sour taste of Chinese salted plums, the texture of a steamed rutabaga, and the scent of something left for months on the bottom of the vegetable bin.

When Tavinho Moura realizes this is my first foray into Mineiro culture, he invites me to return in late March for an ethnographic fishing expedition along the remote São Francisco River. "If you come back when the waters have calmed, I'll take you to a valley that produces the finest *violeiros* [guitarists] in Brazil. That's where they're inspired by the sound of the *urucuia*, a bird whose song can only be heard once you've made a pact with the devil." Is it as an antidote to the temptations of quick wealth that this region should produce a protest music known for its religious overtones, chorale arrangements, and allegorical bent? "All music is regional, even that of the Ipanema crowd," Moura continues. "The problem today is that this country lacks a project, a sense of purpose. In the early sixties, we had the hope that was born through the creation of Brasília. And that gave us the *bossa nova*. Today, there's no new direction, no new music, only imitation. Brazilian music, indigenous Brazilian music, is going the way of the jaguar."

Out in the lush musical wilderness, however, the weapons of destruction aren't bulldozers or brushfires. They're the synthesizer and the electric bass. I discover this when the musicians gravitate to an outdoor patio, behind a corner cantina run by Paulinho Horta, older brother of jazzified guitarist Toninho Horta. At the usual 2 A.M. starting time, an exceptionally pimply band keeps the neighborhood awake with a grating display of heavy metal and searing fusion. They successfully drown out the natural rhythm of succulent mangoes plopping off the surrounding trees. Rock 'n' roll may be an escape from provincialism, but it clashes badly with Belo's star-chocked calm.

Yet a stellar beacon in world music emanates from the dank concrete basement of a posh Belo dinner house. Around the corner from the Cervejeria Brasil is the rehearsal space of Uakti, an experimental quartet known for creating its own instruments from any material in sight. Made up of graduates from Belo Horizonte's classical symphony as well as the short-lived music school founded by Milton Nascimento and Mineiro keyboard man Wagner Tiso, Uakti is the brainchild of an inventor named Marcos Antonio. He's teaching at the university today, but we get a tour from Andres, a blissed-out assistant in cosmological research with a ponytail down to his waist.

The place looks like the laboratory of some mad scientist, except here the test tubes are replaced with experimental sound machines. Andres shows us the fastidious work table where Marcos bolts and screws together his creations—every vise and wrench is well known to Andres, since this shop doubles as his crash pad. A collection of native drums, bells, and bows from all over the planet is piled up in each corner. And then there are the one-of-a-kind Rube Goldbergs on which Uakti taps, pounds, plucks, and toots: marimbas made of plastic tubing, gongs made from gourds and kitchen pots, scrapers reminiscent of washboards, flutes made of bottles and blowguns.

In music, as well as all the arts in Brazil, there is an unquestioned assumption that being "avant-garde" means moving back in the direction of the primitive. Europe or the States are places to imitate, but the Amazon is the place to initiate. While Uakti's name comes from some tribal rite, the primitivity of Andres comes from high intellectual purpose. He admits that he's never even been to the rain forest. "Only in my dreams, only through music . . ." he muses, his eyes glazed over. Andres is eager to play me the track of Paul Simon's Brazilian album on which Uakti provided a sparkly, tribal patter pounded out on xylophones made from flexible plastic piping. "Don't you feel Paul Simon was just collecting you?" I can't help asking. Andres' answer is to ask, "Don't tell me you never hummed a Paul Simon tune? 'Sounds of Silence'? 'Bridge over Troubled Waters'?"

I'm shown up by that innocent receptivity which may yet prove Brazil's downfall. For Andres and his cohorts, music is music. They don't distinguish between commercial and noncommercial. They don't invent or respect categories. They respond. Tapping on a Hindu clay pot, Andres tries to illustrate the difference between various regional sounds. "In Rio, the heart beats in two-two time," he says. "You've got the men pounding on the *surdo*. That's two meters of Africa going boom-boom, boom-boom! In Minas, our *samba* has more swing, it's lighter." The more Andres gets analytical, the more he wants to undercut his analysis with a stoned giggle. The truth that animates Uakti is that anything can be an instrument. Every event produces its own rhythm. In Rio, I even met another wizard of the synthesizer who has constructed a keyboard on which every note corresponds to a sound in the Brazilian environment. Hit a note and you get a parrot cawing. Hit another and you get the sound of a soccer announcer screaming, "Goal!"

I'm reminded of my visit with Hermeto Paschoal, the prodigious innovator of Brazilian jazz fusion. Along with the accordionist Sivuca, he is also Brazil's most famous albino. From his God-given looks, the man could find reasons for unhappiness. Hermeto is obese, cross-eyed, and accentuates his attributes with an unkempt Santa Claus beard and frizzy white hair that lies on his head like a mass of packing excelsior. Yet from the moment I enter his home in a Rio suburb, I feel that I've never met anyone happier. The reason for that is congenital, too. From his beginnings in a small village in the dirt-poor province of Alagoas, Hermeto was a musical prodigy who went about "listening to the roosters, the pigs"—whose porcine noises he has used on LPs—as well as "the waves and the wind in the jungle." Though the saxophone is his primary instrument, Hermeto considers all objects in the universe to be potentially melodious. Expressing an attitude which could only evolve in Brazil, he once told an interviewer, "I can play on anything. If you like, I'll even play you!"

In an attic transformed into a studio by a ceiling lined with sound-deadening palm leaves, I spend an afternoon listening to Hermeto's band. Just back from a European tour, they rehearse complex modernist compositions. Chomping on a black cheroot while he toodles on a synthesizer, Hermeto keeps searching for some new notes. Disappearing downstairs, he returns with a standing wooden coat hanger. In a moment, he's torn each carved arm from its socket. The sound he's needed can only be made by scraping together these drawn-and-quartered parts. When his devoted wife comes upstairs looking for her coat hanger, the band cracks up. They've seen this moment reenacted many times. Hermeto's wife doesn't have to wait for her answer before realizing that another piece of furniture has gone musical.

The name Uakti itself derives from an Amazonian legend about a warrior whose arrow wounds made music as he ran through the woods. "There's music in the forest, among the birds, at the ocean," says Andres of Uakti, reinforcing the connection to Brazil's generous *natureza* stressed by Hermeto, Jobim, and so many others. "You just have to listen and then play back what you hear. Because nature is always singing. Nature invades the soul of every Brazilian and then we just sing it out."

The inherent nature of Minas Gerais sings strongest through Milton Nascimento, whose rough-edged yet honeyed melodies have for two decades cascaded over Brazilian consciousness. An acronym of his two names spells out "Minas," and he has declared in one song, "I am golden, I am you, I am of the world, I am Minas Gerais." Milton was an orphan born in the Rio slums, adopted by a middle-class couple in the Minas trading outpost of Tres Pontas (Three Bridges). No wonder bridges figure so heavily in Milton's mythology—or that his music spans so much of the Brazilian experience. What's most Brazilian about

Milton is his eclecticism—he has been creating "world beat" since before there was such a label. Navajo chants, the forthright *nueva trova* of Mercedes Sosa, the work songs of Mineiro miners, the Catholic mass, Lennon and McCartney (to whom he paid tribute in one early hit), even Jimi Hendrix echo in the poly-rhythmic swirl of a single Milton tune. Spinning impressionistic lyrics that take their cue from Pablo Neruda, weaving from low moans to a quavering falsetto, is a voice that a *New York Times* critic aptly called "the greatest single pop instrument in the world."

"I'm doing a bit of singing these days," admits Fernando Brant, Milton's early lyricist, "but there's always a problem. My partner was just too good a singer. My songs have already been sung by the best." Grudgingly, Brant admits that his words were often written ahead of Milton's elliptical melodies. But he doesn't ap-pear the least bit envious of this local boy's vault to international stardom. I don't get the feeling any of this crowd want to be anywhere else but Belo's cozy taverns.

Yet the setting where I caught up with Milton could not have been farther from the idyllic landscapes his music conjures. The Impresão Digital, Brazil's state-of-the-art recording studio, is a concrete bunker, an aboveground fallout shelter, set down a dirt road at the back of three stark, water-stained twenty-story public housing turrets in the southernmost reaches of Rio. There, I walked in on Milton and his band trying to lay down a final version of "Txai," a song written in tribute to the Amazonian Indians. While the keyboard player and bassist played in the console room, their instruments plugged straight into the board, Milton and his drummer went about their business in separate chambers. The singer's familiar call flooded a dozen studio speak-ers, but I could hardly see him, hunched over a mike in an antechamber protected by opaque soundproofing. The mood of the session was, of course, Brazilian casual. A yeast was needed to keep the track from sounding flat and lifeless. For some reason, this song wouldn't rise. Milton appeared willing to take suggestions from anybody in the room—including the drummer's two precocious preteen kids.

Frustrated, the singer paused to book some plane flights and consult a manager about an international tour. Though Milton affects a youthful sprightliness with a floppy white cap worn atop his forcefully molded African features, he has become prematurely heavy. No musician I meet appears more weighed down by the responsibilities of stardom. That may be because he is the most visibly black of all Brazil's pop pantheon. Along with Chico Buarque, he is also the most politically engaged. In Brazil, I learn that Milton perfected the art of tra-la-las, and filled up albums with wordless melodies, because of the military dictatorship's censors. His tune "Bailes da Vida" became an anthem of the 1987 campaign for direct elections. At one Rio rally, it was sung in unison by over a million people. A call for artists to "go where the people are," the song is not so coincidentally a nostalgic evocation of Milton's early years in Minas as an unknown troubadour. "It's true, life was simpler when I was another singer in a bar," he admitted with a sigh. "In the old days, I could be more spontaneous. I never dreamed that the music would take me here. I know that I represent people who don't have a microphone. This causes me to lose a lot of time and energy, but it also gives me great inspiration. To me, the best part of the work isn't being so professional but trying to find harmony with people all over the world."

In one of his songs, Milton refers to fan letters he receives from "Rio, Paris, Spain, and Shangri-la" and ponders why so many strangers should require the solace of a "Brazilian voice." In person, he did not offer an answer—perhaps there isn't one that can be put into words. He was too preoccupied with an arrangement that didn't work, a new campaign to save the rain forest, his commitments to Amnesty International. When Milton's band went off to consult over lunch, I made my way to a bare-bones snack bar beside a dirt terrace. A dozen bored black girls stood behind long marble counters, poised to prepare *queijo quentes* (grilled cheese sandwiches). I wondered whether these women were troubled by the fact that so many idols of Brazilian culture pass so close to their dreary dead-end workplace. I had the feeling that Milton himself was plagued by a superstar's jet-setting isolation from the common people. Back from his meal, however, the song he's recording suddenly took flight. "You see," Milton told me, "Brazilians make the best music once they have eaten!"

A moment later, he fell asleep on a couch set against the sixty-four-track console, oblivious to the perfect reproduction of that Brazilian voice heard throughout the world—a voice that is first and foremost Mineiro. "As for how my music is affected by growing up in Minas Gerais," Milton had explained, "well, you can hear the church everywhere. I love the sound of many voices together, the choir. But the main influence of Minas was that I could always go into the hills where there was nobody around. In those hills, I could scream as loud as I liked until I found my own voice."

To find the voice of Minas Gerais, I obviously have to get out into its rolling topography. So I take a Sunday bus ride along a lush ravine which once gave forth modest amounts of gold. At the end of the trail is Sabará, nearest of the state's half dozen "historic cities." This perfectly preserved Portuguese colonial enclave has become a poor town that looks like it, too, could be easily scrapped off the hillside. Yet down each dead-end, one finds a church: evidence of all the rococco sanctity that a gold rush could buy. Sabará is a town time has forgot but souvenir vendors have remembered. But I have hardly disembarked into a silent *praça* ringed with palms when a mighty noise comes rumbling out of the hills. As if on cue, a band of *sambistas* is strutting down the cobblestones to commence a wobbly loop around the whole place. Never mind if they're disturbing the peace of the Christmas season. This is practice for Carnival, the holiday that really counts.

Before I know it, I've fallen in line behind five or six drummers, all men in rubber thongs and feathered caps, shorts about to drop off their shimmying midriffs. Some have doused their faces in flour. And there's a single, obligatory transgendered gent, big shoulders covered with sparkle, bearded in a ballerina's tutu. In no time at all, I'm handed a shaker, and after a single uphill block, I'm made the honorary *porta-bandeira*, flag bearer of a flag that belongs to the county of mirth. I hoist an oblong velveteen banner embroidered in fake stones with the name of this raggedy, middle-age band: Paraiso dos Moralistas. The Moralists' Paradise. This sardonic comment on their hometown was chosen some forty years back, after a prudish local general banned the group's original title, a slang term which translates as "Home of the Cocksmen."

A lot of these fellows don't look like they can get it up anymore. They've been working on their sloppy drunks since last night—but they still know how to enliven a Sunday with some supercharged percussion. What do they all do during normal business hours? Their Mineiro *samba* is more lilting than Rio's, though anything would slow down in these guy's hands. The roly-poly carolers stop to chug down quart-size bottles of beer at every familiar haunt that will have them. The brass section, one trombone and sax, happily move from "Jingle Bells" to "Over the Rainbow." One scraggly old farmhand, proud of his Italian surname, makes me a gift of his whistle tied to a leather strap. "You are now among the children of God!" he declares. If so, what a tolerant God He must be!

Worn down by dancing in the midday heat, everyone repairs to a backyard cookout. Not only do I get the best spot of shade, but I'm plied with home-brewed *cachaça*, charred hunks of sausage and steak. Yet down to a man, everyone apologizes for the "economic crisis" which is to blame for their paltry food, minimal costumes, and the fact that much of their town's *patrimonia histórico* is unrestored and heading toward ruin. Once more, I must find it in me to forgive the general disarray. Once more, I find the use of the word *bagunça* to be purely pro forma. The one thing for which no one apologizes is making music their true labor and sole organizing principle. Everybody—black, white, children, old folks, bankers, peasants—is having too good a time wallowing in this mess.

I have to get back to Belo for tamer celebrations. A child psychologist whom I met in Rio has invited me to spend Christmas with her huge Mineiro brood. As the only one to graduate from college, she is decidedly the family "black sheep." But my hostess does have one thing in common with her seven siblings. Her name starts with an "R," as does Roseangela, Renaldo, Rogerio, Rosemary, Rosany, Rosalice, and Roberta. There's a gloomily un-Brazilian air to this lanky and languorous lot, nearly all nine squinting through thick glasses. None of the above, not even the married ones, have moved farther away than the next block. Passing down the hall at any time of day or night, I glimpse a few grown sisters in nighties sharing a bed, combing out one another's hair. In every room, no matter if it's nap-time or spat-time, there's a television going. Maybe all large Latin families share this atmosphere where high jinks and familiarity mingle with a familiar despair.

Next door to this lower-middle-class family's low-lying ranchero, the ruins of some neighbor's modest Brazilian dream sit as devoured by time as the baths of Caracalla. Not that anyone in the vicinity is going hungry. Bubbling on the stove at all times, there's *tutu mineiro* (a kind of bean glop), plus rice and various shrimp stews. It's "hep-u-sef" from two gargantuan refrigerators, and the provisions in the pantry make this seem more like a kibbutz: great sacks of onions and potatoes, industrial-size canned vegetables and condiments. Breakfast means clearing a space amid a table covered with opened jars of creamy cheese, stale rolls and fruit flies. The scene is completed by two burly *mulata* maids. They are so recently hired that my hostess does not know their names. Nonetheless, both seem utterly entrenched, waddling barefoot from the hot stove to the laundry lines to their double-decker bunks set up in a single square barracks. The maids don't go home for Christmas. Maybe they don't have a home. They certainly don't have a Christmas. Part of the family, they are part of no family—it's just another example of the way Brazilians mix egalitarianism and autocracy.

Like everyone else, they defer to the brood's mother, a Latin Ma Joad, small, feisty and hawk-nosed, with eyes clenched for disaster. It's she who has clearly kept the clan together through her untutored version of "tough love." But it's her husband who dominates the stage. This patriarch reminds me at once of a retired British army colonel. He is a dashing figure for his age, walking about briskly in khaki shorts, with a most correct posture, occasionally combing a brilliantly silver mustache. His tanned face exudes health, his bald head is spotted with sun. He holds my attention, and that of all the children, through a slow vanishing act. This old gent is so distinguished that it takes me some time to realize that he does absolutely nothing all day. Except when his pals drop by to play bridge, the head of the household strolls from kitchen to backyard to bedroom in what he calls his *itinerario*. This board-game hop always includes a stop for a nip of *cachaça*. Do not pass go, do not collect a million *cruzeiros*.

My friend's father once owned a string of gas stations, and a farm in the country, which he sold in order to fulfill a dream to run a bakery. But he did it just at the moment when it was deadly to have assets that were liquid. A sudden devaluation of currency and several leaps in inflations turned his life savings into useless paper. He's awfully good natured about being a broken man. Nodding toward the crude shower he's installed in the backyard, he refers to the fact that Minas Gerais has no coastline by joking, "That's what we call a *praia Mineiro*." A Mineiro beach. I smell the liquor on his breath when he corners me to announce, "The only way I resemble the rest of my family is in the whites of my eyes."

As a result, his house has become something out of a García Márquez novel—one of those grandiose Latinate dreams crumbling before everyone's eyes. Tiles are chipped in the shower, the linoleum needs replacing, there are gaping cracks in the concrete. "After all," one of the Rs tells me, "this house is nearly thirty years old!" A true inhabitant of the New World, she says it like that makes the place a Gothic cathedral.

The hallways are dotted with crucifixes—the impaled Jesus a surrogate for a father nailed by his gas-station deal. In such a setting, the Christmas feast proves less than fervent. At least, the children are coaxed into turning off a glitzy Christmas concert with the insipid crooner Roberto Carlos and kiddie star Xuxa as an odd pair of harkening angels. "On the fifth day of Christmas, my true love gave to me . . ." Five billion in debt relief. Ma Joad says Grace before the turkey and ham and macaroni salads. There are at least twenty of us holding hands. Honoring tradition, the husbands of the various sisters proceed to tease the two bookish brothers about whether this will be the year they manage to land girlfriends.

Before the various children begin their free-for-all for presents, the patriarch shows me his special additions to a tree loaded down with tinsel stars, ceramic angels and popcorn. They are wise and edifying sayings, some religious, some philosophical, hand-typed on strips of paper taped to the branches. "This is my idea for Christmas," he tells me with a quiet pride that suggests this is his year's main accomplishment. "Can you guess who said this one? Savonarola. This one is Abrão Lincoln." Our honest Abe. "Here's John Donne." Never mind if none of his children or grandchildren ever bother to ponder the quotes or play the guessing game. No matter if the toys under the tree are all plastic ray guns, GI Joe missile launchers. Or if father's forever slipped off—or been pushed off—his toehold on respectability. In this house, there will be no fall into barbarism.

Christmas Day at the Belo Horizonte bus station means dozens of Mormon missionaries. These eager crew-cut pups have been sent direct from Utah in shoes. Their Portuguese consists entirely of the phrase, "Onde fica McDonald's?" Where is Big Mac, pardner? I also get to observe a number of Brazilian families accomplishing their holiday partings at an agonizing Brazilian pace. Every nephew and niece, aunt and stepson, have to kiss one another on each cheek—or on a patch of air approximating the cheek region—at least two times and preferably more. As the joke goes, you kiss three times so you will have children. You kiss four times so you get along with your mother-in-law. You kiss five times so that you're son won't be gay! "Beijo! Beijo!" The Brazilians even say this when they hang up the phone. These are the kissingest cousins you'll ever see.

Three hours' ride south of Belo, the city of "black gold" sits like a blanket of white stone and orange tiles casually tossed over the landscape's roiling black-green contours. I'm on a pilgrimage to Ouro Prêto, a mecca of Brazilian civilization. This most opulent of the mining towns and best-preserved colonial relic in all South America has been designated a "world protectorate" by the United Nations. The oval squares and grand churches, the stone steps and levels, make for one big Baroque Panorama, the name of a hippie inn where I lug my pack. I've heard a rumor that a Christmas fair here will provide me with lots of local folklore. Instead, I find Ouro Prêto completely closed up, shuttered, *fechado*. Not even a gem shop has bothered to stay open.

Eventually, I am directed to a local folk singer who invites me into his shack and hands me his card, "Jacob e Toninho, Todos os Tons." Meaning "all the tunes" that are fit to spit. He jokes that Ouro Prêto's annual saint's day, once a venue for many local singers, has become so infested with criminals and drug dealers that it's been dubbed "The Festival of the Policemen." In order to scratch out a musical living in these isolated parts, he has been away from his family every weekend for the past ten years. Once more, though, this humble man shows not the slightest intention of giving up the guitar cradled in his lap. I notice that Jacob is branded with immense prenatal scars on both shoulders, as though predestined to life in a harness.

As the sole tourist foolish enough to arrive in Ouro Prêto on Christmas Day, the place is mine. The steep cobblestone alleys, all mine. The sculpted masterworks of the legendary cripple Aleijadinho, all mine. The vistas and *praças*, all mine. The silence of the dark hills, all mine. This is Brazil's Christmas gift. This feeling of being utterly out of synch with the ordinary—not only a man without a country, but without proper hours, decent urges, schedule, or sense—is one of the real treasures travel bestows. Isn't travel, after all, one of the few human activities where we knowingly, willingly, and continually go into situations where we're at a complete disadvantage? Where we never have enough advance intelligence or useful phrases? Travel is a prescription for awkwardness, embarrassment, and always being a step behind—our backhanded compliment to the wisdoms found only through blissful ignorance. Only by becoming strangers on purpose can we, without trepidation or premeditation, break all the rules without knowing we are going to break them. Only then can we stride forcefully toward our next dead end, wrong turn, blank wall. Go without blinking into the void.

Next morning, I find Brazil's oldest working gold mine back in operation. Across the road, there's a huge manor house straight out of *Dynasty*. I don't know if the owners still visit this mine, but the workers have moved on. So have the black slaves who once chanted while they dug, "They call me Mineiro, Mineiro I'm not. I'm a Jongo singer, Mineiro is my boss!" There are no significant veins left, so most of the money is made on the curiosity of people like me. I get to ride to cool depths—the coolest place I've been so far in Brazil—on a rickety handcart which feels as if it could snap at any moment and fall to the core of the earth. So I can dip a miner's pan, I am led to an underground spring at the tonsil of one gaping cavern. Back up top, I put my dish of dirt through a sifter and am shown the few flecks I've uncovered. Probably fool's gold.

Could it be that the transcendent music of Minas Gerais can only be produced once you've labored for gems and had them slip through your fingers? You don't have to get too far beneath the surface to strike a vein of pride and self-sufficiency. Now I know why Milton Nascimento said that growing up here enabled him to unearth his real voice. To find mine, I will need more than the extended weekend I've allotted to this vast territory. "So you've only got five days!" one musician observed. "But tell me, exactly how long will those five days last?" They will last as long as I listen to Brazilian music—which suddenly seems to be far less about hip shaking and far more about a fierce connection with one's own shaggy patch of *terra*. "The people in Minas are just like the mines," Fernando Brant cautioned me, speaking for the music as well. "You have to dig deep, but once you do, you come up with riches."

Music to Read By

MILTON—Milton Nascimento (CBS)
ANIMA—Milton Nascimento (Verve)
CAÇADOR DE MIM—Milton Nascimento (Philips)
MINAS—Milton Nascimento (Philips)
TRAVESSIA—Milton Nascimento (Sigla)
NATIVE DANCER—Wayne Shorter with Milton Nascimento (Columbia)
 **UAKTI**—Uakti (Verve)
ANDALUZ—Beto Guedes (EMI)
DIAMOND LAND—Toninho Horta (Verve/Sound Wave)
ONLY IF YOU DON'T WANT IT, YOU CAN'T DO IT—Hermeto Paschaol (Intuition/Capitol)

MUSICUS INTERRUPTUS

Something is very wrong with this picture. Fifty thousand citizens have gathered to celebrate the 1554 founding by Jesuit priests of São Paulo dos Campos do Piratininga, today the fourth-largest city in the world. A band is blaring from a movable platform parked on the oval, palm-laden Praça da Sé. But the immobilized mob merely stares in amazement. These Brazilian masses—many of whom actually clutch placards of political protest—appear to have lost all impulse to move or sway. "Que é isso?" asks the Paulistas' distinctive declarative. What is this? "Que puta festa!" the locals here like to cuss. What a motherfucking party! Not a soul singing along. At the core of an economic machine which produces 60 percent of the nation's wealth, there is a prosperous silence. The question I'll hear agonized Paulista intellectuals ask themselves is the question São Paulo raises: Are making music and making money mutually exclusive acts?

"Every *cruzeiro* you earn in São Paulo," goes an old saying, "is a *cruzeiro* you could have spent in Rio." That basic bifurcation between work and pleasure still applies to the two big cities of Brazil. Beside the devil-may-care Cariocas, Paulistas fancy themselves as punctual, get-it-done New Yorkers. This city is great at cataloging, documenting, and packaging culture—visiting the Memorial, a library of Latin America housed in a low-lying hangar designed by Niemeyer, I get headphones and listen to old-time *samba* greats in my own soundproof cubby—but it doesn't generate much. Like New York, São Paulo is one giant sycophant, sponging off the vitality of other places. There's nothing indigenous here except coffee beans and profits.

In visual terms, the closer analogy is Los Angeles. Here, too, grimy freeways link urban sprawls of unearthly quiet; shopping malls have been raised to cathedrallike status. The neighborhood where I'm staying bears the lovely name of Aclimação—and anyone could quickly become acclimated to its sunlit parks full of spoiled kids in strollers, its winding streets dominated by billboards of bald-headed, immigrant businessmen. It takes me a while to figure out that these men are all running for the presidency of the Corinthians, São Paulo's top soccer team—perhaps

Brazil's most meaningful election. In São Paulo, a modern survival-of-the-fittest game is set on a deceptively balmy and habitable playing field.

Like both L.A. and New York, São Paulo is energized by its communities of refugees—especially the millions who have migrated from Brazil's own poor Northeast. Liberdade, the enclave peopled by descendants of Japanese laborers drawn by false promises to Brazil's plantations, contributes red *torii* gates, sukiyaki dives, and a few blocks of sterile efficiency. Bixiga, a kind of Greenwich Village where Italians draw the young with mounds of cheap pasta, offers clubs for jazz and acoustic folk. With a little more digging, I find a few sunny blocks of displaced kosher butchers. Can there be wailing cantors in the land of *samba*?

I have to search for evidence that São Paulo isn't entirely tone-deaf. On a hunch, I look up the musicians' union and come upon one of the remarkable sights of my journey. Seven stories below the hiring hall office, the sidewalk is packed with off-duty guitarists, unemployed drummers and substitute singers. Seated on the hoods of parked cars or spilling into snack bars pumping out *mate*, a sweetened grain drink favored in Argentina, small groups of middle-age men clutch scores and arrangements as though they are holding deliveries of crack. Some look grizzled and unshaven, prematurely aged from years of freelance scrounging, holding onto a fading glamour with dramatic black topcoats and cowboy boots. Yet few appear downcast. They have turned this single side of a small park into a swap meet for ideas, equipment, and new licks. They even divide the block into genres. To the right are the apprentices of *sertaneja*. To the left, the on-the-job trainees of *forró*, the Northeast's speedy polka. Nearly all of these men have come to the big city from the rural interior. Most will eventually find a gig or two along the back roads of São Paulo state. They are fortunate, admits one of these unusual unionists, to live in a country that still has an insatiable need for melodies which emanate from live human beings. No jukebox can replace what they do. Among this town's organized labor, they know that they are privileged. After all, a musician out of work is still a musician.

From the *boca do luxo* to the *boca do lixo*—puns which lump "the mouth of luxury" with "the mouth of trash"—São Paulo's sixteen-plus million citizens do not lack for entertainment. This weekend, the main action is a country-western festival teaming Brazilian and North American acts. The headliner of the finale concert is Kenny Rogers, flown straight down from Nashville. Brazil's biggest city is actually the capital of country. The same music and life-style introduced to me in Minas Gerais as *caipira* (roughly "cowboy") is taken by Paulistas to new heights of commodity fetishism. There is a town out in São Paulo province full of boutiques where everything is imported from Texas. Nearby, you can find Americana—founded by refugees from the Southern Confederacy. São Paulo also has the dubious distinction of being the hometown of *brega*. These are wretchedly kitschy love songs that ooze from the bars. At one steakhouse, I'm treated to an awful amateur contest in which contestants outdo one another to sound like Vic Damone. The winner gets a fifty-pound bag of rice.

A Saturday-night party is thrown in my honor. Suggesting round midnight that we head out for a sampling of live music, I'm told: "Are you *louco*? It's much too late!" Then all the guests proceed to gab in the living room until just after dawn. "Que é isso?" What gives? I am learning how to read Brazilians' sometimes circuitous, often obvious, attempts to keep from giving anyone a direct "No." My hostess is an earthy black journalist who wants to impress me by spinning her collection of Bessie Smith blues. Strange, to be in Brazil listening to Billie Holiday squeeze all the pain out of the antilynching tune "Strange Fruit" and to see a roomful of people going wild over Duke Ellington solos the way I soak up Chico Buarque *boleros*. Does the ear also love most the thing it cannot have? Or is all this craving for "the other" a natural by-product of modernity?

Sunday afternoon is meant for the outdoor crafts fair in Embu, a colonial relic in the southern suburbs billed as a charming bohemian enclave. But not so quick: Embu has an extensive population of homeless children and one of São Paulo's highest murder rates. According to one outraged resident, Embu's mayor declared this "the ecological city" only to celebrate with a barbecue of rare and endangered birds. And this place is known worldwide for being where Dr. Josef Mengele, the hunted Nazi, was found buried. "Que é isso? Que puta cidade!" Poncho-cloaked whistle-tooting Andean exiles provide music to buy dolls and trinkets. I drop in on the workshop of a sculptor who complains that his impressive cast bronzes of Yêmanjá and the other Afro-Brazilian gods have been banned from the town square by the local Catholic pastor. His float for São Paulo's weak imitation of a Carnival parade, depicting former president Sarney flying over Brazil like an uncaring tourist, was smashed to bits by police.

If I can't find a native Paulista musician, the next best thing is Dominguinhos. This master accordionist and singer meets me in a narrow convenience hotel near the venerable train station, Estação da Luz. He appears perfectly comfortable in the modern hotel, with its giant plate-glass windows overlooking the once-fashionable Avenida São João, now a bazaar of electronic gadgets, plumbers' fittings, and hobbyist kits reminiscent of Lower Manhattan's Canal Street. But José Dominguinhos de Moraes is typical of northerners who have found prosperity in the South. A stocky *mulato* in baseball cap, with tightly curled hair and a cherubic face that's all dimples, Dominguinhos grew up in a tiny village of the *sertão*. Beginning when he was eight, he played the *sanfona* (accordion) in a musical act with his father and brother. Fortunately, he was soon discovered by the king of Northeastern music, Luiz Gonzaga. "In a hundred years, we won't have another man like that," says Dominguinhos about his mentor. "He was the one who had the courage to bring the Northeast to the South."

Dominguinhos's own journey must have taken great courage.

It took twelve days on the road for him to reach the promised land. "I came to Nilópolis and worked in a laundry. When I first saw the lights of Rio, I asked myself, 'Is this a *festa?*' " Eventually, he was legally adopted by the great Gonzaga. And he ended up accompanying, and influencing, many of the bright lights of urban Brazilian music from Tom Jobim to Johnny Alf. Yet Dominguinhos still identifies with other Nordestinos. "All the skyscrapers you see, the metro, all the hard tasks, were done by us." He tells me, somewhat wearily, that he has turned down many offers to play in New York. "But I don't like to fly and I'm too old to impress anyone." As usual, he howls about his treatment at the hands of Brazilian record companies. "They act like they're doing you a favor to record you. There's no health plan, no retirement benefits. They keep saying this country is in a crisis. But I'd like to know. If the money isn't in São Paulo, where is it?"

There is certainly enough spare change to lure troubadours from the farthest hinterlands. In the course of the next hour, I meet nearly every one in town. First comes Marcia Ferreira, a spunky blond drenched in makeup who has come to the hotel bar to pose for some publicity photos. With no evident bitterness, she informs me that she is the original composer of "Chorando Se Foi" ("Crying Is Gone"), the *lambada* tune made famous by the French group Kaoma and purportedly credited to the fictitious alias "Chico de Oliveira." Ferreira is not the first or the last who will make this claim. She backs it up by describing her years of experience as a disc jockey in Brasília for the national radio station beamed to distant regions of the Amazon. Marcia Ferreira's current pose may be as a peroxide blond in a tight miniskirt, but she has been a tough, political organizer. "I learned the needs of the people in the rain forest from millions of letters to our station. I stood with the *serengeiros*, the rubber tappers. I can tell you about Chico Mendes. But he wasn't the only one murdered. There have been hundreds that the world will never know about."

The struggle over land rights and the rain forest's resources seems a million miles from this comfy hotel surrounded by skyscrapers. Marcia Ferreira, like all the rest, is here on a stop of a concert tour. Everyone in the guest register is a musician. Having already seen too much of life and Brazil, these veteran minstrels have no reason to venture out. Besides, a steady rain has begun to fall on the Avenida São João. So they combine tables in the adjoining dining hall and begin passing around beers and guitars. I spend the rest of my last day in São Paulo entranced by this indoor attraction, having found the music at last. I am astonished by the beauty that emerges so readily from these professionals playing solely for themselves. I am downright amazed by the range of their repertoire, the effortlessness of their plucking. It's a sight I will see many times in Brazil, in airport waiting rooms, bus stations, lobbies. To pass the time, there is always this fallback. The act of making music is as natural as breathing.

What is it about this strange tinkling, this rattle in the cosmos, that moves us so? Why should this most available form of abstraction so affect our concrete emotions? There is no force on earth which goes more uncredited or unexamined than the power of music—that primal art requiring but a single set of vocal chords and a pair of stones. Imagine the money lavished on CDs and concerts or raised for good causes, the consciousness raised through a form of culture that leaps across boundaries more readily than any other! The uncountable number of ears perking up at any moment to radio favorites, the multitude of hearts consoled! How to properly label this commodity which makes dictators cower and pimply-faced Romeos spend their cash? Music is ever the messenger: an ancestral, extraterrestrial medium of tomorrow. It is the cry, a collective sigh. Enlivening us down to our toes, letting the air out of our woes. Provoker of tears, always right before our ears. Hard work to play, hard play that works—scrupulously structured momentary spontaneity. A beat ahead of the story, an adagio behind glory. Call this the *samba* of traveling music, my high notes on low notes, a rhyming reason for what has carried me off on this subequatorial dance. Like the barmen and room-service waiters and off-duty bedmakers who've gathered to listen, I never want to check out of this hotel.

Music to Read By

AQUENTA CORAÇAO—Chitãozinho and Xororó (Som Livre)
ASA BRANCA—Assorted (Rykodisc)
AQUI 'TA FICANDO BOM!—Dominguinhos (Continental)
JACOB DO BANDOLIM—Jacob do Bandolim (Acoustic Disc)
MARCIA FERREIRA—Marcia Ferreira (Continental)

IT HAPPENS

A *conteceu.* "It happens." So the native speakers are fond of saying in a land where almost everything does happen sooner or later, beyond your will or willy-nilly. When it happens, acceptance is a far more treasured skill than interpretation. So here, without getting thematic, is what happened to me over four days. A cut-rate tour package of who, how, and where. Since none of us ever gets very far from our own noses, no more pretense to travel writing! Just the facts, ma'am. That happens to be more than enough in Brazil.

It happens that I turn forty in Rio. This happens not to be as romantic as it sounds. It happens that there is a birthday dinner at a Chinese restaurant facing the Lagoa. It happens that there are Chinese restaurants everywhere. It happens that none of the waiters are Chinese and the food tastes like none of the cooks are Chinese either. Which is all right, since it happens that most of the guests at my celebration hardly know me. One is a dentist from California who happens to own every Brazilian record minted, with each song marked great, good, or poor with the systematic care of dental charts. It happens that there is no cake. It happens that we do not even get fortune cookies. A Brazilian fortune cookie would probably read, "You will have uninhibited sex with a slinky *mulata*." Or "You will finally learn to dance."

It happens that my toastmaster is a highly determined Israeli adventurer, usually clutching beach sandals in one hand and some highbrow *nouveau roman* in the other, who chooses Brazil for his annual escapes into primitivism—preferably at a discount—and has chosen me to accompany him on a jaunt to his determined fantasy, the beach resort of Pôrto Seguro, located at the southern end of the state of Bahia. It happens that the final guest is a travel-agent who tells us that she has pulled strings to procure two tickets on the Brazilian-made Bandeirante turboprop that will be making the trip up the coast tomorrow morning. (It happens that every flight in Brazil is always sold out, but if you happen to show up and even if you happen to be number eighty on the waiting list, you will happen to get on.) It happens that I am not enamored of such small aircraft with so spotty a safety record, especially when I'm boarding one merely to reach a beach. It happens that I spend my birthday convinced that it will be my last.

When we arrive at Aeroporto Santos Dumont, named after the Brazilian bon vivant who happens to have invented flight around the same time as Orville and Wilbur Wright, there happens to be a delay in takeoff. Our plane, noticeably unformidable, sits on the runway but we cannot board. It happens that the luggage, duly weighed, weighs too much. It happens that passengers are being told that several of them will have to volunteer to be left behind. Then it happens that we are loaded, overweight luggage and all, onto the same flight the staff told us it would be unsafe for us to take. It happens to be a cross-your-fingers airline, another Brazilian shortcut.

It happens that we land in Vitória. It happens that we make a stop in Espiritu Santo. It happens that I don't want to die in some town that would make my next of kin ask, "What was he doing there?" It happens that we hit an air pocket just before entering a fat, moist patch of cloud and fall a hundred feet in a second. It happens that the pilots, who don't bother to close the door to their low-tech cockpit, turn to the passengers with a laugh and a shrug. *Turbulência, excelência.* "It happens," wrote Pablo Neruda, "that I grow tired of being a man." It happens to me on airplanes. It happens that my intrepid friend feels airsick. It happens that he leaves his girlfriend's camera under the seat. It happens that we are coming down along a section of coast that is one long beach and that this could be almost any section of coast for as far north as we can go. It just happens that along this section, there is an opening at the mouth of a jungle river, I happen to see it now, which the Portuguese explorers figured would make a secure harbor. Christened Pôrto Seguro, this happens to have been the first European landfall in Brazil. It happened on Good Friday, 1500.

It happens that nothing much has happened to Pôrto Seguro since then. Not until the *lambada*. It happens that this may be Pôrto Seguro's only export of any worth, its revenge on the *conquistadores*. It happens that this area has become a popular party town for Brazil's college students, with the wildest, if not the most indigenous, Carnival. So it happens that, though the *lambada* was first danced far to the north, it was here European backpackers got their first sample. It happens that the brochures now call this the Lambada Coast and the airfield is called the Lambaporto. It happens that we find a lambahotel. It looks like a motel on the outskirts of Phoenix except that there happens to be a family of sloths living in the courtyard. Real sloths, not the more common metaphoric breed. It happens that these are nearly indistinguishable in their hairiness from the umbrella made of sun-faded palm leaves in which they've taken up residence. Black eyes and claws are all that stand out, until the sloths try to rearrange their indolence and then you see that sloths happen to be able to move only one claw, one limb at a time, do one thing at a time. It happens that they even shit slowly, expelling dark pellets. It happens that I wish I could have stayed at home, slothlike!

It happens that my friend wants to cool off in the swimming pool. It happens that there is no water in the pool. It happens that this town is no longer a town. It is one of those shells of former organic life turned into a tourist zone. It happens that the historic ruins of Pôrto Seguro are sequestered out of town. It happens that the dirt streets are lined with bars, money changers, bikini shops, *pousadas* that are just two-room crash pads strung with hammocks. It happens that my friend, who rarely admits to such things, happens to be a trifle disappointed. He's long had the fantasy of purchasing an equatorial roost on-the-cheap in nearby Trancoso. Is it because the name suggests a tranquilizer? It happens that Israelis are the number-one nationality of tourists in Brazil. After their stints in the army, an escape here is equally obligatory. It happens that my friend is a man without a country, unless you count hedonism. He wants the best of everything the world can provide, but he also knows how to lower his standards. In his Quixote quest for the best beach, backside, beat, book, or buddy, I am Sancho Panza. It happens that I fall comfortably into the role.

It happens that we ride the ferry across the mouth of the river feeling like two Lord Jims. Too bad we're only going as far as Arraial da Ajuda, which happens to be a typical coastal town with its one faded village lawn and tiny plaster chapel set on the bluff. It happens, though, that half of São Paulo must be on the beach. It happens that Brazilians do not take to the sea to find nature but to find other Brazilians. It happens that they're all playing paddleball, cracking lobsters, and hanging out in droves near the *batida* stands. This does not bother my friend, a master of cocktail schmoozing wherever the party, in street clothes or string pants. "Looking good is better than being good," is his motto. "You're only young once," he happens to repeat, "but you can be immature forever!" It happens that once the sun sets, everyone heads for more imbibing along Pôrto Seguro's Pasarella das Alcools. The Promenade of Alcohol! It happens that I've been in a lot of towns which could use such bold attempts at self-marketing. It happens that where I come from they call this the Bowery. But it happens that the stars are out and a sea breeze is blowing. It happens that saloon row is just a hundred yards or so from the big dance floor provided by this town disguised as a party.

Once people tire of refreshments, it's time for—you guessed it—the Lambateria. The *lambada* happens to be more than a passing fad in Brazil, perhaps because they happen to dance it so much better here. Because fads tend to become institutionalized, monumentalized in a country with such retention skills for anything of the moment, such an aptitude for the fleeting. The Lambateria is all bark, roofed-over, and big as an ice rink, with a full grandstand on one side for those who would rather just gawk. It happens that there is much to gawk at. It happens that the male dancers are dressed like flamboyant karate masters, in floppy, silky, harem pants tied with thick sashes. Flat Chinese shoes. Nothing on top but their aerobicized chests glistening and heaving. It happens they are all black belts when it comes to leading a well-timed spin, a three-step rocking to and fro. But the pairs do not keep their loins as tightly locked as Northerners have been taught. These kids have too many moves to be limited to the sexual. It happens that this is ice skating in the land without snow, a resemblance emphasized by the pleated Sonja Henje skirts adopted by the gals so that the centrifugal force of their whirling lifts up hems to show everything underneath but for a slash of panties. How is it that buttocks and thighs retain their mystery when so routinely exposed to the light? It happens that the most sensuous action takes place at torso level or above. Beauties flirting with the beastly, the teenage girls toss back their long manes with an equine rearing and whip them purposely across the bare shoulders of their sultanic escorts. Down at the Lambateria, it's *muito lambada*, as I happen to hear the crowds shout. I'm *lambacansado* just from looking. It happens that there may be a few oddballs in Brazil who can't keep a tune or don't have perfect pitch. It happens that there is no one in Brazil who can't dance.

It happens that we are off to Trancoso in a VW bug taxi which grinds through wet dirt for an hour. It happens that the old *taxista* takes us first to the high-priced cabanas on the outskirts of town, hoping he'll get a commission. It happens that he demands a second fare by the time he drops us at our chosen bungalow. It happens that my friend won't yield to his demands, but it is lucky that he eventually does. It happens that this desperate driver doubles as Trancoso's chief of police. Not a very vigilant one, for as soon as we've checked in, it happens that a steward attached to our inn trots by on a white steed. Armored with nothing but cut-off shorts, this shining knight on horseback brings a baggy of marijuana. He promises us eager local girls, too, but those he can't load on the back of his saddle. Welcome to Bali West, Koh Samui, Cozumel, Goa, Transworld Trancoso! It happens that there are a thousand such towns scattered throughout the Third World, wherever there's an empty beach and a baking sun, all going through the same chronology of bespoilment, the familiar ravages of an unregulated interchange between pale and tan, restless and rooted. It happens that Trancoso's beach, down a steep and nasty hill, goes for miles. There is a lovely stucco church, rounded like something out of the Greek Orthodoxy, but the lengthy square rolled out like a green carpet is lined with wildly painted-up pizzerias. It happens that the town is a grimy arrangement of shacks and jeep trails hacked in the jungle. Fruit stands with names like Nova Jerusalém. With a gleam of triumph in his eyes, Don Quixote strips to his swim shorts and declares that people come here not for "what is here but for what is not," to revel in the lack of all they ordinarily have.

It happens that we have not entered the forest primeval but the Black Forest. Our innkeeper is a fastidious German hippie living out a tropical reverie while at the same time attempting to balance the books of his Pousada Calypso. This Hegelian in Hawaiian shirt happens to be named Heinie. His *frau* is a Brazilian of German extraction, from Blumenau or one of the numerous Teutonic enclaves in the prosperous South, a blond lady speaking Portuguese with a clipped Stuttgart cadence, who wanders the grounds with incongruous Brazilian lassitude in a show-all bikini, occasionally pausing to breast-feed her new baby. Over the nightly barbecue of horseflesh or worse, we discover that there happen to be enough Germans staying at this inn to constitute a new branch of the Goethe Institute.

It happens that one is an overpale *Übershickse*, who can't take more than an hour a day in the sun and has run out of traveling money. It happens that another is a bearded and saturnine Wolfgang who naturally goes by the Brazilian handle of "Lobão" ("Big Wolf.") Wolfgang is a radio producer back home, but also a Brazilophile to outdo all Brazilophiles, for he comes here every year to collect experiences, artifacts, and compact discs with Germanic precision. It happens that he also does an efficient Germanic job of letting go of his Germanness. It happens that he ran away from home to escape a Nazi father. It happens that he is a tireless crusader against racism, in Germany or Brazil. But it happens that he has come to Trancoso to work devotedly, fanatically, at doing nothing. *Aconteceu.* He teaches me to say it. "It happens." He has learned the Brazilian shrug along with excellent Portuguese. "A lie is only a truth that forgot to happen," he happens to familiarize us with this most Brazilian of sayings. "The best time to be in Brazil?" he asks. "It is always tomorrow." And when tomorrow comes and it rains for two days, my Israeli friend and I enter into intense colloquies with Lobão beneath the downpour. It happens that we discover the sort of intimate friendship which can only take place between people who are far from their ordinary circumstances and bound together by the camaraderie of outsiders chatting to kind kerosene light. My Israeli friend may not find his dream house, but he has found Lobão. And I have found Lobão's collection of tapes. Have you heard Obina

Shok, my friend? Can I turn you on to Marisa Monte? We could be in Berlin or San Francisco, except that the sounds blend perfectly with storm against thatch. It happens that Brazilian music sounds even better when you happen to be listening to it in Brazil.

Thanks to Lobão, it happens that we stroll nervily into a village bar late one night. Candles on crude picnic tables before wooden benches keep the dankness lit. A number of scruffy exiles from all parts of Latin America are fearlessly strumming guitars and belting out protest songs, paeans to *la lucha* and Che Guevara. It happens that we have taken a time trip back to the late sixties. It happens that this time has never died in Brazil, perhaps because its battles have yet to be fought. But there is nothing grim about the atmosphere here. It happens that a love of life permeates this concrete hole to such an extent that things nearly get maudlin. It also happens that everybody in sight is drunk on *cachaça*. It happens that the proprietor and lead inebriate is a wild man who tucks years of wiry hair growth under a kerchief and wears nothing but a mid-length Japanese kimono and shorts. It happens that his feet are caked with decades of mud and bar drudgery. This bearded androgyne is not just wasted but permanently on his own higher plane of incoherence. It happens that he was once a philosophy professor in Buenos Aires, or so he claims in perfect Portuguese. He wrote a thesis on existentialism. He considers himself an expert on the absurdity of life. Obviously, he settled in Trancoso to do some firsthand research.

"Absurdo!" he keeps shouting, a reference to the thirty-six tabs of LSD which he claims to have taken in twenty-four hours, the kilo of coke up the nose. He always had *uma cabeça forte*, he boasts. A strong head, but apparently not strong enough. "I went to a psychiatrist once," he tells us, getting cozy and punctuating his ravings with infectious cackles. "But I told him, you are the one who has a problem! You have to find a way to live off my madness!" It happens that this exile is picking on us because he has recognized some fellow wayward intellectuals.

"Who is there in this town to discuss *Being and Nothingness?* To debate Kierkegaard?" As though to punctuate his point, it happens that a villager enters making his nightly delivery of an armful of pineapples. After the barkeep gets through with some spirited bargaining, he rolls his eyes toward us in hilarious anguish. "Pineapples! I want to talk Sartre and all they talk is pineapples!"

And it happens, as it does in such cases, that this oblivious fellow is just numbed enough to be something of a seer. He notices me in the corner, ever the observer, Sancho Panza, knight-errant of discomfort. "My friend, I see that you have an *alma fechada!*" A closed soul. I can't deny that when it comes to hippie beach towns. "You need to drink some *cocomelo* tea!" That's the weird kind of mushroom, something brewed up by Timothy Leary. "You must have visions to open your closed soul!"

And, slowly, my soul uncloses. It happens in the ocean next morning, when I notice that, for an instant, I have begun to relax. It happens with the help of a couple of *batidas de maracuja* (crushed passion fruit, black seeds and all) stirred up with *cachaça.* It happens when my Israeli friend nearly steps on a poisonous snake slithering in the mud outside the Calypso. It happens when I, too, am surprised in the darkness by a horned bull's head lunging out at me. All the children who follow behind laugh at me and whoop it up, for this is not a real bull but a villager playing hobgoblin to signal the start of the town pageant for the Folia dos Reis, sometimes known as Epiphany, celebrating the arrival of the Three Kings. A parade happens that night, a halting, crazy, martial affair, with snare drums to drive on the processional which takes four or five hours to cross a few hundred yards to the church. It happens that the Three Kings have cotton beards and paper crowns. It happens that one of the kings is black, one beige, one our retarded marijuana bearer. It happens that one wears Mickey Mouse ears. It happens that they are accompanied by an honor guard of girls whose spread arms are butterfly wings, followed by maidens-in-waiting dressed like prom queens.

It happens that what is homespun is heartfelt and my friend is right. The lack of things—package tours, Pepsi sponsorship—is what we have found. Senses quickened by abundant nature and abundant opportunity for testing self-reliance, Don Quixote has found his illusory paradise. Never mind that Sancho Panza has to pay off the dealers and panderers in order to maintain his partner's purity. Dress-up bulls career and charge through the night, primal demons chasing out all fear. And it happens that the mayor, our *taxista*, tells the crowd that this has been Trancoso's greatest pageant ever. Before continuing the proceedings over at the cattle pen that doubles as a modest Lambateria, the townspeople clap wildly in agreement, perennial believers, like birthday celebrants eager to blow out the candles. "They are all children," Lobão concludes after years of research, without a drop of white man's condescension but perhaps a tad of envy. Trancoso, as seen by a child, is one muddy paradise on the bluff. It just happens that the lies these people tell themselves to stay happy are truths that forgot to happen. It happens that word reaches us, through the town's single pay phone, that the airline has recovered my friend's lost camera. It happens that nothing is lost, as long as your soul is open. Everything can happen in four days in Brazil. And it happens that we must all become explorers in reverse, aspiring to find as little as possible.

Music to Read By

LAMBADA BRASIL—Compilation (Polydor)

HIGH-CRIME SAMBA

There are destinations where dreams are your best guidebook. In your sleep, you swoop down birdlike over a city of tombstones. The cobblestoned plaza echoes with the hammering of coffin makers. Behind a cathedral trimmed in milk chocolate, a cemetery runs all the way into the jungle. Death is this town's leading industry. But once you land hard upon this rocky, morbid world, your vision provides you with a way out. At the very end of a pier jutting out into a harbor, a square shaft emerges directly out of a calm sea. Businessmen in three-piece suits are attempting the short leap from the pier to a surfacing elevator car. Some drown, their attaché cases floating away. Some frolic beneath the shimmering surface. In your dream, you press a button in midair, happy to know that this underwater elevator can only go down.

Then you arrive where omens count more than homens— that's men! Exploding with foreboding. Every stranger in danger. No town for mere tourists, logicians, or honkies! There's too much of everything where everything Brazilian began: too many con games and back-parlor priestesses, too many trade-route influences and too much vengeance, too many false facades and too much neglect, too many muttered incantations and too much left unsaid! Where the occult is ordinary, unseen powers rule every transaction and there's never enough ways to ward them off. Coming cold to Bahia is like staring straight into the sun. Gaze unshaded at Bahia's eclipsed worlds and risk permanent trance! If you can pack an extrasensory flak jacket.

On every street corner, the vendors offer protection in the form of carved wooden "fingers of God," good-luck charms disguised as clenched fists; strings of thick beads whose full strata of colors, *blue to black, summon forth the vigilant deities cum bodyguards called orixás; all manner of talismans and amulets, coral and cowrie, strap-on seashell armlets. You must have a fita, the popular length of red ribbon imprinted "Souvenir of Our Lord of Happy Endings." Your first stop is a pilgrimage to the most beloved Church of Senhor do Bonfim, consecrator of Happy Endings, so you can add your piece of shiny color to an inner sanctum where every saintly statuette is so blanketed that the piles of fabric look like accretions of stalactite. You brush aside more such strands of superstition when the street urchins try to run alongside and drape you in unwanted ribbons, tying them around your wrists with the properly mystical number of twists.*

Strolling around the old center of Salvador, you head for the main square and find a cathedral: towers of baroque delirium, tombstone gray, milky chocolate trim. Then you hear the hammering. You notice the first alley off the main square is lined with open-air workshops where the coffin makers ply their trade. Behind the church is the graveyard of the first missionaries. Reeling in horror toward the waterfront, you discover that you are high on a bluff. Déjà vu leads you toward the dominant feature of this city built on two department-store floors: an ungainly, exposed white shaft called the Elevador Lacerda. For less than a nickel a ride, this elevator hauls much of the populace between the business district and the port, from high sky to dappled sea. Any cheap Baedeker might have warned you. But you feel that your personal orixá must be Alfred Hitchcock. You have found your Toblerone cathedral, your coffin makers doing their thing, your elevator into the sea!

Is that why you fail to notice how quickly downtown's banks and offices are emptying at closing time? What lulls you to linger beside the Bay of All Saints' wispy, tranquilizing dusk bay? How do you happen to wander just a half block off the main boulevard, down a diagonal avenue lined with shuttered record shops, hardly an infamous dark alley? How long has bad luck been tailing you? Or is it that you happen to be walking through a dream? Three youths are charging at you from one end of the block. You turn your head and find three more demons are sprinting just as hard from the opposite direction. They surround you and pin your rag-doll arms to the wall. These predators cannot be for real: a Mickey Mouse gang, hair raffishly falling in their eyes. The ribbon peddlers just grown up enough to take their revenge. You could put up a struggle, but you're not eager to see what protective charms these demons are carrying. They strip your pockets clean, leave your world inside out. They find the watch which you had removed so it would not be noticed. Because you are outside time in Bahia! They make off with little more than the scrawled inspirations in two pocket notebooks. You should be wearing a sign: "Foreign Writer Carries Only Small Change."

"Tudo! Tudo!" you begin shouting. How fear breeds fluency! They've got everything. And everything is not tudo bom, the Brazilian motto. You can see passersby less than ten yards away. From this day on, you will carry a Carnival whistle around your neck. If you ever toot on it, will anyone distinguish an SOS from musical exuberance? Out of disappointment over their haul, the two lead bullies aim sharp knees at your gut. One leaves his calling card in the form of a loping, fisted swipe that lands square on your forehead. You have your badge of honor, your mark of initiation, your lump to show a desk clerk who has seen his share of lumps. You yourself have seen it all coming. You don't need this hotel priest to tell you that you need protection.

So this is your happy ending—a little less cash for spending. Of this town you'll be the toast, with your survivor's boast! Chime in with a tale of contrition, to a national chorus of suspicion. What would people discuss without this latest topic, this cancer that's tropic? Everybody's doing the high-crime samba. Better get ready, don't cry to your mamma! Best to chant in time to this catchy rhyme. Where the only thing catching are schemes that are hatching. Only sheer cunning keeps this country running. Where they excel in pickpockets, not nuclear rockets. Everyone knows the reason for the new dance this season. Step careful, pardner, latch that bag tight! Watch your left and right, stay home at night! Clutch your bag in the day, put that camera away! Abducted in a taxi, woke up without a kidney. Tend to your security or someone will mess up your purity. That lovely socialite, disappeared from sight! You must admit they're creative, in mayhem innovative. They pull off their kidnaps like joggers do laps. To take your purse, a whole play they'll rehearse! Leave your lotion in the ocean, attempt no pursuit when they nab your swimsuit! Followed into the waves, they'll even take your tan—those knaves! How else to show social concern, except to yield all you've earned? These boys from Brazil really mean you no ill. You'd do the same for hire if things were so dire. So be thankful for this happy place, where you only lose cash and not face! In this realm of equality, everyone can grow up to be a casualty. Everybody's doing it. Everybody's ruing it. Brazilians need something new to keep them supple. Once they stop moving they know they're in trouble. Try the high-crime samba! And don't cry to yo' mamma. When it comes to prevention, God has his intentions. And He's not talking. Like everybody else, He's out there stalking.

▲▲▲
Bahia

If Brazil has contributed anything to the world, it is this mixing of blood, this racial democracy.

—Jorge Amado

I SING THE TRIO ELECTRIC

In Brazil, fame is a word closely allied with familiarity. The country's heroes aren't put on a pedestal, they are put on a first-name basis: from soccer star Socrates to activist Lula, singers like Alcione and Toquinho. Flying into Salvador da Bahia, I find myself on the same jet with one of the few Baianos known by a single word. In the pantheon of Brazil's most-storied province, there is only one Osmar.

"Osmar, Osmar, O Carnaval veio trio elétrizar. . . ." Reclining in a coach seat, returning from a São Paulo conference in his honor, this septugenarian is all too happy to inform me about how he earned his distinction. The voice may be faltering, but he still manages to sing his own praises. "Dôdo, Dôdo, antes de gringo, a guitarra ele inventou. . . ." Before the *gringo*, he invented the guitar! Along with his late partner Dôdo, "white" Osmar is credited with having perfected the first electric guitar and creating the local aggregate that put the instrument to immediate good use—namely, the *trio elétrico*, a movable band which is the prime institution of "black" Bahia's Carnival.

"Of course, we started out as a *dupla elétrico*, since there were

only two of us. This was back in 'forty-seven, just after the war."
These days, Osmar makes it onto the airplane with the aid of a
cane. Yet he gets caught up in a boyish, breathless enthusiasm
whenever he talks about his pet patent. His egg-shaped face is
guileless and just brown enough to make him look as though he's
just come back from a morning's surfing. What's left of his silver
hair flows in free locks down to his shoulders. Like many of
Brazil's great cultural figures, he would never be caught wearing
more than a pair of sandals, homespun pants and a blue-and-
white-striped fisherman's shirt. Imagine Ben Franklin in tropical
repose!

"My partner Dôdo was an electric technician, he fixed radios.
I ran an auto body shop and I was always handy at fixing things.
At the same time, my first love was music. My father had been a
mechanic and a musician, too. He wrote fifty original songs. So
it was natural that we would combine our talents, fiddling around
in the garage. And we came up with this." I can't believe it. From
the carryon bag under his seat, Osmar whips out one of the most
precious artifacts in the history of Brazilian music. In his thick,
laborer's hands, he holds a nicely polished, foot-long guitar bridge
severed off its body, with electric pickups under the frets. This is
the actual prototype *pau elétrico*, as it was dubbed. Of course, it's
the red-tinged color of *pau Brasil*, the wood for which Brazil was
named. "This is all we played on at first. For a long time in my
garage, we perfected the feedback, learned the proper spacing of
the pickups so we could apply it to my mandolin. Some years
later, we heard that people in the United States were also creating
the electric guitar. Les Paul and others. I remember Dôdo and I
went to what was advertised as the first demonstration of a *violão
eléctrico*, which someone had brought up from Rio. We thought
from the name that this 'electric guitar' could play by itself!"

But somebody had to match the new instrument to a style of
playing that was equally, compellingly, *elétrizado*. "Soft, gentle
music was much in fashion then. At that time, we had been
playing *chôrinho* mostly"—a genteel sound derived from the verb,

to cry—"with some *valsas* and *boleros*. But Dôdo and I noticed what a stir had been made at the past Carnival by the Vassourinhos, a *frevo* group that came down from Recife." The irony is that Bahia, birthplace of nearly every Brazilian sound, would learn to celebrate itself through a beat borrowed from the North. "This music really made the crowds wild. It was so quick and sharp. And with *frevo*, you could really show your virtuosity. I mean, you had to be good. You had to be a Paganini of the *povão*." In other words a maestro of the masses, for *povão* is *povo* (people), with an ending implying that little people combine to make something very big. "What we did then really took courage. I don't know how we did it. Because up until then, Carnival in Bahia was a tame affair. It was more for the elite and the middle classes. Small bands played *pifanos* [wooden flutes]. There was no wild dancing, no nudity. People threw confetti at one another. The homeowners would set out their rocking chairs to watch the parade pass. They'd chain down the chairs so they couldn't be stolen. But at a certain point, we said to ourselves, 'Why not try it?' And we rigged up my old jalopy. An open two-seater. We put a loudspeaker on the back and set out."

The rest is musical history. "Once we struck the very first note, it was an apotheosis! We were mobbed by people dancing on all sides! They almost turned the car over. *Meu deus!* We lost the sound many times. And then, the police came, ordering us to stop. The elite was against us. They knew that the Carnival would never be the same after this, that there would be no place for them. But the people were shouting, rioting, ordering us, 'Toca, toca!' So we played again. We quickly ran out of our repertoire. I think we even sang 'La Marseillaise.' By the time we got to the Praça Castro Alves, there was such a mob following us that I was sure we'd be taken to prison. Horses reared and drivers were thrown. The mob shoved one another into the *acarajé* stands"— Bahia's deep-fried bean cakes—"and many people were burned by the hot oil and cooking fires. We had lost our brakes by then, lost all four gears, but the people kept pushing the car. Nothing stopped them. They didn't allow us to parade again for two years. But by then, we had a Chrysler. And the *trio eléctrico* was established.

"It's amazing," says Osmar with genuine astonishment that he had affected the world. "All I wanted was to drink my *cachaça* and find a better way to play in Carnival. And now I will be remembered for the launching of this *fenómeno Baiano*! Now, my four sons all play in the Dôdo and Osmar group, carrying on the name." This proud papa breaks once more into song at ten thousand feet. "'Não precisa do rock, so precisa do toque, Envolvente e legal, para meu Carnaval!'" You don't need rock, you just need to strum—or, in a typical double-entendre, to take a "toke" of marijuana. "Thank God, I wasn't born up north or I might have invented a missile. Here, at least, we have a country of peace."

A true man of the South, the typical Bahian mix, Osmar presents a European exterior. Yet his assumptions favor the immediacy of pleasure over obedience to abstract progress. He serves instinct, not logic; his heart lies not with any hierarchy, but with the simple values of the masses, his *povão*.

"Carnival is the celebration of those who suffer and have no rights. It lets out all the social vapor. And where there's more steam, more pressure, there's better singing, more jumping." By this formulation, I'm not sure that Osmar should be so proud of how much oppression his hometown has to blow off. Still, the wheelchair that's waiting for him at the gate only underscores a personal electricity which has outlasted his invention.

But I will soon hear Osmar's musical descendants complaining that Bahia's civic charge-up has reached a point of potential short-circuit. Each year, the amplifiers are more powerful, the *trios* expanding far beyond the original format. The bouncy, good-timey sound introduced by Osmar and the boys is slowly being squealed and bent in the direction of heavy metal. Simultaneously, Salvador's wealthy class—a few outnumbered whites drawing on centuries of experience in manipulation—are reestablishing their hold on much of Carnival's movable turf. Increasingly, the bands are sponsored by local and multinational corporations that cover the expense of outfitting their trucks with the proper amount of voltage and hardware. Atop platforms loaded with neon advertising, the musicians become little more than spokesmen. Membership fees keep rising for the *blocos* that dance behind the *trios* in roped areas, waving pom-poms and wearing color-coordinated sleeveless frocks called *mortalhas*. Exorbitant costs for the costumes have turned these blocks into roving country clubs. These charges aren't necessary to cover the electrified Carnival's utility bills. They are meant to discourage the intermingling of Bahia's rich and poor wrigglers.

"In the past, there was a clear difference," says Caetano Veloso, one of many Bahian musicians highly sensitized to any changes in their community's leading cultural institution. "Blacks, young people, and the poor would be in the streets, following the trucks. Rich, boring people would stay indoors attending Carnival balls. But since the mid-seventies, the street Carnival became very famous. So the bourgeoisie started to get a bit jealous. They found this way of putting up money and backing the *trios elétricos*. The music became vulgarized. They took the indoor Carnival into the streets." Moraes Moreira, spiritual heir to Osmar and the very soul of Bahian Carnival, puts it more bluntly. He calls recent developments "the condo-ization of the public space."

The crowds, too, have joined a planetary trend toward mindless rowdyism. The first thing I notice on the ride into town is a campaign designed to discourage increasing violence during Carnival. Billboard likenesses of various local music idols ask, "I'm the type who plays safely, are you?" Fortunately, I'm planning to stay only through the limited mayhem of the Feast of Yêmanjá, an annual placation of the powers of the sea. Before I can begin to worry, the provincial tourism board's sunnier advertisements hit me with the equally rhetorical, "Aren't you glad to be in Bahia?"

One stroll out the door of my hotel makes me answer in the

affirmative. I've arrived just in time for a municipal concert to promote world peace, staged before the Barra lighthouse which sits between two sandy lips of beach. As a postcard sunset shows a strata from orange to blue, an adoring mob stands before a flimsy bandstand, festooned with Picasso doves on white pennants. Gilberto Gil, the city's self-proclaimed "minister of culture," rouses the crowd with his bouncy hymnal of Latin unity sung in, God forbid, Spanish: "Soy Loco por Ti America!" Olodum, the black nationalist Carnival aggregate whose tribal percussion signaled a new direction for Brazilian music long before Paul Simon recruited them as backups, has brought a single contingent of disciplined percussionists. Dressed in angelic white knee-length African robes, these choirboys turned drummer boys blast at the starry heavens with single-minded synchronization. One resplendent elder with microphone spins a melody line that rises above the urgent din. The words are ghetto Portuguese, the melody a Muhammadan prayer. For a finale, I get to hear Armandinho, Osmar's brawny and long-haired son doodling maniacally on his dad's invention—a true Paganini who works out so hard on the frets that he has to wear two sweatbands around each pickin' wrist.

Salvador in February's summer balm is a perfect place for a party and this is the perfect partying music. You'd hardly know from this part of town that Bahia's city by the bay is a cultural crucible in need of serious salvation—that's been going downhill since 1763, the end of its two centuries as the capital of Brazil. The songs don't tell of the shameful dilapidation of the Pelourinho neighborhood, once the core of colonial Brazil. None of the music admits that 80 percent of the population of 2.5 million is considered unemployed or underemployed. Distressing reports tell of a rapid increase in lynchings—nearly two a week in 1991—by crime-ravaged citizens taking the law into their own hands. Transcendent on its white bluff, Saint Salvador of the Bay of All Saints sinks in the mire of its spiritual density.

"You don't want to go there!" I heard over and over in Rio.

"There's too much street crime, too much craziness, too many . . . well, too many you-know-whats!" Coming from Cariocas, I took these first hints of overt Brazilian racism in the spirit of a pot calling the kettle black. Anyway, I can no more investigate Brazilian music without including Bahia than I could country-western without Nashville. This is the cauldron in which Africans and Europeans perfected the recipe for Brazil's spicy cultural stew, cooked up with palm hearts and plantains, dried shrimps and chilis, oozing dawn-red *dendê* oil. The region is credited with being the mother of all beats: *lundu, maxixe, marcha, samba-reggae,* and the *samba* itself, brought to Rio by migrants from Bahia. The recent roster of Baianos who've become pop innovators begins with *bossa nova*'s number-one voice, João Gilberto; includes pioneers of the irreverent *tropicalismo* like Caetano Veloso, Gal Costa, and Gilberto Gil; proceeds to a new generation's symbols of black militancy, such as Margareth Menezes.

No wonder the lyrics to so much Brazilian music are little more than a rhythmic roll call of Salvador's native lore. Not just musically, but in every way, this is one of those rare places which come exactly as advertised. On every street corner of the historic center, you can actually find the fabled Baianas, the world's most high-fashion food vendors in flowing lacy getups of Sudanese origin, their long skirt called a *saia*, their white blouse a *bata*, and matching turban, the *torso*. A glitzier adaptation of this outfit gave Carmen Miranda her Hollywood persona. Squatting under broad umbrellas to their eternal frying, the dignity of these off-duty cultists rarely seems compromised by the need to move their greasy merchandise. These resplendent cooks offer trays of coconut sweets and freshly made *acarajé*, doughy bean-cake snacks stuffed with *carurú* hot sauce or pasty *vatapá*. As Dorival Caymmi's famous tune disguised as a recipe begins, "To make a good *vatapá*, first find a black Baiana who knows who to stir. . . ." Another Caymmi classic, popularized by Carmen Miranda, asked, "What is it that the Baiana has? / She has grace like nobody else / How well she swings those hips!"

The markets are crowded with trade beads, lace and carvings, spices and baby chicks dyed all colors, even piles of surplus drums and bells. Though you can't quite find "a church for every day of the year," as the Baianos claim, there are fifty-eight of them, straight-backed and austere, leftover from the days when Salvador was nicknamed "The Negroes' Rome." In the main squares, brawny teenagers demonstrate the traditional combat of *capoeira*, a West African martial art banned by the slave owners. Today's practitioners use their most intimidating spins and contortions to extort higher tips from passing tourists. Accompanied by a twangy single-stringed harp called a *berimbau*, self-defense is transformed into—what else?—a muscular minuet. In Brazil, even combat is turned into dance. In Bahia, even dancing becomes a duel between elemental forces, death and lust, decay and creation kickboxing it out.

"It's very Oriental in a sense, it's Taoist," Gilberto Gil will observe. "Salvador is a place that looks like it's dying but where new energy is always coming out." Yet Salvador, a source of pride as the vanguard of Afro-Brazilian culture, is also where the Carnival is most segregated. The celebrations vaunted as the most "popular" and "characteristic" in the country reflect a characteristic color bias. The segregated nature of the *blocos* is one reason blacks responded by forming their powerful drumming ensembles, the Afoxés, and Afro-*blocos*. The groups that roll down the Avenida Sete do Septembro from the posh beachside neighborhoods are nearly lily-white. They are met by blacks strutting up the hill from the Pelourinho and other rundown sections of the old colonial town. On neutral ground, they do mythical, musical battle. Battalions of bouncy blond kids in sneakers and Roman togas frontally assault black phalanxes in sandals and splashy, geometric African robes. Bahia, judged by its Carnival, is not so much a melting pot as a musical race riot. Osmar's *pau elétrico* versus the congas of Oxalá.

Certainly, there is great social contact among ethnic groups, an equality of the confused in a city peopled by, as one history book lists, "prisoners, deserters, Jesuits, Jews, gypsies, prostitutes, Indians." Not necessarily in order of denigration. Most Baianos don't think the situation is quite as incriminating as it appears in a town where most everyone is pretty much brown or beige—and racial identification is more a matter of income than attributes, ideology rather than genealogy. "Money is the great whitener," the Brazilians say. Though there are terms for every gradation of skin color, overt discrimination is often treated as an irrelevant act. During World War II, when a German company dared to advertise for "Aryan" help, their office was playfully vandalized by dozens of non-Aryan applicants while the police enjoyed the show. But few dark-skinned individuals ever make it to the halls of academe or the corridors of power. And Bahia, where blacks dominate most, is also where blacks are most kept "in their place."

Gilberto Gil, an idol of all races as a musician, had no chance at all when he attempted to run for higher office. "The elite isn't ready to accept a black mayor in Salvador," Gil says about his recent exploratory campaign. "By percentage, it's really difficult to find entirely white people in this city. What are they, 15 percent? So they manipulate, they inform the process, they spread stories in the press. They fought hard against my candidacy, not so much on policy issues, but because I didn't fit with them. And people end up doing what the elite wants them to do." While the races have commingled since slavery days, there's a spectrum of colors as rigidly gradated today as in this eighteenth-century schema: "The white man is a gold chain (also heaven), the *mulato* (part black) is silver (earth), the *caboclo* (part Indian) is a reliquary (purgatory), and the negro is a leather cord (hell)."

Even the choice of a hotel in Salvador is racial. I've wound up in Barra: a characterless strip of pizza joints, fruit stands, and money changers which clings to the first open stretch of beach at the western end of the city. There are dozens of districts like this in Brazil, possessing the single saving grace of relative safety. Yet Barra and its shabby environs *are* Bahia to the college students who congregate here in the days before the Feast of Yêmanjá or the Brazilian calendar's many other excuses for a party. The vacationers rarely stray from the sidewalk cafés or the beach—though the waters are clearly marked *Imprópia*, polluted by high levels of mercury and other factory wastes. It is in Barra that the various *trios eléctricos* park their huge truck beds and practice year round. Most weekend evenings, the neighborhood is turned into a giant pep rally. The cause for a school cheer is simply being alive and able to dance until dawn in the tropics. Mobs of restless youths cover the steps, walls, and ballustrades of the shopping malls like human moss. Muscled and tan, they wear Nike shoes, Benetton shirts, Vuarnet shades. It's a Brazilian imitation of Fort Lauderdale on spring break. Or could Fort Lauderdale be a Yankee version of this? In black Bahia, I first learn that there are so many blond Brazilians.

One evening, I follow the preppy set over to a ball at the nearby Bahia Tennis Club. The retaining walls of this exclusive enclave have been painted with crude, barely distinguishable caricatures of Brazil's "men of the year." President Collor, depicted as a cunning fox with greased-back duck's-ass hairdo, is paired with an avuncular Gorbachev. Bearded Lula exchanges smiles with a generic Ugly American who must be George Bush. The open-air auditorium is packed with bobbing blondies. I'm just past the door when I'm befriended by an heir to a Bahia sugar fortune. He wears baggy shorts, penny loafers, and tortoiseshell glasses. A university grad, he presumes that I agree blacks are "animals." When he invites me to join his parents in their luxury box overlooking the crush, I expect to be served champagne and canapes. Daddy passes around party favors in the form of a week's bottled supply of the preferred Carnival drug, *lança perfume*. This inhalant, sniffed from kerchiefs or shirttails, produces a half-minute "rush" that makes the heart pound, hearing waffle, legs go rubbery. Since it's popular in Brazil, I presume there is also some intensifying of sexual pleasure. This landowner looks and acts like a Mafia chieftain. Tattoos snake out from under the sleeves of his polo shirt. He seems just as hungry for a wild time, just as reckless and spoiled, as his son—or the unruly "darkies" the son despises. Another irony of Salvador's separation of classes is that they share values and vices. Where there is really no such thing as a "high" culture to protect, the life-style of Bahia's rich isn't any more refined than the life-style of the poor. The rich just have the means to do it up right.

At the party, I meet Ceiça, who learned her English as an undergraduate at UCLA. She knows a guitarist in one of the *trios elétricos* and promises to get me a ride atop their bandstand the next afternoon. I arrive at noon because Ceiça says that her friend's band will be setting out for Barra by one. But she has a hangover from the previous evening's festivities. She must have a shower first, we must all eat some beans and rice, tuna salad, papaya. Ceiça lives in the penthouse of a heavily guarded smoked-glass tower along a promontory of Salvador's winding coastline. The view from one of the three family dining rooms—though no family appears to live here beyond this medical student and numerous guests—affords a peek at several colonial churches, more beaches, and a cluster of tin-roof shanties that has sprung up around the base of her building. "Distribution of wealth," Ceiça admits, "is Brazil's biggest problem." Given this vantage point, she should know.

This bouncy little rich girl tells me her father is a "farmer" who "runs a number of gas stations." Somehow I think his occupation has lost something in translation. By the time we get to the *trio*'s staging area, the truck bearing her friend has already set off. We try to catch up, weaving our way around surfers and strollers. But this future M.D. pauses to shake her fanny each time she picks up the rhythm of the faraway band. In three blocks, she shimmies into at least a dozen of her hundred favorite acquaintances. Each must be greeted with a kiss on both cheeks, sometimes a triple kiss. "Beijo! Beijo!" Ceiça cries out that all-purpose greeting in a society where everyone aspires to dispense affection like Dinah Shore or some tooth fairy. Watching a Brazilian in a hurry is a bit like watching an undertaker doing stand-up comedy. It's a contradiction in terms that cannot be breached, a parody of forward motion.

By the time we overtake the *trio*, they are already in mid-set. Ceiça's friend signals between strums that I'll have to try again the next day. With perseverance, I get my crack at climbing the ladder which ascends up the side of the band's truck through the balanced black blocks of amplifiers. This close, I can feel each thud of the electric bass reverberating in my chest cavity. Riding a *trio eléctrico*'s slow-moving juggernaut, sandwiched between a half-dozen groupies waving pom-poms, a couple of bodyguards, and one of the three percussionists, I discover what's true about most everything in Brazil. The view from the top isn't as compelling as the vision gained in the midst of the pack.

Along with an intense headache, I get a feel for how difficult the work of a Carnival musician must be. Given that the work is seasonal, the *trios* have got to take as many jobs as they can get, at whatever meager rate is offered. Yet even in this warm-up, the trucks inch along at a block an hour, and it can take them up to twelve hours to cover the main parade route. Most of the bands are then kept busy until dawn at balls and block parties. Nonstop frenetic energy is required. There are no "slow dances" in Bahia, no thirty-minute sets. Luckily, the guitar pluckers are brawny longhairs who wear rungs of sweatbands like medals earned in battle. Their playing looks as unrehearsed as it is, for want of a better word, electric.

"In Bahia, so many people want to sing that we say a person isn't born, they just have their debuts. Music is elemental to us, like air and water," observes Moraes Moreira, court jester of Bahia Carnival and the leading pop alumnus of the *trios*. In the late sixties, Moreira was a founding member of the Novos Baianos, a band that tried to synchronize native rhythms with the worldwide youth counterculture. Maintaining his independence even now, he speaks to me while seated at the control panel of what he claims is the only musician-owned recording studio in Brazil. Moreira is probably the ultimate Baiano, a melange whose golden Portuguese face, black mustache, and hangdog eyes are topped by shoulder-length hair tied into stringy braids from which beads dangle to match a multicolored African skullcap. Strapping as a football tackle, he dresses in floppy pants of Japanese *yukata* fabric, a loose tunic and an accumulation of seashell bracelets on each arm. In Brazil, a party animal is not just a party animal.

"The idea of Novos Baianos was to make a conscious decision to share everything," Moreira explains. "Everyone in the band had to live together and create a family out of something other than blood, to become brothers in ideology and harmony, to share everything: our hopes and pains, food and hunger, and playing *futebol*, too." It was seven years before Moreira decided he needed room for his individuality, joining Dôdo and Osmar in becoming the "first singer of the *trio elétrico*."

"I sing the body electric!" as old Walt Whitman once sang. Moreira prefers to find his inspiration in *o povo elétrizado*—those "electrified masses" for whom he is playing no matter where he tours. "Bahia," he argues, "has a spirit without frontiers." Even when Moreira played in Japan, "You should have seen the people *pulando* (jumping up and down), showing that Carnival is something we all carry inside us." Like so many of the musicians I meet, Moreira combines a naïve idealism and a sophisticated vision that transcends all boundaries. "The more regional, the more universal!" he shouts, stating a secret of high art which Brazilians appear to carry in their bones. "I don't play MPB"— the *musica popular Brasileira*—"I play MPP. That's Popular Music of the Planet!"

His declaration reminds me that even old Osmar does his dreaming in worldly terms. "My goal now is to bring the classics to the *povão*," I remember the founding father telling me just as our place circled over the Bay of All Saints. "One day, we hope to build a truck that will carry an entire orchestra and amplify great music for miles! I want to help perfect the *trio sinfónica*. Did you know that last year we did an experimental performance with members of the Bahia Orchestra? You should have heard it!

The *Blue Danube Waltz elétrizado!*" And why not Beethoven's Fifth plucked out in double time on the half-stop of a fretted *pau elétrico*? Or a hot party lick like the *Flight of the Bumblebee*? "You should have seen it! Ten thousand people jumping up and down in the street to Ravel's *Bolero!*" Now that must have been electric nirvana.

Music to Read By

TRIO ELÉTRICO—Dôdo and Osmar (RGE)
CIDADÃO—Moraes Moreira (Columbia)
SOY LOCO POR TI AMERICA!—Gilberto Gil (Braziloid)
CAPOEIRA BAHIA—Bira Almeida (Renown)
CAYMMI'S GRANDES AMIGOS—Dorival Caymmi (EMI)
GAL CANTA CAYMMI—Gal Costa (Philips)

I AM FOREVER

I have not come to the Pelourinho to see how I look in a turban. The future of Brazilian music begins at the base of Salvador's Little Pillory Hill, deep in the pit of Brazil's dark past. Beside the whipping post which once dominated the view of the colony's first capital come the latest variations of lashings on the drum. From the streets where Bahia's sugar queens were borne in gilt-edged palanquins by teams of bewigged servants emerge the latest trends in black consciousness—with new rhythms and heroes to match. "Valeu, Mandela!" ("It was worth it, Mandela!") proclaim the spray-painted graffiti on the sides of the sky-blue Church of Our Lady of Blacks, built by and for slaves. On the side of the modest Museu Afro-Brasileiro, as much a comparative display of musical instruments as anything else, some current Afro-Brazilians have scrawled "Show Reggae Negritude. Haile

Selassie Lives!" What lives here is indisputable evidence that this was the end point for the largest forced exodus in the history of mankind.

Is that why my Nikes slip and my knees buckle each time I trod through the leafy Terreiro de Jesus and negotiate the bumpy Rua Alfredo Brito? Would there were topographic charts to warn tourists that the route to Brazil's beginnings is decidedly, prophetically, downhill. What this country needs is a cartography of consciousness, a Rand McNally of Awareness! Maps impose a tyranny of dimension, where all streets look created equal. Boulevards as solid as dotted red lines, named after Portuguese barons or drawing-room poets, may be mere mud lanes, dead ends of the soul, or alleys opening onto unsurveyed states of mind. Isn't there some sure scale to indicate when a road is cluttered with shanties and when it is touched with divinity? What keeps me off balance is that I am boring through the glittery layers of Portuguese culture, Catholic culture, plantation culture, slave culture, artisan culture, a more recent hippie culture, a lumpen and even criminal culture. But mostly, the Pelourinho sends me skittering toward Africa.

"It was a long night that took long to become day," a Baiano poet has described the resolve born of blacks' one-way passage here, "so strong when rising that it dazzled the eyes of the people, so that people were turned into things. Up in the heavens, at this moment, Xangó woke up. 'Oh, my father Oxalá, forgive this son of yours. I promise you to make on this soil of Bahia a Negro paradise shaped after the African Eden!' " A first glance at the Pelourinho does not indicate that they've fulfilled their vow. With its hanging laundry, pastel façades, and colonial delusions of grandeur transformed in degrees of rot, this is certainly the most photogenic set of square blocks on the planet. Here is Lisbon in the tropics: an architectural storehouse splashed in extravagant Latin shades. The side streets are studded with gift shops peddling bargains in leather goods and a glowing output of primitivist art. Iron balconies are crammed with caged parrots and a wild profusion of plants. Stone mouldings of sculptural excess frame windows which show only jungle growth reclaiming gutted palaces. But look beneath the palaces speckled with moss and you'll see far more than another mouldering ghetto. Step inside every doorway and you'll find living masters of all the African arts: music teachers, wood carvers, fabric printers, jewelers, healers, fighters, psychics.

"It's all so consanguineous, so strong!" proclaimed Dorival Caymmi, Salvador's longtime laureate in song. "Bahia is a Negro city, full of atavisms!" An eighteenth-century French traveler wrote, "There can be few towns as curiously peopled as Bahia. If one didn't know it was located in Brazil, one could, without much imagination, take it for an African capital, the domicile of a powerful negro prince wherein the pure white foreigners' population goes entirely unnoticed. . . . Everything that runs, shouts, works, everything that carries and moves is negro."

But exactly which sort of Negro? The racism that runs through all the Americas causes us to distinguish between German, Irish, or Italian Europeans, while we lump together Africans with far greater ethnic and religious differences. Among the blacks who populated the north of Brazil were Sudanese Moslems, Nigerians from the Yoruba tribe, Mandigueiras from the Guinea Coast, a lesser amount from Dahomey, and a surprising number from far-off Mozambique, plus the Bantus from what is current-day Zaire and Angola who predominate around Rio. Until some years after Princess Isabel's 1889 abolition of slavery, Brazilian blacks identified strongly with their various home *nações* (nations). But identifying tags such as "Congo," "Monjola," and "Benguela" came to serve as human brand-names and were abandoned as vestiges of a shameful past. Dozens of African languages have been passed down, largely through their use in music and religious ceremonies, including Nâgo, the main tongue of Bahia and the *candomblé* houses.

Just off the Pelourinho's main square, the descendants of slaves have gathered for one of black Salvador's binding rituals. A haphazard line of young males waits with touching patience outside the azure-trimmed colonial rattrap which houses the clubhouse of Salvador's most revered Carnival society, Os Filhos de Gandhi. Yes, the illegitimate sons of Gandhi, here pronounced "Ganjee," as in Mohandas K., founder of modern India, reside in not exactly nonviolent northeastern Brazil. In 1949, just about the time that Osmar and the "electric trios" were plugging in and souping up Carnival, the darker-shaded masses decided it was time to make their first organized stab at participation. A directorate drawn largely from Salvador's dockworkers heard about Gandhi's assassination and decided to fashion their marching troupe as a tribute to this small, nut-colored man who had stood up to the white power structure half a world away.

The choice was inspired: Gandhi as defiant rebel satisfied the iconographic needs of the group's rebellious rank and file; Gandhi as peacemaker reassured the white populace as to the intentions of this unpredictable addition to the dancing throngs. Better yet, the organization has lasted some forty years because the Indian motif works so well as theater. Imagine five thousand lean and hungry blacks, sauntering down sixteenth-century cobblestones wearing white toweling folded into a one-piece robe, white turbans stamped with the group's logo portrait of Gandhi clutching a shepherd's staff, strings of blue trade beads, blue socks, and white sandals. It's a sight that would leave Salvador Dali gasping—all wrong, and at the same time, very right.

In a moment, I'm being swept along into the small lobby, past the locked case holding a plaster holy cow idol, then downstairs to a concrete yard that's been transformed into a giant haberdashery. Seated on folding metal chairs, a dozen men are having the hand towels shaped and pinned into individually sized headdresses. But what do these followers know about the historical figure whose blue portrait in beggary is displayed like a third eye in the center of their wrapped foreheads? I cannot resist a quick polling. "Gandhi was an African chief," one son answers. "I think he must have been some sort of god," says another. Now it's my turn to become an honorary Indian. A volunteer lady barber beckons me into a chair, her wide girth shaking with laughter. The result makes me look like one sick Sikh. Or am I Yasir Arafat getting a permanent? A momentary peek into the mirror tells me I do not qualify to march with this oddest association of brethren.

To fit into the throbbing heart of black Brazil, I need more than a fitting. Across the square, Salvador's original, sky-blue City Hall, used as the movie home of Bahian author Jorge Amado's *Dona Flor and Her Two Husbands*, houses SENAC, a state-run cultural association. Each night, SENAC sets out, buffet-style, an introductory course in the highly seasoned Bahian cuisine that is unabashedly African. Here, tourists can learn to identify a *moqueca de peixe* (fish stew), *ximxim de galinha* (chicken in peanut sauce), finished off with a coconut pudding (*quindim*). Set in an outdoor amphitheater amid a backdrop of the district's red-tiled roofs, I find SENAC's "cultural presentation" staged without pandering or commercialism. For once, the "native acts" seem less a vehicle for obtaining foreign currency than a means of preserving the rituals which serve to underpin a community's sense of continuity. Passed down through five centuries with remarkably little alteration, dances and songs from West Africa are taken up here by an enthusiastic new generation of Baianos.

During these teenage recruits' tame and predictable round of *samba de roda*, a country dance done in a large circle, tears suddenly well up in my eyes. I hope nobody will notice. Or that they chalk up my sniffling to the hot sauce. What gets to me, after a lifetime of supporting, idealizing, and occasionally fearing North America's ex-Africans, is that I have never seen black people so genuinely at peace with who they are. By comparison, the expressions of Afro-American pride I'd seen back in the States seemed exaggerated poses, cast in bitterness. In Brazil, any ambivalence toward blackness, the agonizing conflicts over where and whence to somehow return to some hallowed ground, has been muted. Despite their abominable treatment, Brazil's slaves escaped mass deracination. They carried on what mattered most, even if that meant covering up the figure of Oxalá with one of Saint Anthony whenever the Portuguese master strolled by. Being in Brazil was not a source of endless calamity and self-abnegation, but the opportunity to step onto a grander and more prosperous stage. Brazil is seen not as some prison of alienation but as a marvelous gift of history. The theme *sambas* of Rio's Carnival continually return to this notion. "The Negro came and the flowers bloomed," is one of the lines to which I'd swayed. I'm not surprised to learn that SENAC's folkloric group is chanting Yoruba words that mean "I am forever."

Somehow, the chain remains unbroken. That is because the situation of Brazilian slaves and North American slaves was different in at least three major ways. First, the Brazilians were not forcibly separated from others who spoke their language nor were they forbidden from maintaining their past on their own time. The origin of Carnival itself may be in the advice expressed by an eighteenth-century Portuguese Jesuit: "You should not make it difficult for them [the slaves] to choose their king and to sing and dance as they desire on certain anointed days of the year." According to Gilberto Gil, the pop star who has become the chief lobbyist for Bahia's blacks, "The slaves were given lots of cultural space. Since the colonizers had already managed the Indians easily, their only problem was to pacify the slaves. At the same time, the slaves had no place to run away to."

Yet Brazilian historians admit to at least fourteen major episodes of rebellion. Courageous blacks established *quilombos*, backwoods communities of runaway slaves. The short-lived Republic of Palmares, founded by the rebel leader Zumbi, is among the most-celebrated subjects of Rio's *samba* schools. At the same time, Brazil's geographic proximity to Africa ensured the slaves' continual cultural replenishment. Due to a tricornered trade route which linked both sides of the Atlantic to Portugal, some freed Brazilians reinvested in African businesses. Even today, there is a decidedly Brazilian architectural flavor to both Lagos and Luanda. In the musical arena, too, the influence was not just one-way. As early as the 1700s, dances evolving in Rio and Salvador were imitated back in Angola.

Finally, the Portuguese who conquered Brazil had already lived under dark-skinned rulers for hundreds of years. Having been occupied and civilized by North African Moors, they carried less baggage of white supremacist thinking. "The Portuguese were already a little African themselves," observes Gil, "from the Moorish influence, and they brought the slaves inside their houses. They were into sex with them. They could be cruel, but not like the other Europeans." Certainly, in sexual terms, they were the world's biggest fans of dark flesh.

"The first African *bunda* [ass] that the Portuguese saw and it was all over," is the summary of Brazilian history I got from the feminist filmmaker Tizuka Yamasaki, herself a uniquely Brazilian hybrid. On Brazilian plantations, no connection was more intimate than that of the master and his *sinhazinha* (black nanny). The familial caring which marked life on plantations in the American South—that symbiosis allowing the powerful to admit their weakness and the weak to reveal their power—went several steps further in this true South. "I am ugly, but I am also affectionate," went one pathetic slave saying. "The seasoning looks ugly, too. But it makes a dish taste good." Some Portuguese squires developed such a taste for blacks that they could not perform sexually with their European wives unless an item of slave clothing was hung in the room to produce an alluring slave scent termed *budum*. Slave girls were regularly used as prostitutes, according to the hierarchical formula, "White girls are for marrying, *mulatas* for whoring, Negresses for doing the work." Not surprisingly, Brazil became known in the 1700s as the world capital of syphilis—just as it may soon gain that distinction for AIDS—where white landowners acquired the disease even from their black wet nurses.

"Brazil is a very original construct," summarizes Gilberto Gil, chatting in a cozy condominium den far removed from the Pelourinho. "The Portuguese who arrived here, most of them were underdogs, second-rate kind of people, bandits suddenly given lots of land and honorable titles. And even with industrial evolution, that whole structure has been maintained. Yet, from the beginning, there was no Europe here. No nearby neighbors to impress, no Spanish airs. All those factors together made the situation here hard and loose at the same time. And Bahia is the symbol of it all."

Bahia's hottest symbol is Olodum, the first and most openly militant Afro-*bloco*, its name derived from a Yoruba word for "God of Gods." Every time I walk through the main square of the Pelourinho, I find one or more of their drumming units practicing for a celebration of the Carnival group's tenth anniversary. They need hours to perfect the tight coordination which propels their earth-trembling, martial beat. Sticks and mallets fly in a synchronized show worthy of the Texas State marching band championships. Many of the recruits are literally little drummer boys, but that doesn't stop them from getting maximum bang out of the deep *surdos* slung across their shoulders. The drum casings are dazzling in black, yellow, and green stripes representing Mother Africa. The point is to show that black people can march as one, firm and unified.

A drill sergeant named Mestre Neguinho conducts his troops like a streetwise Zubin Mehta. Twirling the tiniest of batons in huge, confident hands, this maestro looms even larger thanks to a mass of bushy dreadlocks which flow from the back of a blue baseball cap. I doubt this son of Bahia knows that the B on its crown stands for Brooklyn Dodgers. His headgear is merely meant to match his T-shirt advertising Spike Lee's *Do the Right Thing*—both purchased when Olodum was brought to New York for a performance with Paul Simon. Apparently, Mestre Neguinho doesn't mind achieving a hip look with the aid of imperialist accessories, so long as they are black accessories. Olodum's new beat, he growls in my direction, may be called *samba-reggae* but it has nothing to do with *samba*. That's all old hat, a commercialized pose. While I hope he'll draw a distinction in terms of a four-four beat, Mestre Neguinho will say only that his rhythms express "pure black consciousness."

Olodum's drills, half martial and all style, are strikingly similar to the early maneuvers of U.S. Black Panthers in their berets and leather coats. Marked by a wood placard with letters carved into the shape of seashells, their second-story headquarters has the feel of a political command post. "Steal not a needle or thread from the people!" went the old Maoist dictum cribbed by the Panthers. Here, Olodum is setting an example of a black-run enterprise that's orderly, efficient, and devoid of corruption in a corrupt land. I hear a stream of rhetoric cribbed straight from the late sixties' Black Power advocates. "But we're not separatists," explains Peter Leão, as in lion, one of the group's founding artistic directors. "We're happy that more whites than ever come to Pelourinho because of our shows. We don't want blacks to be seen as something apart, something monstrous."

Olodum's office is but a few doors from the Sons of Gandhi, but their attitude is a generation away. According to Leão, the peacemaking symbols of their illustrious forerunners have lost all social meaning. But I'm not sure what Olodum's music has to do with their most recent slogan, printed on bolts of African fabric and plastered on T-shirts. "From Atlantis to Bahia, the Sea Is the Highway!" Leão, whose ex-slave grandfather is still alive at age 106, argues that movements "start first in Salvador because the culture brought from Africa has not been dispersed through too much industrial development. Also, we're a port and we've got this hunger to be in solidarity with the rest of the world." It's the sound, not solidarity, that has won a following for Olodum. Yet Peter Leão insists that his group's radical departure in cadence is a cry against racism and a show of black pride to the entire nation.

"We started with six of us and now we have over a hundred drummers." The great majority are male, but, in a recent stab at tackling male chauvinism, Olodum has been actively recruiting women. "Here is the first woman selected by Olodum to sing during Carnival!" Leão points to a shy young lady with tightly braided curls whose preparation for her debut is doing most of the office's secretarial work. "We have so many people who still want to join us. And now, we have so many imitators. But we're not worried, because everything we do stems from a solid base of research." Is it ethnography or just plain posturing? From the posters around their office, this organization's reigning deities include Tutankahmen, Amnesty International, and, of course, the Jamaican guru of reggae Bob Marley. I even buy a cap imprinted "Olodum—Malcolm X."

Do people here know that he's not a renegade king named Malcolm the Tenth? It seems a perfect illustration of Brazil's ongoing colonial predicament that the country's most conscious sector has to take inspiration from afar. Even their nationalism is imported. "What you see in Bahia about Mother Africa, Jamaica, black power, funk music, these are all general expressions of the black diaspora," Gilberto Gil explains. "The new Afro-*blocos* are part of this energetic attitude, a sign that the community is developing its own ways, its own fashions. It's just like rap music in the States. It's the same in Jamaica or here, where suddenly culture becomes an important means to take community life into our own hands. That's why up in Harlem, you might hear them quoting Fela or Bob Marley or even Gilberto Gil. You know, there are lots of black North American tourists coming to Bahia now to try and check up on specific aspects of their roots. It's becoming an ordinary interchange. And while Rio's Carnival is for Germans or white Americans, Bahia Carnival has become a point of reference for black people in America and the Caribbean. We're building a network."

Gil, whose song about the Sons of Gandhi first spread their fame through Brazil, is a man of unbounded ambitions. Born in Salvador's Tororó district, but raised in the Bahian hinterlands as the son of a schoolteacher and country doctor, he is that rare, educated black with the confidence to have become a spokesman. His musical roots are as one of the founders of *tropicalismo*, the eclectic, rock-influenced, Dada-espousing musical movement of the early 1970s. "As for Brazilian music," he says, "let's just say that it's very seductive, sensual, smart, well done, and intelligent." Gil's albums are a perfect example—often brilliant pastiches of topical references and universal declarations. He was also among the first to put a *reggae* lilt to Portuguese lyrics. "You can see, from the spread of *reggae*, what the power of Brazilian music would be if our lyrics were in English. We'd have the money, the promoters, the international audience. Because English, not Portuguese, is the colonizing language now, the language of power."

As Gil has turned more of his attention to pursuing political aims, his music has gotten more popular—some argue, too commercial. But he still writes ditties that go, "We feel what the masses feel the masses want to scream!" The hit on the lips of Salvador's blacks in recent days is Gil's "Provocation Samba" with its refrain taunting Michael Jackson for being able to survive "not only because he became white, but because he became sad." Gil doesn't seem to have been slowed even by the recent death in a car crash of his eldest son, also a budding musician. Speaking of his "profession of always being good," Gil confesses in one of his songs, "I can't forget that to be in a hurry is the enemy of perfection. . . . If I always take jets, at least I've learned to be the last one off the plane." Gil seems sanguine about all developments, a creature of boundless ebullience.

"During my two years as chief of culture," he continues, "I tried to sell the idea that we had to take better care of our architectural wealth, our inherited black traditions, restore our houses of *candomblé*. I also tried to improve relations between Bahia and some places in Africa, established a sister city in Benin, and so on. After that, I became a councilman and I considered running for mayor. We know a political dimension is there in the music, but we can't let it spoil our individuality. I fight hard to keep this institutional role from spoiling the way my being manifests itself to me. But this country is very tribal and we have to play roles here." I feel like Gilberto Gil is articulating something I have felt from the start, but dared not speak aloud. "Let's face it. The reason Brazil is musical is because Brazil is an African country. And African people are very musical, they create music for working, to teach the children, to make love or make war. The musicians are tribal chiefs, that's just what life made you. Just like in Africa, we keep the history of the soul, the body, the mind."

Like in Africa, political organization lags far behind music. How long will it take before Brazilian blacks find their first home-grown leaders? Forget a Malcolm. So far, this nation that's got some African blood coursing through more than half of its citizens' veins has yet to produce a Booker T. Washington, Thurgood Marshall, Frederick Douglass or even an Adam Clayton Powell. As for a black president, or even a candidate like Jesse Jackson, Peter Leão offers me the same answer I've received from Djavan and other black pop stars. "This will take twenty years at a minimum. That is going to come long after it does in your country because we're still educating our people to participate. Look how few blacks make it to the universities!"

If anyone, aside from the soccer star Pele, could become that first black president, it would be Gil. But aside from musicians, the only widespread symbols of black discontent are renegade figures from slavery days: the muzzled runaway Anastasia, the uprising leader Zumbi and the archetypal Xica da Silva, who seduced a Portuguese governor into setting her up as a queen. Maybe she's not allegorical at all, and the Brazilian notion of a "movement" really is coital. Here, the main battlefield remains cultural. The drums may thunder like artillery, but they are not the first salvo of some general uprising. As usual, the only part of Olodum's message that seems really original, truly Brazilian, is the music.

And music appears to be the only issue serious enough to fight over. Just look at how Salvador's new musical movement has been carved into competing camps. Like various sectarian coteries, each Afro-*bloco* has its own ratty storefront, its distinct constituency and ideology. Olodum is the big daddy because it came first and because of its central location in the Pelourinho. Muzenza insists they are the purest Jamaican sound, the true heirs of Bob Marley. On the steps of their clubhouse, a bare shell of a house in the bleak ghetto misnamed Liberdade, boys in nothing but shorts are tuning this season's set of drums and painting them orange. These look like the same instruments used by Rio's *samba* schools, but no, explains one of the Muzenza kids, Baianos call the snare drum a *caxa de guerra* (war box), the mini-tambourine is a *tarol*. The older groups, like the Sons of Gandhi, call their rhythm *afoxé* and still use maracas and the *agogô* bells.

Headquartered just one dirt street over, the Ilê Ayê block is known for being the most separatist. They do not allow white members. The opposite is true of Ara Ketu, an organization whose location, closest to the white institutions downtown, is more than symbolic. Named after the Nigerian Ketu tribe, whose descendants are numerous in Bahia, this aggregate is unusual enough to be led by a woman. "You don't work against racism by being racist," argues this earnest and rather humorless teacher, who gave up her career to research African music in Zimbabwe and Senegal. Thus far Ara Ketu is the only *bloco* to include electronic instruments in their marching orchestration. The band leader considers her company more of an ethnographic laboratory than an organization of activists. Yet she is quick to boast that Ara Ketu has started a school for children of the street. "Those who pass this life in repose do not live," she quotes Castro Alves, Bahia's official bard. The leader of Ara Ketu also proudly shows me a register of guests that bears a handwritten endorsement in English from Jamaican singer Jimmy Cliff: "You are the rising sun. Let your light shine to the world."

Whatever that light, it is sure to be used and channeled by others. Just as Bahia once gave Rio the *samba*, so this raw fount of black invention is making new rhythms which will infiltrate and reenergize Brazilian popular music. "The blacks got together and invented these things that are very fresh and creative," composer Caetano Veloso explains. "It's like watching a river, a waterfall. You can't deny it. When you hear Olodum or Muzenza playing, you know better what you have to do. It's more than a direction, it's an insight." Already, Gal Costa and other mainstream performers have added ferocious Bahian drumming corps as backups to their repertoire, à la Paul Simon. Along the way, white singers are sure to make fortunes—leaving blacks to ponder a more direct path of subversion.

"The examples of revolutionary moments here are very few and never really happened," Gilberto Gil reminds me. "Every time, the people's resistance is passive. That's what creates this astonishing incomprehensible situation that you find here: people under pressure, in poverty and misery, but at the same time, they manage to have their own style, they don't bother the people on top, they just say, 'Those fools, they're crazy!' We just curse them a lot, *filho da puta* and so on, we talk very badly. But we don't mess with power. So we live in two worlds: one very hierarchical and one not at all. Hard and loose, very tight and very free."

The "minister of culture" has made more vivid for me the cultural schism in which most Brazilians live. It's not enough to posit Brazil's traditional political apathy in crude Marxist terms, some rigid equation in which social responsibility is equalized by the escapism of Carnival, where music and dance automatically absorb all the fervor which should go into larger causes. Who is to say, anyway, which cause is larger, which goal is more real— freedom guaranteed by a piece of legislation or freedom felt in the moment? Why shouldn't Brazilians retreat into a rich heritage of customs and beliefs that have nothing to do with "Order and Progress"—their flag's motto—or upward mobility? The nonlinear and the nonrational offer instead a mobility of the spirit.

"When people talk about a 'new world order,' a hegemonic American situation," says Gil, "I just smile and think, 'Poor fools, it's finished.' From my point of view, Bahia is a good example for the planetary, multicultural future. We are rapidly coming into the other world that speaks another language. That's it: a world where politicians are going down, where music is more and more important."

I've had to come to Bahia to fully enter this world unmarked on any map. It's a world where a guy from New York City can get his head wrapped like a Hindu holy man in the name of Mother Africa. A world in which rhythm, that supreme medium of the momentary, is the chief mediator. Where song is the storyteller, the headline maker, the cinema and the telegraph, the daily scandal sheet and the literature. A world where music is the surveyor and the long-range planner. Music is the first, second, third, and fourth estates. The legislature, music; the moralist, music; the king and the upstart, music; the judge and witness, music; the archivist, music; music, the calendar, the chronology and the clock, not so much marking time as keeping it, hoarding it through the drums' unceasing now, a four-four forever.

Music to Read By

DA MÃE AFRICA—Banda Reflexus (EMI)
OLODUM: TEN YEARS—Olodum (Sound Wave)
AFROS E AFOXÉS DA BAHIA—Compilation (Polygram)
ELIGIBO—Margareth Menezes (Mango)
THE ETERNAL GOD OF CHANGE—Gilberto Gil (Tropical Storm/WEA)
REALCE—Gilberto Gil (Tropical Storm/WEA)
SOM LUXUOSO—Muzenza (Continental)

~~~~~~~~~~

THINKER WITH GUITAR

Over there is the house of Caetano's aunt! Look, that's the primary school of Caetano!" A very black Baiano, elegant in a red polo shirt, points out the landmarks to the pilgrims making their way through the stony streets of Santo Amaro da Purificação. Until our bus unloaded moments ago, I had no idea that this two-hour Saturday evening run out of Salvador carried anything but weary shoppers returning to the villages of the tobacco-growing zone known as the Recôncavo. But I'm not the only one traveling where the music leads. This time, every fellow passenger is heading to the free concert given each year by Caetano Veloso during his hometown's Feast of Purification.

I should not be surprised by the hold exerted on Brazilians by Caetano Emmanuel Viana Telles Veloso. For twenty years now, this curly-headed sliver-thin intellectual has endured as the leading troubadour of Brazil's love-hate relationship with the modern world. There is no exact North American counterpart: not quite Bob Dylan or Leonard Cohen, somewhere in between John Denver and Jim Morrison. Along with fellow Baiano Gilberto Gil, Veloso spearheaded *tropicalismo*—a musical rebellion which synthesized the "psychedelic" sounds of the late sixties with native Brazilian styles—earning them arrest and exile during the darkest moments of military rule. Sometimes Dadaist, sometimes doggerel, both populist and effete, Veloso's concrete poetics have been ranked by some critics in the same league with Fernando Pessoa, the reclusive turn-of-the-century bard who is to Portuguese what Baudelaire is to French. "My country is my language," wrote Pessoa, rewritten by the tradition-conscious Veloso in the lyric, "I like to feel my tongue brush against the language of Luis de Camões . . . I know that poetry is to prose as love is to friendship." One composer colleague's lyric coined the honorific verb *caetanear*, "to Caetanoize." A greater and more sincere tribute to this quiet singer's sense of the popular pulse is that, wherever I go, no matter what the social strata of my guides, sooner or later I hear someone say, "This street was in that Caetano song," or "It looks just the way Caetano described it," or "If you want to understand, I'll have to play you Caetano."

But how does an icon like that come from a town like this? Half sunken in muddy topsoil recognized for its fertility since the earliest days of Portuguese settlement, Santo Amaro hardly looks like a prime stop along the musical trail. Not a single car interrupts our plodding pilgrimage along the dark, stony arcs of what passes for a main street. The pack's route to the concert feeds through a series of oval greens, clean but treeless. I count three bell towers, a granary, a couple of bakeries, one "Hotel Amaro" indistinguishable from other two-story peeling facades except for its discreet wooden shingle. A first wafting of sound turns out to be the village brass band, rehearsing in somebody's living room, all in uniform, shutters flung open. Everyone else must be in the *praça*.

I had presumed Caetano was a scion of the town elite, but our busload's chatty guide points out various Veloso family haunts that reek of mildewed civility. Some walls are covered with recent anti-Caetano graffiti, engendered by the singer's opposition to a corrupt plan to carve Santo Amaro into several jurisdictions. "And that cross," this local expert goes on, "is the grave of Dona Veloso." He's got everyone believing that Caetano's grandmother is buried right in somebody's front yard. Then he shoots me a wink.

"Please, friend, spend the night with us! There is space on the floor at my cousin's house, men in one room, women in the other. . . ." They're used to putting up Caetano fans in this town. My new friend also insists on treating me to supper at a tavern on a side street off the main square. In honor of the rare foreign guest, the proprietor moves his one enamel table outdoors—in fact, smack into the middle of the street. We are brought a tin plateful of black beans and my first sample of the tough, preserved meat called *carne de sol*. "How do you like horse?" asks my host. I fight off an involuntary queasiness, figuring this is another of his pranks. Then the barman returns to ask the same question. The two of them have conspired to fool the *gringo*. Everyone roars at the look on my gullible face.

Around the corner is a town celebration that's far more recognizable to me. Beneath strings of bulbs, dozens of stalls offer the usual long odds on dropping a coin into a bottle or hitting it on some spinning, spangled mandala. The menu would be the same at a midsummer gathering in the middle of Iowa: fresh popcorn from the many traveling *pipoqueiras*, cotton candy and corn dogs. Brazilian hot dogs, popular throughout the country as *cachorros quentes*, are canned sausages steamed all day in a tomato broth and topped with a soggy salad of shredded carrots, onion, and cabbage. But no county fair back home would offer paraplegics performing 360-degree spins and impressive double-wheelies in their chairs for tips. Nor would you see a roving troupe of *capoeiristas*, practitioners of Bahia's martial art in white headbands, doing their contortionist karate duets for a crowd knowledgeable enough to rate every looping kick. This being Brazil, the carny booths surround a cathedral. Aside from the wavy woodwork around the main doors, Santo Amaro's main monument is starkly functional. As always, the church is painted a color which could only be called pallid, like skin in shock. Stars of Bethlehem made of red and yellow bulbs dress up the double bell tower. Directly across the front steps is the sound stage erected for Caetano's concert: an outdoor house of worship for a no less ubiquitous Brazilian faith.

Of course, there's no scheduled time for the show to begin. If there were, nothing would begin until at least two hours later anyway. What hurry is there on a tropical night with families on the stroll, young toughs gambling and drinking, the pious patiently gathered around their church, the groupies savoring the anticipation of singing along to their favorite pop hymns? The festivities all lead up to Sunday's *procissão* of purification—an annual airing of the church's saint figures hauled about on believing shoulders. For now, though, everybody is waiting for the singer's entourage. Around eleven, there's a stir on one side of the *praça*. At the head of the Veloso family, ambling casually along with friends and various aides-de-camp, is a proud grande dame dressed in black, her gray pigtails wrapped in a neat bun. This has to be Caetano's mother. She shares the same hooked Indian nose, the deep-set Portuguese eyes with her daughter, the singer Maria Bethânia. Now I spot Caetano's equally famed sibling cowering beneath her trademarked black locks parted in the middle. I can't believe this is the Brazilian Edith Piaf, the same husky-voiced supercharged torch singer I witnessed holding an audience in thrall for three nonstop hours at the Olympia in Paris. On stage, Maria Bethânia always goes barefoot and projects the image of an unfettered, passion-buffeted child of nature. In her hometown, she reverts to the shy younger sister.

At the back of this anarchic procession, shielded by a TV soap opera ingenue who has become his latest wifely protectress, comes the Crown Prince of Santo Amaro. Or is he the town Brahmin, moving with blue-blooded deliberation in white jeans and matching Bengali tunic? Caetano holds his guitar with one hand at knee level, in case someone failed to notice his entrance. But he keeps his gaze on the cobblestones, with an instinct for self-protection easily misconstrued as haughtiness. The air of nobility is increased when the singer's court takes up a leisurely surveillance on the front porch of a house separated from the autograph hounds by a high wrought-iron cage.

Eons later, a huge black gent in a Good Humor suit mounts the stage. "Since before I was born," Caetano will tell me, "this same man has given drama to the life of a simple town." The town crier now booms across the square, the tobacco fields, the Bay of All Saints beyond—to clarion the impending appearance of "O grande poeta Santo Amarense!" After such an introduction,

Caetano's act can't help but be an anticlimax. He strums through an abridged version of the all-acoustic set I'd seen him perform back in Rio to hushed and appreciative aficionados. At the birth of the image-busting *tropicalismo* movement, Caetano often appeared in sparkly eye shadow and Oriental robes, cultivating an image at once pure as a sage and polymorphously perverse. In Rio, he sported a striped Oxford shirt and the gray vest of an investment banker, albeit unbuttoned. The collegiate audience went gaga over lines about how "the anthropologist Claude Lévi-Strauss detested the Bay of Guanabara." Santo Amaro's teenagers are less attentive. For Brazil's ever-replenished young, Caetano, pushing fifty, is a bit old hat. The groups of stocky, *mulata* girls holding hands in circles want something to make them kick up their white tennies. They chatter and snicker above Caetano's associative word play and his many allusions to world politics. He's too cerebral for his hometown crowd but he does his best. Local boy makes good making music.

"Oh, I was terrible, wasn't I?" Caetano's greeting is a rhetorical question asked from a recuperative couch in the front room of the family sanctum on the square. "Excuse me, but this is my mother's night. My saintly mother!" She is hovering close, though her son's curls have begun to turn gray. Now wearing a bright orange jumpsuit, he looks much younger than his years. His frame is the sort which cannot hold fat. His lithe arms were made to bear silver bracelets, blue trade beads, *candomblé* charms. He is not just the perennial hippie, but the unsullied golden boy. "I don't feel professional in Santo Amaro. It's not a real show, these people, that confusion! It's a lot more difficult for me to sing in Bahia than in Rio or São Paulo. I feel naked. People look at me like, 'Come on! What else can you show me?'"

With the ease that only comes with fame, Caetano Veloso shows me how hard he works to avoid the seductions of fame. "If a show of mine is to be admired, it has to be for itself, it has to have magic. The Brazilian audience expects a lot from you, but I enjoy the intimacy." The singer speaks in a soft, Edwardianpolite English honed during his two-year exile in London. But he is all Brazilian. "I've always been honored to be among Brazilian musicians. As a child, I knew thousands of songs. My mother would sing me the older ones, but more often, I learned them from the radio." The relative sophistication of Brazil's mass communications breeds sophisticates in the strangest of places. "So I wanted to be part of the tradition. I *had* to be part of it. Thank God, it's because our music goes so deep. Because musically, I am mediocre or poor. I have imagination, maybe, but that unbelievable musicality that you find in Djavan or Hermeto Paschoal, no." He is referring to the albino wizard who plays every instrument known to man and some that aren't. "In fact, I decided to leave this profession twice. But my college friends were all big *bossa nova* fans and talking with me was useful for them to develop their ideas. So I decided I'd help them up to a point and then go off. I wanted to paint and to make movies. But I found the visual-arts environment very deadly. Pop music in Brazil is so vital that I was caught. I kept saying I was going to give it up, but Gilberto Gil said, 'If you leave, I'll leave, too.' To me, Gil is music itself. So music was saying, 'You're not allowed to leave me!' "

At each stop along his chronology, Caetano draws a finger across his hips and mutters, "I don't know, I don't know." If there is anything pat about this man, it is his refusal to be pat.

"The same year we began the *tropicalismo* movement, we buried it. We went on television with the coffin of *tropicalismo*, because the whole point for us was to be free of all traditions. We had no idea it was going to be such a scandal. The Leftists said we were Americanized. Compared to us, *bossa nova* became entirely Brazilian all of a sudden!" Up until the late sixties, purists had railed at Jobim, Gilberto and others for their cool, jazzified sound. "The critics thought we were rock and rollish. But you listen now and it's amazing. It doesn't sound like rock at all. It was hippie, because we had long hair, but you can't identify us as just part of the world counterculture. It was less and more than that, a different thing. We were influenced by the Beatles, but the Beatles after 'Eleanor Rigby,' when they became sophisticated. We were interested in making comments on Argentinian tango, Brazilian *brega*, that's bad-taste music, everything. We didn't like all these ideas we'd inherited about respectability. *Tropicalismo* was breaking with these things. It was turning *bossa nova* inside out."

Only a Brazilian musician can speak about musical forms like objects held in one's hand. But I think I know what Caetano is getting at. His generation had to find a new way of responding to the Vietnam War, ecology, LSD, Eastern religion, the increasing interrelatedness of the planet through mass communication. At the same time, they wanted to preserve what was life affirming about being Brazilian in a way that came out louder, raunchier, less stylized, and with fewer black-tie pretensions. "*Tropicalismo* was the Brazilian response to modern life, when we got the irony of modernity," Veloso's leading coconspirator, Gilberto Gil, explained to me. "You know, modern life is quite funny and tragicomic. Because we are all controlled but we are controllers, we are victims but we are the executioners. The good things are immediately taken over by the bad, the bad informed by the good. It's like Coca-Cola: we know it's poison, but when it's hot on the beach, we love it. We swallow the good and the evil. *Tropicalismo* was the first moment when we had a consciousness about this simultaneity, this fragmented reality. From then on, though, everything, all the values, could be thrown out on the table. Brazilians could consider everything like a modern society should. We could discuss so many things through music! Every matter, every subject. Not just love affairs and shallow sentiments. In Brazil, we go deep, we go philosophical."

As a premature punk, Veloso shocked one national song festival by entering a tune entitled "E Proibido Proibir"—"Prohibiting Prohibited"—and shouting, "You all want to police Brazilian music! Gil and I are here to do away with the imbecility that rules Brazil!" But the sixties were no time for revolt in Brazil, not even in a cultural form. Unlike his counterparts in the developed world, Caetano's wild phase coincided with the height of military repression. "The military weren't critics. They didn't put the *tropicalia* advocates in jail in 1968 because they thought our sound wasn't Brazilian enough. They did it because the music was too anarchical, violent, dangerous for the behavior of families, for relations between the younger generation and their parents, respect for authority, religion. Maybe they were right. Maybe what happened during the sixties was youngsters' rubbish, neoromanticism. I was so naïve. I believed that good things always have good results. We wanted to liberate everything! And suddenly one morning, we were put in a cell."

It's odd to hear Caetano speak of this surrounded, imprisoned, by the safety of his large family. "In my house in Santo Amaro, I grew up with ten women. I didn't know about military feelings. For me, it was almost unbearable psychologically. I was in the same prison as Gilberto Gil, but I couldn't see him. We couldn't have a lawyer, we didn't know anything. I spent one week in solitary, sleeping on the floor, next to the toilet. Then I was moved to a cell where there were so many people, not everybody could sleep at the same time. Most of the prisoners, if they weren't too bitter to be kind, were very warm. They would say, 'Don't be afraid. Let's pray!' And I would pray with them, though the soldiers often took away their rosaries."

Two months in jail was followed by two and a half years in chilly England. "As soon as we were released, Gil and I decided it was best to go into exile. At the beginning, I just felt depression. But being in London from 'sixty-nine to 'seventy-two, I saw Rolling Stones concerts, the most interesting phase of the Stones, fantastic performances, Jimi Hendrix at the Isle of Wight, you don't forget that, Led Zeppelin, T-Rex, and many others." In England, in English, he penned the classic "I Miss Bahia." "After exile, I remained solely in Bahia for three years. I was so homesick. Even now, every year during Carnival, I'm there, in the middle of the people. The *trios elétricos* always invite me, they call me. 'Come up if you're there, Caetano!' I climb the truck, sing one song, get hoarse. I love it, really. It's savage, Dionysiac. And Carnival songs are very spontaneous, what rock 'n' roll has always tried to be. Like 'I can't get no satisfaction!' The words are very simple, very strong, but not pretentious. A good Carnival song is like that, made by an old fat black man."

Like Caetano's own classic paean "Chuva, Suor e Cerveja." "Rain, Sweat and Beer"! Caetano's tone is suddenly more animated. The love of music has brought him back from the deflation of his performance. "I feel excited by the idea that I can do anything I want in a song, talk about anything. I remember, I was in jail when I first saw the photo of Earth from the moon. Given our tradition of love for the Earth, the transition to ecological subjects was almost unnoticeable. And I love names, my songs are full of names." For example, a line that goes: "The sun scatters into lovely Claudia Cardinales." Or, "The oval moon of Esso illuminates the kisses of poor sad . . . lovers in our Brazil." Or the chorus, "Love is blind, Ray Charles is blind!" "In an American newspaper, some critic in Philadelphia or somewhere wrote, 'He's got a pallid voice and he does lots of name-dropping.' I laughed a lot, because I always put in names, a serious author or an obscure literary character or a street in São Paulo. That's why I'm very surprised that anyone would like my music who doesn't speak Portuguese. My references mix high and low culture, low and high. I belong to that generation that wanted to break the hierarchy, to make a mess of everything."

Twenty years into that murky artistic struggle, he remains true to the cause. While draped in the outer trappings of rebellion, his face shows that self-acceptance has been attained only at great cost.

"During the sixties, some pop idols were suddenly considered political or literary leaders. That's an illusion which I don't want to take part in." The days of issuing manifestos have been replaced by a subtler form of struggle. "When I play around the world, I have my professional, technical level. But the first time

I went to sing in America, at Carnegie Hall, the sound system was rubbish. Why? Because if you're a star, you have fourteen channels for your voice. Don't you, Madonna? I was crying after the show. But the American critics weren't bothered. In the U.S., it's clear. Everything is money. It's brutal, but it's very efficient. You produce lots of perfect saxophone players, lots of perfect black female singers, millions of dancers who move their legs exactly at the right time! Maybe it has to be like that. But maybe we can provide a better way."

Perhaps the Brazilian way is to make sure that the machinery of mythmaking is prone to breakdown. Now one Brazilian myth is doing what he does best in his songs, extrapolating from the personal to the societal. "It's strange, this becoming a modern democratic nation: you almost see the thing, in spite of so many difficulties! But the historical development of the Brazilian people is such a mess!" To illustrate, Caetano refers to the recent elections, in which voters "intuited that we needed a representative of modern liberalism"—but wound up instead with young President Collor, a "caricature" of what is modern and liberal. At the same time, Brazil has undergone a transformation which the singer could hardly have imagined when he was in prison. "Whatever the social problems we still have to face, it's an undeniable improvement to give up the dictatorship. Still, you wake up and see that you live in a very complicated, very frustrated country. Sometimes it's really depressing to feel that you're part of such an impoverished life. I do not accept the way things are physically in Brazil. And even in my music, I always think of it, and I want to behave in a manner that would make possible, or at least not make impossible, the change."

Caetano's definition of change is peculiarly Brazilian. "In Brazil, we've never been able to create a big, strong healthy nation. Maybe that's why we like music so much. The U.S. is what Brazil should have become but didn't become. And yet these things are very subtle, very complex. Maybe we have the spiritual values you seek. This is something that's not measurable. I don't want to be mystical, I just know it's true. Remember, Christ said, 'The poor, you shall always have them with you.' If I want Brazil to be completed as a nation, it would be in an entirely different way from the States. Something more to do with the Holy Ghost than with the Son—or the Father."

Does he mean a world that's more about process than final solutions, less linear, less authoritarian and more like—yes, more like music?

"I don't know, I don't know. João Gilberto—our greatest artist, the one with the deepest vision of all this—said once that Caetano makes *acompanhamento do pensamento*. How would you translate that? I keep company with my thoughts? That's all. I'm a songwriter and I can sing my songs—much better than tonight! I only know that you cannot go on playing *chôrinho* in a world dominated by rock. There is no denying the world you are living in. You must learn to love it with your own true love."

Tonight I must learn to love the fact that the guide who offered me a room for the night is nowhere to be found among the smoochers and inebriates under the canopy of *festa* fireworks. Learn to love with my own true love the all-night bellhop of the Hotel Amaro, whom I wake by banging on plate glass. He shows me to a room I must learn to love: a dank, windowless torture chamber where a fan recirculates crotch rot toward my lumpy cot and a mistaken trip to the toilet leaves me with all-night visions of a caked-on feces smear. It's just another Caetano song, this learning to love the ubiquitous dry biscuits that are the only item available the next morning at the town bakery. Learning to love the many stops on the bus ride to Cachoeira, heart of the Recôncavo, where dreams of industrial glory, a rail line, sugar mill, iron bridge, sink into the tropical mire. It must be a Caetano song, this town named "Waterfall," where I readily love with my own true love the five or six aging pals who spend their Sunday in a hole-in-the-wall *botequim* passing around a single half-strung guitar, worn *conga* and bottle of *cachaça*. It must be a Caetano song that these tobacco-pickers know every melody of Rio's Pixinguinha and Noel Rosa from the twenties, loving "the classics, only the classics!" I can see Caetano taking his turn, reveling in the musical democracy, Caetano who once sang that while Brazil may be a little absurd, one must admit that it has "perfect pitch." I return to Santo Amaro just in time for the grand *procissão*, an annual cleansing of the dusty town done with a light once-over tour of Catholic figurines. And I love with my own true love the sight of Caetano's mother on the cathedral steps, beaming with the same pride she'd shown for her son at the exhumation of gilded porcelain patrons from the nave's shelter. It's something from a Caetano refrain that Santo Amaro's same booming announcer has seized the microphone to offer his running account of "our magnificent São Bartolomeu, our Lady of the Sorrows!" The town crier announces each sainted statuette in the same grandiloquent tone which Brazil's leading singer had received the night before, with his own true love, nothing more but certainly nothing less. Making me recall, with my own true love of recall, the last saying of Saint Caetano of the Sorrows as he was beckoned back to his family and fans. "I can't say if we really have a natural equality in Brazil. Maybe it's just that we're incompetent for everything, even for being stars."

Music to Read By

ESTRANGEIRO—Caetano Veloso (Elektra)
CINEMA TRANSCENDENTAL—Caetano Veloso (Philips)
UNS—Caetano Veloso (Philips)
CAETANEAR—Caetano Veloso (Fontana)
MEMORY OF SKIN—Maria Bethânia (Verve)
SIMPLESEMENTE—Maria Bethânia (Polygram)
25 ANOS—Maria Bethânia (Polygram)
BETHANIA, CAETANO & AMIGOS—Maria Bethânia, Caetano Veloso (Fontana)

SAINT OF ALL BAYS

S alvation in Salvador is no dry affair. In this port city, everything begins and ends with water. That's why I'm staying through the sixth of February, the saint's day that belongs to Yêmanjá—Bahia's patron mermaid, Yoruba goddess of murky change, tides, and temptation. In the meantime, I come upon numerous ritualized *lavagems*, spring cleanings of church steps, squares, and docks, accomplished with holy juices from earthen vases on the turban-wrapped heads of Baianas. It's hard to know exactly when these Spic 'n' Span processionals will suddenly set out. One is signaled by drumbeats, yet another by the hoofbeats of ponies doing a double gallop down the beachfront. The main water bearers are *mães de santos*, matriarchs of the *candomblé* houses—in this town, even the janitors are anointed—along with fledgling sisters and tiny trainees' daughters. Gliding along in their wide skirts of white cotton matching the summer's antiseptic light, they look like kewpie dolls from another planet. The vases they tote on their heads, holding sprigs of lilacs and lilies, are as rounded as the hidden curves of the priestesses. Bodies turned to airy mystery, their layers of lace are the purest sight in Bahia.

They dump the flowers and dribble the scented waters over the threshold of the nearest House of God, no matter if it's nominally Catholic. Once monotheism gets its animist blessing, the spectators press forward in hope that a little moisture will get sprinkled their way. "Tia! Tia!" they all cry, "Aunt! Aunt!" Ancient blissed-out hags with no teeth, their all-seeing eyes behind glasses thick as mason jars, are glad to oblige in the distribution of liquid. Their role is to discern which supplicants deserve a drop or two on the nape of their necks and which need a full dousing. As the day heats, the ladies in lace are replaced with municipal fire trucks that hose down souls indiscriminately. All Bahia takes a shower with their clothes on. In the end, everyone shampoos in sanctification.

I presume that the yearly attempt to placate Yêmanjá's oceanic temper is launched in the main harbor, with the populace rolling up their pants legs and wading as one into the Bay of All Saints. I envision the launching of a giant flotilla of grace, flimsy yet unsinkable, paper rowboats dotted with burning candles, laden with tiny beribboned offerings for the goddess to unwrap with sure, soggy hands. But this is just another of my colonizing wet dreams. The main celebration actually takes place before a concrete House of Yêmanjá, modest as a log cabin, set at one point of a small cove beside the mix of hillside shanties and trendy dance clubs called Rio Vermelho. This site must have been chosen by some fortune-tellers throwing seashells. The beach is too small, the promenade too small, the temple too small, the neighborhood too small for the barmen who hastily hammer up their *barracas* for selling fried shrimp, for the mob of devout offerants, the many ladies-in-waiting to the sea spirit and that less delicate throng which comes out whenever there's an excuse to slosh up against one another's sweaty backs, rough elbows, odors. Food is love, so they say. But in Brazil, I've concluded, love is overcrowding.

Returning every few hours or so through the hottest of all the days I'll spend in Brazil, a quintessential equatorial bake, I hope to catch the boat launchings. Instead, I chart the increasing density and drunkenness. In the early morning, priestesses have taken up chanting in the shade of a temporary thatched shelter. Some of the older ladies puff cigars while doing slow 360-degree turns to spin themselves toward trance. The line of those who want to give gifts to Yêmanjá already spreads a half mile down the promenade. Enduring the sun in their holiday finest, black women clutch huge bouquets to their breasts. With all the offerings, the thatched hut begins to resemble a florist's shop. But I see little action on the beach except for barefoot kids with their crab nets. Some *candomblé* congregations, their white hems stained with sea and sand, eat sloppy picnics of spaghetti with their hands.

By midafternoon, it takes an hour to push my way a hundred yards from the coast road down to the water. Seagoing vessels are indeed being loaded, but they are dinky old rowboats filled artlessly with bushels of flowers. With contingents of Olodum and Ilê Ayê prancing about, there is much chanting and some drumming. The beach is a minefield of broken bottles, paper cups, crushed flowers. Returning at a slightly cooler hour, I find those few worshipers left by the waves either reeling with booze or scanning the horizon for the silhouettes of ships sent out some time ago. The local authorities, so I've heard, have to send out their own convoy to police the sea. A predictable crew of thieves actually swims or rows alongside the boats, aiming to retrieve the more valuable offerings before Yêmanjá snatches them up. It's bad luck if the tides send the whole mess back to shore.

Up on the promenade, more readily understood games of chance are doing great business. The party is in full swing, *lambada* music blaring. The *barracas* are full of diners. Every desperate vendor sells the same *caipirinhas* and *caipiroskas* (fruit juices mixed with vodka instead of *cachaça*). Where one fellow manages to earn a *cruzeiro*, thousands try an identical tack. Brazilian culture, at street level, is remarkably unified and, by the same token, not much different from the stalls and hustles of Mexico and India. Every sign is in the same script, every menu with the same fare and prices, every con game pursued to its crude finale. In the end, the most depressing aspect of poverty is its lack of imagination. So many millions, all over the world, with so little aptitude for anything but the imitative! Like the bullying mothers passing on to their wide-eyed and efficient little daughters the sum of their knowledge in the easy manipulation of a few bowls and charcoal-heated grease. So many schooled in a shortcut to barest survival which turns out to be such a hard way to go! How long will it take to bring this world out of its colorful mire of self-defeat when it has to be done one shrimp fryer at a time? I can't help feeling dampened by the lack of sanctity to

Yêmanjá's day. And yet, though nobody ever seems to be in charge, everything that must be done gets done: every blessing and every quick-buck affront.

For some daft reason, I keep searching for my own priest to unravel the occult mysteries that regulate the most ordinary transactions in Bahia. And I keep coming up with a single, compelling name: Geronimo. I'm told that I can find this local balladeer holding down an invented desk job at the city's leading cultural foundation, named after the early Bahian poet Gregorio Matos. At first glance, I can see why everyone says that Geronimo has his pulse on the local beat. He's certainly not your average civil servant, lounging with his feet on his desk, wearing a nautical blue-and-white cap tilted jauntily to one side, its brim reading "Capitão dos Pôrtos da Bahia." Apparently, the actual chief of the port has given this honor to Geronimo. "And I'm a sailor, of course!" he bellows out. "All my songs are about the sea!"

Geronimo is a picaresque straight out of a Jorge Amado novel, the classic figure of the charmed and charming Brazilian *moreno*. He's got the charged green eyes—those *olhos verdes* referred to in so many songs—of a Portuguese scoundrel sent off course. His curls are jet black and overgrown, his face scruffy and three days unshaven, his skin the faint brown of a permanent suntan. He is utterly rakish, even without the hat or the verbal barrage, even without having to work at it—though he does. "The reason Bahia has the best music is because we're close to the sea. That's right, the sailors bring sounds that aren't heard anywhere else in Brazil. We've got *salsa* here, we've got Jamaica here, we've got the Caribbean and Europe." Funny, I haven't seen anything of the sort in Salvador's hole-in-the-wall record shops. "We're all smugglers of sound, musical contrabandists. . . ."

Geronimo leans back in his chair with satisfaction. "You know what our renowned Gregorio Matos, that seventeenth-century pornographer, wrote in a poem? Bahia is the place where black people just put their dicks out the window and pee! And things haven't changed much in three hundred years!" Such a joke about blacks can only be made by someone who is an honorary member of the community. "In my other life, I am known as Sarapigembe, the messenger. My role is to preserve and protect the secret life, the houses of worship. Have you read Amado on what used to happen here back in the thirties? The soldiers would shut down the *terreiros*"—backyard congregations—"because they used to shelter troublemakers. Brazilian communists used them as sanctuaries. That's until the police got afraid, until they were overcome by the power! Xangó, my *orixá*, ordered me to become a liaison between the spiritual life and the life on the street. The ancestors gave me the word. That's why I've got to know everything about Bahia. Being an artist, I've got a special duty, I'm a scout. My job is to seduce people!"

I am nodding away like a new convert. "Every house has its own rhythm. Like the *afoxé*. That's a very nonthreatening sound, the rhythm of the waters. I found out quickly that I wasn't going to learn anything about music in the university. That's where they try to make you forget what you already know. We've never learned anything from Europeans in this country. It just doesn't work for us. The Portuguese were stupid besides. They had the land and the money but the blacks did the rest. All we got from the Indians was *farinha* [flour]. Brazil is just a house, but Angola is our real home. So we humbly apologize to Jesus and Mary, but we pray like hell for our African gods to fight for us!"

Funny, Geronimo doesn't look African—but that's the key to Bahia and Brazil. He certainly doesn't talk like a teen heartthrob who'll be performing dance hits from his latest album at a local television studio. I'm thrilled when he invites me there for my last night in Salvador. "You can watch me do my thing. Then I'll take you around to a few spots no foreigner has ever seen."

This gives me an afternoon to look up a young percussionist recommended by Caetano Veloso. "If you want to find the spirit of the new Bahia," he said, "go talk to Carlinhos Brown." But this Brown has no phone and the street address I've been given refers only to an avenue which runs on a ridge above a neighborhood of squatters. I've no choice but to climb down a dirt road that snakes around one side of the gigantic, carved-out bowl at the inland center of Salvador. The houses here are surprisingly grand, with big front porches and iron gates, but they're all disfigured by aborted, ill-matched add-ons. The creek that trickles along the side of the road also doubles as a sewer. One flash flood could wash the neighborhood away. My inquiries about the promising composer of the hit tune on Caetano's controversial metallic LP *Estrangeiro* lead me to the very bottom, the most sprawling place of all. Is this split-level cinder-block mansion, from which little tykes emerge as though out of some bottomless closet, really the abode of this misplaced Mister Brown?

I find the man-child himself across the street, sharing a living room sofa with a couple of boys from his band. "This is my aunt's house," Carlinhos explains. "She's a great lady. Always supports the music." And she's got a VCR, so they can review the moves of a rehearsal they've taped inside a nearby garage. As for his name, Carlinhos explains, "I was dancing at a party and people just said, 'You dance brown.' " He uses the English word. "Maybe like James Brown. Maybe an insult. It's something like the expression 'This blue is you!' " Carlinhos savors this rare test of his Americanisms. Standing at least six-foot-four, with half a foot added on by the standard, cake-dry Rastafarian curls, he is a shy man who exudes a contentment that cannot help drawing others to him. His broad grin stretches nostrils and cheeks already spread to their widest.

"This is our *laboratório*," he explains about the videotape. "It's only a *castanha*," the kernel of the nut, which in Brazil is not often a Brazil nut, more often a cashew. I try to act appreciative of his group's jangling attempts to synthesize Brazilian rhythms with rock. More often than not, this means the Brazilian elements are drowned out by synthesized drumbeats, the *samba*'s soothing vocal delivery replaced by a rant. But the more I watch this videotape, the more I think Brown and his young pals are onto something. I'm witnessing the embryonic struggle to create another strain of universal pop that goes by the term "world beat." Perhaps world music always begins in tumbledown places like this, in unpaved *barrios* patrolled by pigs and roosters. Carlinhos Brown admits as much when he tells us, "The music here isn't about Bahia anymore, it's something for the whole planet."

To that end, Brown wishes he had access to the planet's more developed parts. "Of course, this recording would be better if we were in the States," he apologizes. "There, you have Fender guitars, great instruments, technical support, plenty of music schools to attend." He's not the first Brazilian musician who presumes that his counterparts up North are merely handed free admission to the Juilliard School of Music, followed by a union card and full employment for life. Hasn't anyone ever told these guys about the premature deaths of Bessie Smith, Bix or Bird or Clifford Brown? The martyrdom of most jazz geniuses to junk, obscurity, nightclub sycophants, gangsters, life on the road? By those standards, Carlinhos Brown doesn't seem to be doing that badly. Instead of suffering in some cold-water flat, he remains in the warm embrace of his family. In a padlocked basement, Brown has stashed a keyboard synthesizer, a crude computer, and a brand-new fax machine. "We've all got to be connected!" is his philosophy. And he has no fear of being homogenized by the new technology. "A *sambista* with a computer is still a lot better than a computer with a *sambista*."

"Besides," he continues, "we Brazilians think that a mixture of things, new and old, black and white, is always best!" For an unschooled sophomore just turning twenty, Carlinhos Brown speaks with a calm and probing authority. "I've always been the one responsible for my four brothers and six sisters. I like having them around. You know what we say? Before the sperm, comes the pleasure. After the sperm, a person. But I probably would never have started with music if it weren't for my neighbor on the hill, Mestre Pintado." I heard this frail but sure *conga* player accompanying Gilberto Gil at the concert for world peace. "He began teaching me when I was just seven or eight. He always said

I was his true son. He promised to buy me my first set of drums if I would learn to play."

Now he leads me into a dark shed which extends under the entire length of the generous front porch. If drums are the weapons of Bahia's racial war, then Carlinhos Brown has just revealed a huge cache. "For me, music is on the right side and the world is on the left side. The music is a witness, is that how you say it? It accuses. It sees something no one else is seeing." He handles each of the bongos and *surdos* with love. "I started playing on an aluminum pail. It seems to me that every piece of wood, any old rail, has something to say to us. I like reclaiming the history lodged in things." Is this the same fledgling MTV rocker speaking? During Carlinhos's speechifying, a half dozen neighborhood boys have drifted in. "You'll have to excuse me, because my pupils are arriving now. You don't think I'd have all these drums just for myself? I lead a class almost every night. I like living here, in this place where I was born. I don't think I'd ever want to leave. Why do you need a car when the bus takes you everywhere? Why do you have to buy fancy tennis shoes to give you contact with the earth? Here, we have it every day, because there's no asphalt on our streets. A poor neighborhood can teach so much."

I wonder if he'll still be saying this when he's leading his Afro-funk band on a forty-city tour of the States. We head onto the porch to chart the beginnings of a lurid sunset coming over the ridge that seals us off from the big city. Getting fully relaxed, showing off both for me and his retinue of young admirers, Carlinhos pulls a nearby guitar out of its case and sings "Meia-Lua Inteira" ("Whole Half-Moon"), one of the tunes that Caetano Veloso made famous. The composer's version is rougher and more earnest. "The song isn't mine. It is just sung through me," he says, echoing what many Brazilian musicians have told me. I feel comforted to think that the future of Brazilian music is in the hands of people like Carlinhos Brown. Maybe he'll turn electric, maybe he'll end up in a beachfront condo. But he will always be able to transmit some secret knowledge, always ride Bahia's elevator to the sea.

In a flash, Carlinhos has moved over to a set of *congas* and it doesn't take long before he's comfortably kicking back, summoning the end of the day with a supple explosion of tapping. Without waiting to be asked, a couple of the older boys pull out their skins and join the jam session. The drumming can be heard across the whole hillside, but nobody holds back. Looking around the darkening shanty town, it seems that the key to musical greatness may be having neighbors who don't call the police. It's having neighbors who go and fetch their drums, too.

I hate to leave the class still in session. As I do, Carlinhos Brown pauses to fish from one box a rusted and hand-soldered *agogô*, the classic double bell which gives thinking purpose to the beat of the *samba*. "I want you to take this *agogô* home with you. We say that the *agogô* is the start of everything. The *agogô* opens the way. Use it when you want to start writing your book. When you start anything new. Vai que vem. Come what may!"

Back up at the rim of the ghetto, I hail a taxi to take me higher up another bluff. Geronimo has asked me to meet him inside the barbed-wire gate of the local television station. But nobody is guarding the transmitter. I have only to follow dozens of teenage girls down a cramped hallway to find the one, on-air studio glowing with hot lights. The taping has just started. Geronimo is the guest of honor on a weekly variety show hosted by a local self-promoter who calls himself "Big Ben." With crooked teeth and an obvious toupee, the host looks like a Cucamonga car salesman. He's wearing a Hawaiian shirt covered by a full cascade of leis and barks into a globular mike propped against his chest. Geronimo has abandoned his sailor's cap and donned a flashy satin shirt beneath an emerald-green vest. The outfit makes him sweat like hell under the lights. There's no pancake to remedy the problem. The music itself is Bahian bubble gum, cloying and only a trifle African. I don't hear anything in his lyrics about this

man being a messenger of Xangó. A single camera pans constantly from Geronimo to four amateur ingenue recruits in stretch
leotards who can't suppress nervous grins each time they glimpse
their non-stop bounciness on the monitor. Their cheerleading
routine is set against a full painted drop with floating balloons and
the figure of Rei Momo, symbolic king of Carnival and generalized mirth. Geronimo is my candidate for the job: an experienced
lip-syncher who proves just as moon eyed and mischievous on
camera as in real life. His charm remains unruffled by the lunar
stains under his armpits, revealed each time he hits a high note.

The performance leaves Geronimo drained. Once he and his
manager share some marijuana on the drive downtown, my tour
of "nonhonky Bahia" goes up in smoke. Apparently, the singer
doesn't have the energy tonight to prove he's a psychic. But
perhaps he is, because he lets me out at the foot of the municipal
elevator. The Mercado Modelo, showcase of high-kicking *capoeiristas* by day, is usually dangerous at night. But I don't mind
getting a last look of the stars out over the water. The quick
descent from Upper to Lower City leads down to the eternal
elements which have marked this landfall. A few fishermen repair
nets in their crude dugouts. Speckled faces are knowing beneath
their straw hats. Pleasure excursions to nearby Itaparica are just
unloading. With its thick Portuguese chin thrust out into the
isle-strewn Bay of All Saints, Salvador casts its net for metaphors,
pounds on its drums only to compete with all that sea silence.

"This brother is a musician. Stick with him, because you
know, foreigners can get hurt around here." With that, Geronimo leaves me in the care of a muss-haired, hyper-skinny kid who
just happens to be leaning against an old Chevy in the moonlight.

"Trust old Geronimo. Everyone has to tread careful." The
hanger-on's relaxed lilt suggests he's been waiting for me. "I come
from Surinam, man, so I got to know. It's a spiritually heavy
place. Where we go into the woods and wrestle with demons. It
took seven years for my mother to have me. Seven is the number.
She prayed seven years for a visionary child, a musical child.

That's why I had to come to Salvador. We have all been here many times in our past lives." Somehow I'm not surprised when he adds, "Can you relate, man? I had a dream about this place before I was ever here. . . ."

Music to Read By

RITUAL BEATING SYSTEM—Bahia Black: Carlinhos Brown and Others (Axiom)
DANDÁ—Geronimo (Continental)
AXÉ BRASIL!—Compilation (World Pacific)

RISE AND FALL SAMBA

The first million years, a cove of black sand formed at the mouth of the jungle tributary. The next day, he came downriver, clinging to his overturned canoe. Had he not beached on the far lip of the cove, he could have been flushed out to sea. This was not the official account of the founding.

The second day, he built mud ramparts around the word "discovery." When the natives tried to stop him by flinging papayas, he renamed their tribe "the spoilsports." Why did someone always have to be there ahead of you? He wanted a world no one had trampled, a world with no mothers, no beginning but his. To make peace, he gave the spoilsports full title to his delusions. Then he turned his soggy underwear into a perpetual deed to the cove and issued a proclamation he'd been rehearsing all night. Everything big, said he, begins with a speech to ourselves.

The third day, he noticed a distant patch in the marshlands where he'd been sleeping. This most easily flattened turf, this promising stain, he called a praça. The trail to his washing he named, "Avenida do Rei." The trail to his defecation he called "Rua Dom Pedro Joaquim da Silva Pereira." Since he had forgotten his own name, it was good that he still recalled that of the king. Culture, said he, is nothing but a lifelong test in mnemonics. In the late afternoon, he climbed onto the bluff and took his first survey. He made a preliminary sketch of the proposed main square, allowing room for an ice cream patio and a Shinto shrine.

He decided that a pile of discarded wild onion peels would be the site of his civic museum. The crude map he shoved down his crotch would be its first exhibit. He chopped down twelve totem poles to serve as the museum's beams, the foundation of the first tax-deductible foundation. He spread a few bluegrass seeds that had blown into his pocket on some other continent and called this young lawn "Seaview Park." He killed anything that approached to eat the grass. He was terrified by the creatures flushed from the brush. He named them as he ran. He was already thinking about a zoo.

On the fourth day, he invented a citizenry. They arrived on a steamer, in damaged condition, their skins dusted with cocoa from the ship's hold. He thought it would be a nice touch to stamp their passports personally, deporting known lawyers. He considered trading them in, until one asked him where he could find the duty-free shop. Each citizen came with a set of golf clubs, an advanced degree in conch-shell excavation, a dog tag (left unengraved). All fully insured and indentured. They were very cosmopolitan. That is, few of them recalled their ancestors beyond the last installment of their allowance.

He announced that the first ordinance of his city was death to those who did not breed. This they all did in the shelter of the hills without grunting. In the evening, the State Conch Shell Exporting Cartel was formed. Aside from a world monopoly on confetti, this would remain the sole industry. He was placed on the board of directors, but his only responsibility was to remember.

On the fifth day, he laid tracks so that some people could live on the other side of them. He did not feel comfortable on either side, so he put up his castle straddling all the divisions he had created or would ever create. Between the kind and the nasty, the triumphant and the conchless. If the city ever got a subway, it would run through his basement. He put in coin-operated baggage lockers.

On the sixth day, a public latrine was built on the Rua Dom Pedro but it proved too small, so he enlarged it and called it a jail. A courthouse came next. He forged a trail from the courts to the jail and named it "Freedom Boulevard." In his city, there was great freedom, even unconstitutional license, but only he could lay a new road. City Hall doubled as a bingo parlor. He took the first census by issuing bingo cards.

On the seventh day, massage was legalized (except for persons whose surnames ended in the letter "n"). Ten punches in your bingo card and the eleventh time was free. The far end of the cove became a thatched brothel and go-cart track. The employees were allowed to put half their gratuities into interest-bearing conch accounts so they could one day buy back the cove. Then, in the name of egalitarianism, gratuities were banned. He also banned rents, cocktail sauce, drip coffee makers, jealousy. He closed the first bank and opened the first pawnshop. Every citizen was given the inalienable right to hock his or her woolen trousers. He printed the first postcard, which showed the praça at sunset. (There were no sunsets until the twelfth day.)

At the first restaurant, he was the first chef, until he became the first waitress. With eating out, he initiated the era of communicable disease. The plague came with appetizers, but he was still hungry. The hospital, built on pontoons, floated until it got stuck and doubled as a dam. Electricity gave way to torchlight. The sick became seasick.

The eighth day was his heyday. Conch shells were in demand and he was deep in the dream. He built the first monument, which housed an exact replica of his overturned canoe. He turned every pigeon into a watercolorist and every chess player into a pelican. He inaugurated a duty-free shop (finally), a gymnasium, and a funicular, not necessarily in that order. Housing was moved to the far side of the bluff so that he wouldn't have to put up with any more snoring. It was all held together without nails.

Enough time had passed for the fermentation of liquor. Thanks to secrets received from the spoilsports, it was made from a piny fruit which grew only within the city limits. No place-name is more potent, said he, than the name of its poison. So he cut the tongues out of all distillers. To accompany the new drink, a distinctive rhythm was played on the spines of banana leaves. For the briefest of times, a ballad was sung, spontaneously, which gave perfect expression to the particular local brand of longing. They had arrived.

Rua Dom Pedro was paved with conch-shell gravel. Seventy eligibility technicians died from overwork. Nonetheless, the jail was converted into the welfare office. The mental-health outpatient clinic reopened under identical management as a French café. The plaza burst into red foliation, the petals falling in rows and aisles. The trees were lined with streets.

On the ninth day, new immigrants lined the docks, clutching the postcard with the counterfeit dusk. He traded one up, one new laborer for one used one. Used women got to run the library, as they did everywhere. He dug a moat, which failed to make him feel surrounded. He mixed the zoning laws with the obscenity code until both made sense. He presided over the Chamber of Commerce, which met in the nude but never met quorum. His citizenry could now attend three bars, six fun houses, and a cycle-through spa. Most people walked and few demanded towels. Poets gathered in the welfare office and wrote odes to the one river, as viewed from the one bridge. The coastal range lost its palms to blight, making the silhouette even more dramatic. The zoo got its first cage, donated by the Ladies' Auxiliary. His job was nearly complete, except for a guidebook and the canoe's bark patch. The spoilsports served canapes and denied everything.

On the tenth day, his census showed a drop from previous rough estimates. Conch prices fell on the Antwerp exchange. The dockside warehouses were converted into gift shops, though there were no holidays on which to give gifts. Several films were shot on location, but with no murders in them, they were destined to fail. The cabbies went deaf, their riders blind. Transportation was never the problem some said it would be. The kind forged an alliance with the nasty, though they never agreed on what to demand in the name of whom. Even the Shanghainese began packing up. In an act of despair, he created the first storefront, but the mannequins looked too old, the fashions too new.

On the eleventh day, there was talk of bribery among the

fisheries commission. Health inspectors found code violations in the kitchen of his castle. The museum was now closed on Thursdays, due to a lack of history. Spray paint arrived, along with ethnicity. Rebels jeered each time he tried to swim in the cove, because of his unelastic boxer trunks and who knows what else. He heard they were calling him the benevolent janitor. It's true, said he, all I asked of my citizenry was that they make their own spare keys. When they hung their heads and paddled off, he responded with a salvo of ten thousand postage stamps. The Great Sulk, a commemorative issue.

On the twelfth day, his city was put up for auction. His castle went for a half dozen littlenecks. He knew those coin-operated lockers would be good for something. The spoilsports would never be good for anything. The praça was leased to the Maryknoll Sisters; the brothel declared a wilderness preserve. One tires of everything, proclaimed his final proclamation, even unhappiness. But nothing could be returned to its original disorder. Nobody had kept the blueprints. He packed the museum into one mildewed chest and, bingo card in order, incognito in a garland of wild onion peels, stood in line for the next steamer upstream.

North

The economy goes well, the people not so well.
  —General Emílio Medici, President of Brazil

CARNIVAL KNOWLEDGE

C all it a commute into the primeval. Boarding the light-rail connection for downtown Recife, I find my car full of a straphanging Amazon tribe. A load of make-believe braves model leather loincloths, fur wristlets, and headdress plumage. Some can't help shuffling their mock moccasins and breaking into a war dance. Others compare body-paint designs. Nobody is shivering from all the exposed flesh nor does anyone giggle at the scene's incongruity. Miniature bows and a brace of tiny arrows click in time with the rattle of steel wheels. Only a few intruders—one overworked maid still wearing a baby-blue apron, a couple of fellow travelers with cheap plaid luggage at their knees—spoil the effect of this mass delusion on mass transit. It's as though one got on at Times Square and found only Apaches.

Anyone crazy enough to arrive in a Brazilian city on the first night of Carnival should not be surprised to find the asylum ruled by the inmates. Carnival began in the seventeenth century with the *entrudos,* rude street games where colonists ambushed one another with wax projectiles full of foul fluids, including human wastes. Eventually, confetti became the harmless substitute for stink bombs. When black slaves began imitating the pre-Lenten party, they just turned up the volume and loosened the dress-up code. Though it took nearly three hundred years for the event to break free from the shackles of European gentility, this was always a grace period in the class struggle, a revenge against reality. What stuns me is the ease by which a populace moves from the mundane to the theatrical; the matter-of-factness with which internal reality is transformed into external mythology.

Nothing like this could ever happen in any other country. If it did, Brazil would no longer need to exist. The closest I'll ever come to my idealized vision of a nation in sequins is this arrival amid Recife's *caboclinhos*, the term used for all these foot-stomping Indians-for-a-night. My subway escorts are but a fore-taste of festivities which are considered more fervent and less commercialized than Rio's or Bahia's, Brazil's other major Carnival sites. When our train emerges onto a final stretch of elevated track, I glimpse an uninterrupted lineup of apartment houses following the gentle outline of the ocean shore, gleaming white against charcoal storm clouds. Recife is no plebeian boom town, but an amphibian monster. An Atlantis with malls! Pronounced "hay-see-fee," derived from the word for the off-shore reef which protects its harbor, main port of the state of Pernambuco since the 1530s, coveted and conquered by the Dutch from 1631 to 1654, this is the fourth-biggest town in the nation. Three million Recifenses, at last count, make this the greatest concentration of wealth and labor on the east coast of South America for thousands of miles in either direction.

Beneath the tracks, vast lots of swampland at the unclaimed edges of downtown have been consigned to the *favelada*, shantytowns as horizontal here as they are vertical in Rio. Job seekers from the drought-stricken backcountry have built boxy lean-tos out of discarded, sliced-up sections of billboards. On one corrugated piece of siding, just above a cut-out door, I recognize the big "L" from the electoral poster that exhorts "Lula Lá!" ("Put Lula There!") The blue band of stars from the Brazilian flag—each representing a state, though the Brazilian ones are scattered like the Milky Way—are dotted across what has become a roof. Recife's squatter encampments are immense collages, deconstructionist statements pieced together from building-block words, "Estado" or "Banco," the nose of President Collor or the slogan of some corrupt *governador*, the promises of politicians sliced up and finally put to good use.

Beyond is what remains of the original port, dotted with colonial church spires sprawling across several interconnected, tear-shaped islets, separated by fingers of ocean which once caused Recife to be misnamed South America's "Venice." Recife could be Mombasa could be Tianjin could be Karachi another monstrous tumor of underdevelopment consigned to the margins of our world view. Like all of the above, this town is a reminder that the dominant experience of the Third World is no longer peasant but urban. As such, Recife functions as the cultural capital of the entire Northeast—Brazil's pious dust bowl, as poor in goods as it is rich in folklore. To this steamy magnet come primitivist masters who illustrate the region's cowpokes and Catholicism through arresting black-and-white woodcuts. In Recife, you can find practitioners of the *literatúra de cordel* (literature on a string): roving oral historians who recite and publish in crude pamphlet form poetic paeans to the backcountry's epic bandits and lovers. And of course, the city siphons from the countryside most of the ambitious devotees of the Northeast's many musical forms. For Brazilians, Recife is synonymous with *maracatu*, both a wild beat and mythical personage adopted mostly by *mulato* farmhands from the Pernambucan countryside. And everyone in Bahia readily admits that their electric trios are powered by musical juice diverted from Recife's pet beat, the *frevo* ("fray-voo"), derived from the verb *frevar*, meaning "to excite."

What makes Recife's Carnival exciting is that Recife's environs contain four distinct Brazils. Crammed along miles of beach to the south, the Boa Viagem district is a staggering row of luxury condos standing as testament to the seventies' "economic miracle." *Centro* is a mix of flashy modernity, abandoned art deco, and outdoor markets packed with umbrellas barely capable of keeping a bounty of fruits from succumbing to the heat. Immediately inland, austere villages set amid semiarid hills give a hint of the vast Northeastern "outback." And if that's not enough, there is Olinda, one of Brazil's original capitals and among its best-preserved colonial relics, quarantined from the twentieth century on a spit north of the city. As storied a Carnival setting as Rio, Olinda's grubby taverns and high-ceilinged mansions are home to this laidback nation's largest community of artists and general layabouts.

Of these distinct expressions of Carnival, the *caboclinhos* are now the least popular. While downtown has been turned into one open-air tepee, the tribal entourages prance past half-empty reviewing stands. Only a few old-timers have brought their beach chairs curbside for a front-row view of the spectacle. A single judge barks out a steady trill of announcements through a bullhorn. It's not easy keeping order at this powwow—or determining which clan should receive prizes for most native nattiness. Teenage kids from the countryside hop barefoot on city asphalt, flap their feathers in a coordinated preening of resplendent wingspans. To keep everything going in time, they pull and release the tiny arrows attached to their bows. Better than turning swords into ploughshares, their archery transforms weapons into instruments.

In a country where endless wilderness has long provided symbolic shelter from the abuses of man, who wouldn't want to identify with the savage? Siding with history's losers is a way of conceding that what's been lost is what's best. Yet fewer and fewer are answering the annual summons to get indigenous. The braves of Pernambuco are as outmoded as the Knights of Columbus. These days, Brazilians prefer to pose as Michael Jackson and Saddam Hussein or at least invoke their Amazonian roots in a more sophisticated manner. Begun in its mass form with the creation of Rio's *samba* schools less than seventy years ago, Carnival is really a fickle, twentieth-century affair. Economic conditions, the media, newfangled fabrics, and fads all impact the group psyche which finds outlet here. Brazil's big bash evolves with the speed of reverie, making leaps in imagery as swift and disjointed as in any dream. Carnival obsolescence comes just as soon as a metaphor ceases to resonate.

By now, this anti-institutional expression is the biggest of all institutions, one long-lost weekend whose oblivion has taken all year to plan. Police lines, publicity posters, parade orders, traffic rerouting, drivers, vendors, and sweepers doing double time—all these are part of a mammoth organizational task in service of a most disorganized outcome. For this one period, efficiency reigns along with the Dionysian figurehead King Momo. In Brazil, it's not some dictator, it's Carnival that makes the buses run on time.

The only tip-off that the Saturday morning before Fat Tuesday may be a bit unusual is that the streets outside my guest house are eerily abandoned. This may be due to the unquantifiable number of Brazilians whose nonstereotypical response to their country's rampant socializing is clearing out of town. More eager Recifenses have already headed toward *centro* for the Galo de Madrugada, a kickoff ritual named for a rooster who can hardly wait to crow. This first processional of *frevo* bands on motorized carts is perversely routed through the narrowest and most hemmed-in back alleys of Recife's warehouse district. Is this the Brazilian equivalent of stuffing a telephone booth? This day, one newspaper headline—in type large enough to trumpet thermonuclear holocaust—claims the guests on hand top one million. In the 100-degree heat, it feels like ten million.

And how do you add up all the folks peering down from balconies, sitting so casually on overhangs that they could be fishing? Or the unaccountable souls strutting half-naked on rooftops? What a mess one sniper could make of this crowd! Fortunately, I'm in a country where people climb to high places only so they can bump and grind a little closer to God. The human gauntlet before me resembles the running of the bulls in Pamplona. Here, everyone is a rampaging *bicho*, the Brazilian term that's closer to beast than animal, connoting a mixture of disgust, respect, and self-confession. The only relief from the various forms of heat is offered with a generalized spritzing—a clear link to the original custom of the *entrudos*—accomplished with hoses, gas cans, and water balloons. The city that showers together, cowers together. Once everyone is soaked to their shorts, practical jokers make their way flinging and dumping fairy dust from sacks of manioc flour. These honorary chickens are ready for fricassee, battered from the roots of their hair to their tennis shoes. In the topsy-turvy world of Brazil, there's no need for blackface, but a general whitening is always *de rigueur*.

An entirely new set of campers occupies the esplanade that evening in Boa Viagem. Brazil's lengthiest urban beach is so mobbed that it looks like the setting for some massive amphibious assault. The black trucks carrying musical groups are stationed along the seaside like permanent fortifications against the tidal wave of barefoot revelers. The food stands extend for miles, hot dogs stewing for hours in tomato sauce and squid-on-a-stick competing with truckloads of fresh coconuts and the chalky dry griddle cakes made by *tapioqueiras*. Much in the manner of Bahia's Barra district, this mostly middle-class enclave is the setting for a Latino *Animal House*. The volume of raucousness makes foundations tremble in the high-priced condos oddly lined up at right angles to the beach. Balconies look mostly onto other balconies. Like the country's precarious prosperity, Boa Viagem is a house of stacked concrete cards about to topple.

As in Salvador, live bands perform atop monstrous boom boxes on wheels. Here, it's strictly *frevo* which pumps the communal heartbeat up to rates of mass fibrillation. The martial rat-tat-tat of snare drums drives the accompanying brass section past double time, triple time into a no-man's-land of notation. Trumpets and trombones cascade like a roller coaster in sound. Old-fashioned *frevo* is Brazil's purest partying music: rollicking and ribald, always slipping off into sharps and flats. The proper accompanying dance, which few locals seem to bother with anymore, is a kind of hippity-hopping clog dance done under miniature parasols switched furiously from side to side. This free use of umbrellas and brass makes the *frevo* closely allied to another African-American expression known as Dixieland. The Recife Carnival is probably the nearest relative of New Orleans' Mardi Gras.

In the environs of the Patio São Jose, *centro's* oldest commons now lined with the hand-painted shingles of restored shops, I stumble on some sights and sounds unlike anything found along the Mississippi. Timeworn pedestrian alleys lead past warehouses to one baroque church after another. On the steps below an overdone façade, a 3-D nightmare of gargoyles and saints amid cascades of surf frozen in stone, a hundred gawkers are following a wandering troupe of *maracatu de tambores*—as in drums. A dazzling display of dueling *congas* shows me just how far north toward the Caribbean I've come. The call of Mother Africa animates the night balm, but the Carnival pose affected by these descendants of slaves is to mimic eighteenth-century Portuguese nobility. Buxom queens in red velvet gowns, princes and consorts wearing buckled shoes, feathered caps, and general frippery, form a dazzling nobility of the street.

The ladies-in-waiting do more posing than dancing. But they are served by a contingent of *candomblé* devotees, dizzily spinning visions in white lace. Their butt-thrusting, head-bobbing evocation of the ancestral gods is presided over by *mães de santos*, black and shriveled as betel nuts beneath white kerchiefs. Then I notice something strange about their subjects. Beneath the layers of petticoats, embroidery, and holy beads, several of these whirling aunties aren't aunties at all. One two-ton belle of the ball, a barefoot dervish spinning furiously, wears a curly blond wig but has obviously forgotten to shave that morning. If this isn't confusing enough, most of these lost Baianas dance with puppets held over their hands. On close inspection, the bobbing dolls-on-a-stick are but miniaturized versions of the dancers, little voodoo entities in white.

To get a taste of the uncorrupted, rural *maracatu*, I've been recommended to an outlying village called Tracunhaem. The thirty-kilometer trip takes another two hours, no doubt less time on days when the driver isn't recovering from the previous night's alcoholic abuse. He stops as often as he can for beer and Popsicles and frequently wipes his nose on the company tie. The landscape we're driving through looks permanently hungover. This ribbon of land, forming a transitional stage between coastline and inland desert, is actually the fertile Zona da Mata. The fields of sugar-cane are barely stubble at this time of year. Most of the rolling hills are brown and painfully unshaded. It is hard to believe that things could get so dry so close to the ocean or that the desolate towns along this route could be so near the big city.

Each stop reminds me of the frontier settlements depicted in the film *Bye, Bye Brazil!* The towns' only contact with the rest of the country came through the television antennae known in local slang as "fish bones." No bones out here, no fish, no sea: just the obligatory church and saloon eyeing each other from separate sides of main streets laid on the far side of the moon. The bleakness of the setting is compensated by the towns' outrageous color schemes, lime-green houses striped diagonally in orange, expanses of pink façade interrupted by baby-blue shutters. So far, the only evidence that Carnival reaches out here is an afternoon dance at an agricultural hall. I can tell it's crowded by the number of local teenagers hitching their horses up at the door.

At first glimpse, Tracunhaem looks no more lively. The bus lets me out at the bottom of a steep slope lined with typical stucco boxes. Three village boys, faces smudged, bare knees scraped as though part of their costume, race out of one house. Without a word of greeting, they start fashioning tiny birds, pigeons, and piglets from pieces of gray clay. Instead of shaking my hand, they thrust their instant creations into my palms. Pottery making is the main industry here, though it's never clear to me if these boys are trying to make a sale or just make me welcome. They are plainly tickled to lead a wayward Americano toward the one *praça* which defines their world.

Up over the ridge, a large crowd has gathered in the shade of the church steeple. Their view is directed toward a small stage erected before a couple of bars. Unloaded from pickup trucks on their rounds from village to village, the next *maracatu* troupe is assembling at the foot of a far cobbled walkway. According to several drunken boasters, Tracunhaem is the most popular venue for the region's wandering dancers. Despite inflation and belt-tightening, an ambitious mayor has ensured his lasting glory by springing for the cost of Carnival entertainment. Most of the *maracatu* are lured here with payments nominal enough to cover gas money, a patronage of pittances for their yearly exorcism. With membership and regalia often passed down from parent to child, being a *maracatu* is a serious matter. The title embroidered on the first troupe's velveteen standard reads Maracatu Leão Tei-moso (The Stubborn Lion). Though there has never been any such animal in Brazil, every troupe is named after some sort of courageous, royal, or wise king of the jungle.

Accompanied by young girls in party dresses with high bod-ices, twenty or so men come sprinting up the hill in fast-rushing, ever-widening circles. Their movements are purposely jerky, threatening and unpredictable. The final phalanx is called *cab-oclos da lança* because they wield and thrust lances festooned with bright streamers. The strips of rags which hang from these poles hardly disguise their seven-foot length and sharpened ends. Staged by men of mixed African and Indian blood, these charges make festive the rage pent up by centuries of double subjugation.

But it's the getup of the *maracatu* which gives me an other-worldly fright. Each fellow wears a cone-shaped wig that adds at least a two-foot extension to his head. These hairpieces may once have been made of rope and fabric, but are now Medean masses of dazzling red and orange see-through cellophane strips. Such punk coifs clash with almost any article of clothing, but especially with the dancers' sequined getups. They each wear armless capes, every inch filled with the shiniest, loudest possible array of em-broidery. Underneath these intergalactic ponchos, the *maracatu* have strapped on their backs rigid wooden boards mounted with a series of cowbells. These bells shake every time the men stomp or shift weight. And each dancer can carry up to forty-five pounds of trappings, most made of velvet and other unbearably unbreathable materials. Just to keep things consistently odd, the men sport painted sneakers and striped soccer socks pulled up over their pants to their knees. For some reason, many hold a fresh white carnation in their teeth.

Every troupe is cut out of the same hallucinatory mold, with the same plastic locks and striped socks. The performance is as ritualized as it is nonsensical. One troupe elder mounts the overcrowded platform to seize the single rasping microphone. He works his way through the monotonal cadences of an epic poem—pausing at the end of each drawn-out quatrain. In a style related to the tradition of *repentistas* (spontaneous improvisers) who make up ribald ditties for tips, these Brazilian rappers summarize the events of the past year. Topics range from the size of the local harvest to the administration of President Collor. "He has a face without shame," observes one rhyming shaman about Brazil's head witch doctor. "Brazil will always have peace because Christ is Brazilian."

However hyperbolic, each bulletin or homily is echoed with an "Amen" of bell rattling. As soon as one *maracatu* chieftain has finished, another oral historian climbs the podium. Each wave of dancers grows more frantic in their wild circling, more resplendent in their plastic plumage. Annual exorcism accomplished, they sprint for the pickups parked in a line opposite the village graveyard. Waiting in the truck beds to be shuttled across barren hills, the dancers never crack a smile. These cosmic field hands recover from another day's tillage by chugging on cigarettes. Aviator-style sunglasses—a recent innovation—hide exhaustion and, so it's said, a trancelike state verging on hypnosis. I glimpse no signs of psychic release, none of the usual Carnival letting down of hair. Their cone wigs rest upside down on hooks set along the panels of the truck, looking like wasps' nests gone psychedelic.

Are these mostly scrawny and sun-ravaged cane cutters supposed to be more befuddled exiles from the Amazonian Eden, Borneo bushmen, one-man bands? Like New York City mental outpatients wandering the IRT in highly evolved delusional trappings? Or are they simply figments of a collective Brazilian unconscious that teeters between high tech and Stone Age? Such a melange of archetypes is enough to make a Jungian dyspeptic. Perhaps the greatest mystery is that there is no mystery at all to Brazil's indiscriminate embrace of influences.

I leave Tracunhaem feeling that I've skirted the literal and metaphoric edge of Brazil's infinite frontier. This is a landscape where nothing ever happens yet everything seems to happen. Here, in its crudest form, I've come face to face with the wonder of Brazilian Carnival—which is irrationality institutionalized down to the tiniest detail. If these villagers ever came through Lower Manhattan, they'd be hailed as an experimental company of performance artists. The *maracatu* dance goes beyond theory, poses, pretensions to meaning. In Brazil, genius prefers to go by the credit line "Anonymous."

Pulling myself away in order to catch the evening's last bus, I'm still clutching the damp clay dove made for me, its wings bent. I share the darkened slope out of town with a last set of cosmic tribesmen stooped under the burden of their disguise, their progress easily traced by the washboard bells. "Shall death not come upon me," goes a *maracatu* cry. "So that I may dance here again!" All the way to Recife, I carry the sound of this human herd's clanging.

Music to Read By

SAUDADES DO BRASIL: FREVO—Compilation (Musical Heritage Society)

⟨⟨⟨⟨⟨⟨⟨⟨

MIDNIGHT MAN

arrive in Olinda disguised as the eternal stranger, weighed down with luggage and misconceptions. After crossing the causeway that connects modern Recife to this fabled speck of old Brazil, my taxi is blocked by a *bloco*, some thousand or more celebrants who make periodic passes through town in matching T-shirts that read Unidos Fudidos (The United Fuck-Ups). Though it's only ten in the morning, partying has seized the steep inclines of this seaside promontory, lined the gutters with beer cups and strewn fruit peels, dressed up the churches in strung confetti trim. Walking the rest of the way toward my reserved inn, I'm transformed into another character in Olinda's constantly improvised theater of the street.

No setting could be better than the stage-set facades of a town christened on its 1537 founding with the Portuguese words for "how lovely!" Olinda's Carnival has nothing in common with Salvador's miles of matching pom-poms or Rio's topless, mech- anized writhings. This is a center for craftsmen and bohemians, not exactly Brazil's Greenwich Village, more like its Santa Fe. As a result, the festivities here are Brazil's artsiest and craftiest, the most freewheeling and loyal to the Carnival's roots in childhood innocence. Painted mannequins are stationed on balconies to look as though they're royalty reviewing the passing rabble. Papier-mâché masks of sun gods gleam in rows atop the red-tile rooftops. Numerous expressionist murals have been painted with V peace signs, Egyptian ankhs, and other leftover symbols of the sixties counterculture. The costumes are equally homemade and far more individualized than those of Rio's *samba* armies. Packed with college kids from around the country, Olinda more closely resembles an American Halloween, minus the K-Mart Franken- stein masks.

I fall in with a frivolous mob surging behind their own marching band and Olinda's renowned variant of whimsy, the *boneca*. This is a larger-than-life doll bobbing wildly, arms swaying, on a wooden pole held above the crowd. From afar, these fifteen-foot caricatures in cloth are the Carnival's most individualized human forms. The lead character in Olinda's annual puppet show is the *boneca* dubbed the "Man of Midnight," a mustachioed Lothario in top hat and tux modeled after a turn-of-the-century philanderer who accomplished all his extramarital activities after dark. In time, he was given a permanent mate *boneca*, the rosy-cheeked, frowsy-haired *hausfrau* called the "Woman of the Morning." Some Carnivals later, they begat an offspring of dubious legitimacy, the "Child of the Afternoon." But the first *boneca* I spot is an obvious Joe Tourist, red-haired and freckled in polka-dot shirt and mountaineering shorts, with a cardboard Instamatic camera yoked around his neck. If I don't get to my hotel in haste, somebody will make a mythic marionette out of me.

As its name suggests, the Pousada das Quatro Contas is a restored eighteenth-century mansion that looks out over the junction of main streets that forms the four most crowded corners of the old town. Brazilian tour groups reserve space here months in advance for the privilege of being in the unquiet eye of the human hurricane. They pay plenty for their five-day, four-sleepless-night package, commemorative T-shirt included. Leaving me a room in a modern basement addition, with windows at street level. Unlike my first taste of Carnival in Bahia, there's no canned music from a loudspeaker to stimulate my insomnia. Olinda's all-nighter offers tantalizing stretches of quiet before the signature refrain of a *frevo* favorite slides from the trombone section and a merry roar signals that the streets have yet to be abandoned.

Keep moving, keep dancing, keep drinking. He who flags and falters is crushed. Again, the lesson that's driven home on all sides is that Carnival functions as far more than some crude social safety valve. That's just a pat formula invoked by outsiders to keep all this madness in its nonthreatening place. It's not as though everybody here feels that they're really supposed to be tackling some other task, which, according to some scale of values, might be deemed more "important." Wine, women, and song—in Olinda's case, *cachaça*, *frevo*, and the handiest bisexual—are not a formula by which to cope with life. They *are* life. It's the rest that's just coping.

Some celebrants play in teams, staging elaborate roving skits, like the satirical crew with a cardboard video camera labeled TV Bobo—Portuguese for "stupid," their comment on the actual TV Globo—led by an inanely slick reporter who sticks out a phallic microphone at anybody who dares to be interviewed. Attentive nurses, boys in drag, of course, carry the corpse of the Brazilian economy on a stretcher. A thermometer rests uselessly in the straw mouth of the deceased. A chart, plunging ever downward, lists President Collor's Plan One and Plan Two as the causes of death. Circus clowns, wearing suspenders and red noses round as bicycle horns, move in tag teams. Gypsies, their heads shrouded like babushkas despite the heat, tell the fortunes of those willing to slow their dancing. The local mythology also features Scheherezades and sheikhs, all veiled and most lugging oil cans that drip blood. Approximations in rubber and foam turn men into strutting penises, condoms, and cottony tampons. The Man of Midnight himself comes to life in the form of an elderly black gentleman who saunters amid the mayhem in frayed tuxedo, top hat, and white gloves. For over forty years, he has been the self-appointed "Lord of Olinda," greeting his subjects with overblown, mock protocol. One of his lordly sons turns out to be my hotel's bellboy.

The writing on every seventeenth-century wall tells me that this town has an uncrowned king. "Alceu, we love! Alceu, you are eternal!" In any other country, one would presume that such a cult of personality is inspired—or orchestrated—by some local tyrant. In this case, Olinda is offering tribute to its resident main man of pop music. Alceu Valença is Pernambuco's homegrown Mick Jagger, who has fused the pose of the modern rock rebel with a deep respect for the folk traditions of his native region. On albums and in concert, he mixes backcountry inflections with frenetic, heavy metal. One bit of Olinda's adulatory graffiti sums up his sound: "Alceu—bom de frevo, bom de rock, bom demais!" Good at *frevo*, good at rock, better than ever!

I catch up with Alceu across town at Boa Viagem, where Brahma and Antarctica, sudsy competitors of the Brazilian beer biz, sponsor simultaneous free shows in the sands. Bare-chested, his shoulder-length hair flowing from under a stovepipe hat, Alceu Valença skips and struts and dominates the stage like no other Brazilian performer. When he dashes offstage, the loyal crowd holds its breath to see how their local boy might reappear. The stovepipe becomes an Uncle Sam disguise, painted with stars and stripes, becomes the bowler hat of Charlie Chaplin, becomes a dunce cap, a backcountry witch doctor's headdress. The presentation is as avant-garde as the lyrics are accessible. In "Morena Tropicana," he extols the virtues of Northeastern ladies, comparing each body part to a tropical fruit. And Alceu's adolescent swagger is contrasted with several volunteer Shirley Temples, tiny tots dressed in pink birthday dresses and white gloves, punctuating their dance by spinning matching pink umbrellas. A few months back, I would not have known what to make of this anomalous admixture of hokeyness and hard rock, this uniquely Brazilian mongrel.

"My music is like the Holy Trinity," are Valença's first words of explanation, appropriate since his strong, plaintive features happened to be framed with parted, Jesus-length brown locks. If I want to speak moderately, I'm pop. When I'm violent and angry, I'm rock. And when I'm feeling like a clown, I'm *frevo*." In a dressing room packed with guitar cases, band members and their girlfriends, Alceu radiates a Messianic charisma.

"You want to know where I come from? I am the grandson of Luiz Gonzaga and the son of Jackson do Pandeiro!" These are the two great popular minstrels of the Northeast's backlands, the great innovators of the country rhythms called *forró* and *baião*. "And if you listen, I can prove to you that Luiz Gonzaga is exactly the same as Elvis Presley!" Alceu began a guttural mumbling: "You ain't nothing but a hound dog" in Portuguese. "And Jackson do Pandeiro is just like Little Richard!" The other musicians shoot me looks that suggest I shouldn't take seriously anything out of Alceu's ever-moving mouth. He illustrates by banging various beats on the wall. One sounds like galloping horses, one like a metronome on speed. "That's the *frevo*, which came from the military bands and our Portuguese traditions. You have to know theory because *frevo* is very baroque. It's our Mozart."

But Alceu's exposition of Northeastern roots has just begun. "The music from the coast has always been more *negra*, from Africa, but that's somewhat of a false distinction. At São Bento da Una, a hundred miles inland where I was born, the culture we inherited was already half Moor. The Portuguese were already mixed up, you might say. Just look at this nose of mine!" It is rather hooked, a good compliment to wide, imploring eyes, a cleft chin beginning to sag. But I don't get what he's driving at until I recall that this area of Brazil is said to have been populated with Novos Christianos. These were Portuguese Jews forced to make a quick conversion when the king of Portugal was made to comply with a Spanish request for their expulsion. So intermingled was Jewish blood among the Portuguese, an old joke goes, that when the king signed the expulsion decree, his first minister asked, "Sire, which one of us leaves first, you or me?" Leaving Alceu Valença to claim five hundred years later, "Everything works on guilt. When my old aunt went to have her yearly exam, the doctor asked her if she was urinating well. And she answered, 'Better than I deserve!' We are all lost Jews in the Northeast!"

Alceu leaves me in the hands of Nilson Barbosa, his producer and chief aide-de-camp. This gaunt and prematurely balding figure, a sort of Abe Lincoln with a suntan, turns out to be an honest-to-goodness Jew. He looks far too preoccupied with weighty matters to manage a musical mirth machine. But he beckons me to tag along for the after-show party in a beachfront penthouse. Finally, I am gaining entree to a genuine Brazilian Carnival bash! This one consists of only five or so couples, give or take a few precocious children, sitting cross-legged on a living room rug and passing the inhaler of *lança perfume*—the etherlike drug associated with Carnival revels for more than a century. In the spirit of thorough research into forms of abandon, I take a few lengthy sniffs. At once, I feel myself cast into a throbbing, echoing well. Sound, sight, legs, and heart waffle. It isn't all that scintillating, this rapid flirtation with total vascular engorgement, eyeballs and eardrums and arteries about to burst. The drug does make more persuasive the call of music. But what do I get for an authentic sound track? Nilson is infatuated, obsessed, with Paul Simon's Brazilian album and keeps placing the needle back on the first cut to savor the way American recording perfection captures the full force of Olodum's drumming. He plays the same two-minute riff about thirty times, pausing to take another drag from the inhaler then reset the needle, over and over until everyone howls for relief.

When I follow Alceu's manager out to the balcony for a breath of sea air, out comes a flood of intoxicated confessions about why he had given up his first passion, filmmaking. "Not a decent feature has been produced in over three years. Imagine that in a country of this size! There's no money for anything now." I find this hard to believe, given the new construction going up along Recife's namesake reef for as far as my stoned eyes can scan. "Oh, but you must remember, this isn't Brazil right here! You know what they say? That we Brazilians live like crabs, always scratching at the sand. You must go to the interior." The record producer shouts at the merrymakers below. "You must know the hunger! The misery!"

But this is Brazil, where social conscience need not interfere with a good party. I think of a story told by a Brazilian friend about arriving at 2 A.M. in the provincial town of Curitiba during the height of the *ditadura*, searching for a meeting of the banned, clandestine Communist party only to be directed to the wildest, noisiest bash in town. Now Nilson leads the way to a private swimming pool. By the time everyone changes into spandex G-strings, the sun is coming up. Dawn at the tropics is never gentle enough for eyes and hearts that don't want to relinquish the relief of the *madrugada*, a comforting middle ground between night and day which so many Brazilian songs extol. From the water, I watch Nilson slump lower and lower into a piece of lawn furniture. Barely leaning over, with the aplomb of a veteran, he vomits onto the tiles.

By thin Wednesday, all Brazil is sleeping it off. The recuperation begins—and so does the planning for next Carnival. Staggering out in the late afternoon, I find that Olinda's revelers have retreated en masse. For the first time, the streets' steep, cobbled flumes lay at my disposal. I finally get an unobstructed view of the many churches flanked with royal palms, the wild murals depicting the idealized Olinda of bronzed peaceniks and dancing clowns. "Paz, Liberdade e Socialismo!" reads a banner painted over the door of a bar. I can stand back far enough to discern that the shopping mall occupied by sandal shops was once the old slave barracks, still outfitted with an auction block for humans. For all its artsy airs, I now see that Olinda is a poor town. One single, uninspired bakery and juice bar, buns and rotting fruit supervised by insect swarms, serves the whole overcrowded hillside. Yesterday's inescapable chaos has been quickly swept up and reduced to heaps of colorful streamers, shed shards of costume. Brimming with color, the piles are offerings left at a shrine. In this town, the trash is flamboyant, Orientalized. In Brazil, even the garbage is grandiose.

I know exactly which house to head for—I have seen it pointed out by fans angered over Alceu Valença's recent endorsement of the school chum running as the ruling party's gubernatorial candidate. "You fucked up! You fucked up!" went the chants of the *blocos* as they passed Alceu's front door. But that door remains unlocked, open to criticism. "O Americano!" a pretty *mulata* announces with singsong glee. The carved doors open into a Soho artist's dream loft. All the beams and brick walls of this seventeenth-century shell have been exposed, the three floors connected with metal firehouse stairs. A few antique dressers barely disturb the grandiose emptiness. Potted plants and Indian hammocks lend a tropical feel. But there still isn't room enough to contain Alceu.

He's been expecting me, though I would never know it from his standard aging rock-star attire of torn blue jeans and nothing else. Valenca goes bare-chested, no matter who drifts in and out. Despite the several dramatic streaks of white in his sixties-style hair, he remains eternally cocky, exuding both decadent decay and a vigor beyond his years. "You know, I wasn't always a musician," he launches in without invitation. "I wanted to be a journalist, I wrote poetry. I studied briefly at Harvard. A great time. I knew all the Black Panthers." Between calls on a portable phone and bites of a pasta dinner, Alceu quizzes me on American politics. "The trouble with America is that it is run by lawyers. It's much simpler to be ruled by generals! I graduated in law. But my career consisted of trying a single case. Soon enough, Brazil lost a mediocre lawyer and gained an ironic rebel."

The singer completes his biography with a tour of his brick walls' exhibitionist exhibit. Along with a collection of Pernambucan masks and the horse-head getups he uses as stage props, there are numerous donated portraits of the star, most of the artwork for his album covers, some framed publicity photos. This is one man who doesn't need a bathroom mirror because he can see himself everywhere he looks. This apartment could be called the Museu Alceu Valença. Here, the art and the docent are one. We're being dogged all the while by the enthralled black girl, a well-endowed teenage runaway who cleans houses in Olinda. "All she talks about is marrying an American and now she won't say a word. When she heard you were coming, she ran and took off her bra!"

Alceu teases her so mercilessly that she retreats into the kitchen. Alceu's wife, most recent in a series, is just as wide-eyed but oozes the self-possession of wealth. In a country where they could choose from an unrivaled bevy of beauties, the musicians I've seen have all opted for rather stolid helpmates. "Alceu told me the first time we met that he would marry me and I laughed in his face," his wife recounts. She is the only one in the house who isn't entranced by Alceu's energy. At one point, he interrupts his lecture to bend over and kiss her, declaring with a wry smile, "I'm her puppet." That must be a relief since he so easily pulls the strings with everyone else.

This includes a coterie of Olinda's disgruntled artists and amateur historians, plus assorted refugees from the Carnival madness. "It used to last three days, then four, now five," Alceu tells me. "So we're working our way to a Carnival all year round!" One fan has walked all the way from Boa Viagem to get an autograph. Alceu invites one and all to watch a videotape—of himself, of course—showing his recent performance at Rock in Rio. One of the few native musicians to perform this year, he is wildly popular with an ocean of teenyboppers filling Maracaña, the world's biggest stadium. I get the reference now when the TV cameras zoom in on one fan carrying a sign that reads "Olinda," then another dancing orgiastically à la Woodstock while holding a miniature bobbing *boneca*. Alceu's voice suggests an angelic fragility unapparent in the flesh.

"I'm the best because I'm a musician and critic all in one!" Alceu concludes, patting his bare stomach, always appearing to feel, to paraphrase his guilty aunt, better than he deserves. "Only I know how many Brazils there are! I am on the road constantly, a hundred and twenty cities over the last year. I've seen the logging camps of Pará, the red earth of Rio Grande do Sul, the far reaches of Rondônia! I've sung in towns where they had to use the only generator for my show. To hear my music, the streets went dark. I think music has this central importance because our society is not yet too homogenized. When Brazil gets too developed, then we'll stop singing. Until then, Brazil will remain the most available of countries!"

When I survey the scruffy types welcomed into Alceu Valença's household, I certainly can't argue with the adjective "available." However, Alceu the Second, nicknamed "Ceceu," hears another message in the sounds of the rabble that his father adores. "Brazilians are so incredibly stupid. They're like a herd of cattle, marching to nowhere." The drummer in his dad's band, long-haired Alceu Junior is as hulking as a Nebraska linebacker and as hip as a New York street kid. Junior dreams—like the flirtatious maid, like many in his generation—of immigrating to the States. But he doesn't lust for security. He wants the best drum pads, the best recording studios, a clean world of high-tech opportunities. "Look at Japan. Forty years ago, they were bombed to shit and look what they've done! Our people have had five hundred years and they're still making excuses!"

Junior stays behind when the rest of the gang gets the urge to find another party. Alceu's spiffy white Chevy leads a caravan down the cobblestones and out along the flat boulevards to a new Olinda that has sprung up along the flat tip of the peninsula. Drive-ins, dry cleaners, the flimsiest way stations of modern civilization line the way toward the town's one five-star hotel which sits at the edge of a thoroughly polluted beach. Alceu and entourage are boldly crashing the mayor of Olinda's Carnival reception. Around the kidney-shaped pool, we find a smug group notable for their lack of dark-skinned faces, a veritable tropical chamber of commerce. I always know that I'm among the rich in Brazil when I catch myself thinking that even Brazilians can be boring.

"You know," Alceu confides after another round of blinding *caipirinha* cocktails, "I often have this dream about going to heaven and finding Christ at God's right side and Karl Marx on the other. And they are giving all new arrivals a written exam! I'm just another guilty son of the village of São Bento da Una! I'm not just a musician. I'm an existential humanist." Should I be surprised that the court jester of Brazilian music talks French philosophy? "Sartre and De Beauvoir, those are my heroes! Power to the imagination! It's the awareness of nothingness that makes us *engage!*"

Alceu's big green eyes indicate that he is too worldly for the world he moves in. Yet if he were ever to turn his back on that world, everything that gives him joy would be shattered. Perhaps he is Olinda's real "Midnight Man," not so much a tiptoeing seducer as one sneaky cat. A blond in a sun dress has come all the way from Florianópolis, a thousand miles or more, to seek an audience. "A kind person, a good person I'm sure!" he whispers once he has satisfied the fan. "But she's just not a member of our tribe!" Before I can figure out whether he's referring to the existentialists or the Jews or the kind with feathers and loincloths, a new arrival makes Alceu leap to his feet. "There he is! Now you can see the one client I ever represented in court. My only litigant! But I can't remember. Please tell me, did we win or lose?"

Music to Read By

OS GRANDES SUCESOS—Alceu Valença (Philips)
ANDAR, ANDAR—Alceu Valença (EMI)
OROPA, FRANÇA E BAHIA: TROPICAL ROCK—Alceu Valença (RCA)

ASS MEDIA

The main sport of Brazil may be football, but Carnival is the Super Bowl of voyeurism. Watching, not touching, is the rule of the day—and the raison d'être for all-night broadcasts. Whenever the local revelers tire, they can always drop out by tuning in. If the party outdoors is beginning to flag, the festivities are brought indoors with the flick of a dial. Even in the realm of pleasure, a majority of Brazilians get nearest to a live body by snuggling up to their living room set. Many of the natives accept what most foreigners would find sacrilegious: that the greatest show on earth may be Carnival's televised version.

In truth, sampling world variants of the boob tube may be the most underrated pleasure of travel. After all, who wants to admit to being an international couch potato? Yet a country's approach to the airwaves can tell you as much about national character as its billboards, its menus, its leaders. Take, for instance, those silky, purring madonnas of Italian weather girls; Chinese commercials that prove the durability of carpets with army tanks; late-night Sumo wrestling broadcasts viewed in contemplative Japanese inns by dropping hundred-yen coins in a slot. And I'm not the only one who sometimes prefers to participate in the global village with a finger on the "mute" button.

Like the Super Bowl, Rio's four-day nonstop half-time show was made for the twenty-inch box. It's amazing that the *samba* schools were invented some seventy years ago—about the same time as American pro football—because both are perfectly tailored to a fifteen-inch screen. Carnival's sexy scrimmage between competing teams, uniformed as much as any on the gridiron, is a linear contest on a well-lit playing field. Through some video alchemy, the grubby Sambódromo, its cold concrete grandstands like stalled freight cars, becomes a place of gaiety and warmth. From afar, football and Carnival are both a blur of colliding bodies. Instead of being reduced within cathode confines, the action is enlarged. Viewers at the event could never match zoom lenses at keeping track of all the crisp formations and very forward passes, the jukes and shimmies, the flagrant fouls and especially those tight ends!

With all its mad jiggling and quicker-than-the-eye shuffling of feet in six-inch spiked heels, the *samba* itself seems to have been made for repeated analysis through slo-mo. When it comes to senseless gyrations, there is nothing like those instant replays! Just as we've come to expect with the Super Bowl, the Brazilian stations manage to cover all the angles: from aerial surveys of the centrifugal rotation of the Baianas' wide skirts to the sprawled, floor-level view up through the crotch straight into the huddle. A moving track shot is mounted on the stadium's wall, just above the level of the parade. No expense is spared. Nor any sensibility. Hand-held "Carnival-cams" take the viewer beyond intimacy to "up close and personal" with the unpadded buttocks of a taxi squad of topless *mulatas*, the whirling moves of the *porta-bandeiras*, the wizard *passistas* doing athletic double time with tambourines balanced on their noses. Directors zoom in on favored sets of nipples, smiles, belly buttons sprinkled with glitter. Cameramen carry out much of their tough assignment sprawled on theirs backs in a constant attempt to get lower than hemlines. Thanks to TV, we are only inches away from the forbidden fruit. A nation's urge to mix and mate is given full frontal exposure. This makes the Dallas Cowboy cheerleaders look like the Muppets.

Costumes, dances, and drumming are all subjected to the nonstop scrutiny of a pedantic form of play-by-play. The expert commentators in Rio are drawn from the ranks of old *carnava-lescos* and new singers, including such notable stars of the *samba* form as Alcione and Beth Carvalho. Strikingly, though, there is still a higher proportion of black faces in the parade than in the announcer's booth. Prominent socialites, soccer stars, and tourism officials are more likely to step up to the mike. A team of rapid-fire interviewers steps into the fray to pull aside sweaty percussionists, a stray pop singer, or politician caught in the act of total abandonment. These familiar Carnival hosts are mostly young and casually dressed in striped fishermen's shirts, no stuffed tuxedoes out here. During breaks in the Rio transmission, a *Late Late Show* which lasts until the next morning, there are live shots of the various festivities around the nation. Cutaways to the usual views of mob frenzy come on like urgent bulletins.

As with our Sunday-afternoon coverage, it's beer companies that offer most of the sponsorship. A bikinied lass raising a glass or two is the inevitable intro video. Brazil's two national networks, Rede Globo and Manchete, spend months showing off each season's new graphics and theme music as though their ratings depend on it. Are people going to tune in *Star Trek* reruns instead? Given that nearly half this Nielsen ratings' test group is functionally illiterate, and some one-fourth live in rural areas which lag far behind the development of the cities, Brazilians are accustomed to accepting televised images as a reliable vision of their contemporary life.

Brazil's television programming is slickly produced, but on clear examination, comes up more than a bit skimpy. To North American eyes, the daily schedule never quite gets to prime time. Evenings are taken up with the wildly popular *telenovelas* and miniseries that North American housewives are allowed during the dreary daytime hours only. The days have passed when such soaps relied heavily on illicit liaisons between master and maid. After exhausting boardrooms or beach resorts as settings for intrigue and adultery, the trend lately has been toward stories of betrayal and bonding amid the cowpokes and cowgals of the Brazilian frontier. It's a bit odd, in the land of the *samba*, to see so much passion presented without anyone ever kicking off their tall boots. Perhaps this reflects a generalized increase in the spending power of city dwellers with country roots. Many of these feature upcoming *caipira* singers as their heart-throbs. Don't call it "Dallas," but the Mato Grosso.

Of course, matches of *futebol* get priority over everything. Variety and musical "specials" are probably more frequent in Brazil, but, given the pool of talent to draw upon, hardly as rich as they might be. An hour or two each day of Brazilian "MTV" airs international videos alongside amateurish imitations by local rock bands. The nightly news hours are relatively sober. However, even here, that Brazilian tendency to improve on reality sometimes yields odd results. In the middle of a live report on pollution in Kuwait after the Gulf War, a film of birds drowned by some other, unspecified oil spill is interspliced and set to a tear-jerking sound track. A study of U.S. military might can be casually interrupted with brief, nearly subliminal flashes of Arnold Schwarzenegger or a Rambo rampage. There is no attempt to disentangle fiction from fact.

Adding a more surreal touch, the bulk of the children's fare features dubbed Japanese monster mixes of martial arts and robotics, Godzilla in Portuguese. Brazilian television, like Brazilian culture, is fixated somewhere around the third grade. It's not just Saturday morning, but every afternoon, that the kiddies get their due. And no show is more popular with children or their parents than the daily marathon of live studio games and hoopla hosted by a lithe and annoyingly angelic blonde named Xuxa ("Shoosha"). Carrying a microphone in the shape of a heart, the off-screen Maria das Graças Meneghel leads a selected group of standing, bounding, bouncing, cheering tots through a variety of indoor sports that look designed, at times, to stymie and humiliate the children. But it's all in good fun, and everybody always gets to kiss the reigning queen afterward. In between whipping up the enthusiasm of this peppy pep rally, Xuxa reads fan mail, drifts dreamily about, or performs some of her latest hits, accompanied by a group of writhing backup singers who, like her, sport blond bangs and vinyl go-go boots.

So great is Xuxa's appeal that a second *Clube da Criança* (*Children's Club*) is hosted by an equally pale and sinewy imitator. " 'Tá na hora, 'tá na hora, 'tá na hora de brincar . . ." goes one of Xuxa's insipid smash hits. "Now's the time, now's the time to play!" Before I ever heard her sing it, I got a rendition of this mindless ditty from one Rio couple's pet parrot, who goes by the name Fuck and has learned to squawk Xuxa's entire repertoire at a somewhat lower register. Recently, Xuxa even rated a real-life kidnapping attempt, causing her to hire a team of eight bodyguards. As one Brazilian cautioned, "This woman has probably sold more records than all the people you are going to write about put together."

After being in Brazil for a while, it doesn't seem at all odd that a country so mired in racial symbolism should have as its most popular figure someone so white and Nordic. It is also utterly appropriate that the nation's number-one child-care provider should do little to suppress her evident sexiness. From the earliest age, Brazilian TV promotes a population devoted to physicality: it's all singing, all dancing, all jumping, all shoving, all bouncing. The preschool message seems to be that if you don't move, you can't live. I never see a moment when the children are being read a fairy tale. In Brazil, it's woe to the bookworm or the uncoordinated!

Given this regular daytime Carnival for toddlers, the real thing isn't much of a change. "The revolution will not be televised" went a popular protest song in the States. In Brazil, a thousand mock revolts are broadcast in living, exploding color. And it's all done without safety labeling or disclaimers. No hypocritical hand-wringing or even a repentant nod toward the admonitions of authority figures or the pieties of the Catholic Church. Considering all I've heard about the hypersensitivity of the powers-that-be to every form of subversive innuendo, the impromptu script of Brazil's favorite miniseries bears not even the marks of self-censorship.

Reaching its crescendo, the Carnival coverage takes a nation's leering eye inside the raunchy balls of Rio and São Paulo. Once, the Black-and-White Ball, the Scala, even the gay balls, were the exclusive domain of the jet set. Today, they appear to have been thrown open to anyone who can afford the ticket price and has something to show off. Given that this is Brazil, the music at these events is shockingly prosaic. Big bands pump up "Cidade Maravilhosa" and Carmen Miranda chestnuts, the tropical equivalent of Guy Lombardo and His Royal Canadians. The setting is nothing much for the camera, a thousand café tables shoved to the side of a dance arena. So the coverage turns into an unending series of screen tests. One after another, the hopeful ingenues step forward for an interview, followed by their big chance to moon the entire nation. It's as though ABC, NBC, and CBS had been turned over to members of Andy Warhol's Studio in the late sixties. This is no naked lunch, but definitely naked TV.

The chatter goes so quickly that I can't always follow along. What's there to say at such moments anyway? I get the drift when it comes to describing someone's inspiration for their she-cat costume, what town in Brazil they'd left behind to carve their mark in Rio, whether they want to be a model or an actress. Many of the women are dressed in nothing but feathers and lingerie, garters and stockings, although the complete nudity of the 1988 Carnival—down to wagging penises painted with polka dots—has led to an edict that genitalia should remain at least nominally covered. They must sell an awful lot of depilatory cream in the days before Carnival. At the gay balls, there's no law against the campiest double entendres. For an hour or so at one of these cargo bays of androgyny, the announcer boldly asks each new guest, "So tell me, boy or girl?" The talk is always small, the behinds large. "Que moca bonita! Que bum-bum maravilhosa!" What a pretty girl! What a gorgeous butt! Where everybody knows how to score a touchdown, the anchormen are free to be dirty old men.

What, exactly, is the source of Brazil's obsession with the gluteus maximus? The *bunda*, "boom-boom," butt, fanny, rear, is somehow more than every girl's "savings account," as local slang calls it. The brown Brazilian ass, European in grace and African in bulk, is a symbol of national identity—openly referred to as "the glorious flower of our miscegenation." This is the artifact which most directly and graphically illustrates Brazil's glory and Brazil's quandary. What other land on earth would allow its mass media to become ass media?

Who can say what this numbing procession of anatomical perfection does to the national libido? Has the climate, the diet, the lack of uncorrupted moral authorities really turned Brazil into the land of unbridled libido? Brazilian song lyrics are explicitly suggestive when it comes to all sorts of acts—and the unregulated ribaldry of Carnival is said to produce a huge rise in the birth rate each year, exactly nine months later. But I never catch anyone doing anything that comes close to open procreation. People appear to go home with those that brought them. I have the feeling that most of the dancers and shakers never get around to anything half as kinky as what us pent-up Northerners do behind our double-locked doors. By showing all this flesh, people seem to be saying, "So what's the big deal, anyhow?" At a certain point, all that anatomy gets discounted, in more ways than one. All the bumping and grinding must serve to siphon off some of the urge. The effect of being Brazilian has, at some point, to be like living in a nudist colony. Sexuality has to be a lot more than what meets the eye.

Soon enough, the videocassettes will be edited and ready for the tourist shops. Brazil's greatest highlight, Rio, in *samba* stereo and full multiracial color. Brazil's Super Bash is never one-sided, a letdown, or a bust. But every Super Bowl has its winners and losers, and so does the Carnival. The coverage isn't concluded until the afternoon following the climactic showcasing of Rio's *samba* schools of the first rank. This time, the transmissions to an entire nation are claimed for hours by the announcement of the Carnival voting. The finish may be the most fascinating exposition of Brazilian culture during the entire five days.

The judges, mostly high functionaries in the Rio Tourism Bureau, are as white-skinned as those they are judging are black. They dress in linen suits just like high-class pimps. Is there a more technical term for someone who lives off the exploitation of pleasure? They have long, distinguished Portuguese names: Doctor Roberto Antonio Figueiredo Maçeo da Silva Mendonça, all flashed on screen. With pomp and seriousness taken to interminable Brazilian lengths, each announces the score he has given in each of ten categories: theme song, costume, general coordination, originality, and so on. As the scores are toted up onscreen by computer, which never occurs without glitches, teams of reporters are stationed at the tables crammed with the presidents of the schools. These chain-smoking godfathers await the moment of judgment, chatting breathlessly about their chances, comforted by wives with beehive hairdos. They look even seedier than the sycophants on the podium: sun-avoiding lizards plucked from the dingiest, smoke-filled Las Vegas lounge. Everyone in the country knows full well that they are criminal *bicheiros*, from the *jogo do bicho*, Rio's version of the numbers racket. But nobody cares. After all, someone has to pay the bills for all this spectacle.

Back in Rio, I'd been tipped off that this year's winner would either be Mocidade Independente de Padre Miguel or the more traditional Salgueiro. In fact, the voting comes down to the very last round, with exactly those two schools separated by one tenth of a point. With the final tally, the camera switches to Mocidade's president embracing his spouse. Next, the network cuts directly to the school's Zona Norte rehearsal space, where the faithful have thronged for a last burst of exaltation. With word of their second victory in a row, the Carnival erupts once again. The drums pound, the masses bound on waves of delirium.

From such frenetic moments to the testing grounds of *futebol* fields to the enforced memorization of ten thousand Carnival standards, there is an ideology afoot in this land. Judging from Brazil, it would appear that wild abandon is not necessarily an innate skill. This transformation of licentiousness into a life-style is calculated. The sad truth is that spontaneity comes no more naturally to human beings than does browbeating or angst. People have to be encouraged from an early age to want to get this crazy this often. The coverage ends with a last rendition of the winning "theme *samba*," the ecstatic gloating of this year's champion. No accomplishment could be more proud. No moment in the nation is more solemn. Then they turn the airwaves back over to the kiddie shows.

Music to Read By

SAMBAS DE ENREDO '91—Assorted Samba Schools (RCA)
BATUCADA—Mocidade Independente de Padre Miguel (JSL)

THE PARROT'S PERCH

The first time I was in prison, they wouldn't believe I was a musician." About to take the stage for a sold-out concert, Geraldo Azevedo recounts, "My jailers brought me a guitar and asked me to prove it. The officer was impressed and he sent away the soldiers. So music is what got me in trouble—but music is also what saved me from torture!"

You cannot touch on the first subject in Brazil without bumping into the latter. Alongside music, I'm learning, torture must be counted as Brazil's most sophisticated art. In this field, too, a few Brazilians have been most prolific. Characteristically, they couched their activities in humor and blessed their creations with colorful nicknames. *Pau de arara*, the "parrot's perch," was a means of hanging a victim upside down. The "Chinese bath" involved hours under water. And when victims were made to stand with arms outstretched, holding telephone books for days, this was named after Rio's leading tourist attraction, Christ the Redeemer. During the *ditadura*, the dark period of military rampage from the 1964 coup d'etat through the mid-eighties, many thousands were murdered, raped, manhandled, broken. Thanks to the marvelous Brazilian inability to keep a secret, Catholic activists smuggled meticulous documentation of over 5,000 cases out of government offices, one file at a time.

I can't believe that this wandering minstrel could be among them. With his cherubic mass of gray curls, piercing blue eyes, half-white goatee more cute than sardonic, Geraldo Azevedo looks the perfect aging hippie. He wears flat Chinese slippers and a sky-blue Indian tunic. In an antiseptic dressing room with mirrors big enough to check the makeup of visiting opera divas, he appears too slight to carry a show by himself. Yet he exhibits no jitters. Hunched in on himself with total concentration, he tunes his guitar with flicks from witches' nails. In the rest of Latin America, his allegorical lyrics, soft folk melodies, and pyrotechnic skill as a *violeiro* would brand him an exponent of the so-called Nueva Trova (New Song). In Brazil, where distinctions are less readily drawn between music spiritual or political, sounds trendy or traditional, Geraldo Azevedo is just another Saturday night troubadour, playing the provinces.

The homespun singer jokes that he knows what it's like when the amount of money in your pocket feels like "the tongue of a mosquito." Thanks to a soft, commercial sound and sheer staying power, Azevedo is doing a lot better these days. He has won recognition as a leading participant in a popular series of recorded *cantorias*—the Northeastern term for an informal singalong. No matter how long he has lived in Rio, Azevedo is identified as a Nordestino. So tonight he works the Northeast circuit in João Pessoa, the point on the Brazilian bulge closest in nautical miles to Europe and Africa. A few hours' bus ride from Recife, this capital of the immense state of Paraíba is but another sleepy coastal town. There's a beach packed with the single-sail *jangadas* of the local fishing fleet, barefoot peddlers carrying coolers full of cocktails served in scooped-out pineapples, deserted hotels, mysterious lagoons, statues of heroic horsemen, pompous courthouses. "Independence Square," Azevedo had pointed out on the way over, "and we still don't have our independence!" On the outskirts of town, crowded by the banks of open sewage pits, are the tin shacks of the new arrivals: "Houses so small they shake when people have sex!"

But Geraldo Azevedo is glad to be here, pleased to temporarily sate his countrymen's insatiable appetite for live sounds. "The music chose me, I did not choose it. I am a child of the *sertão*, from Jatoba, just outside of Petrolina and across the river from Juazeiro, which is where João Gilberto grew up. It's the sort of town where people still go in the streets at night, stand outside the window and sing *serenatas* to their sweethearts. My mother was a teacher and taught the ABCs to all the kids from the neighborhood. She was a very inventive woman and liked to dramatize her lessons with singing and dancing. Everyone in the family played music. From the time I was four, my brother and I would perform sketches and travel around the district with her."

I can't imagine a more perfect preparation for a touring musician. "Still, I came to Recife to study architecture. I was surprised when I became more and more drawn to the music department. I was even more surprised when I was invited to go to Rio with other local songwriters." Sooner or later, all Brazilian musicians must make the trek to the nation's artistic testing ground. In Rio, as in Hollywood, oddball artistic types from all over the land make it big singing paeans to places they were all too eager to leave. "Rio is like the window of a music shop. Everything you want to choose is there. But I wasn't prepared emotionally. It was a difficult adjustment for me. I still had thoughts of becoming an architect and made my living doing engineering drawings. But I just got so involved in the music. And then I was arrested."

By now, I have heard many Brazilian life histories pause at this point. The break in chronology comes with such suddenness. In fact, each personal tale reflects the cruel abruptness of the 1964 military coup. So complete was this interruption in national life that it is difficult for me to imagine that Brazil had ever been a "normal" country. In the light of what was to come, Geraldo Azevedo singing ditties to his mother's pupils seems as innocent as that period of hope which had led to the building of Brasília and to the flowering of *bossa nova*. Back then, there were contested elections, active trade unions, a radical peasant movement, a socially conscious Catholic priesthood, all the morbid symptoms of a people attempting to solve their problems. North Americans are encouraged to think of their Latin neighbors as naturally tending toward dictatorship. But the putsch of 'sixty-four, executed by a military made jittery by the increasingly populist rhetoric of President João Goulart, need never have happened. Even those most committed to a state of emergency did not believe it would be necessary for long. But the generals were carried off by that fatal Brazilian overexuberance, a kind of Carnival in reverse.

"Confronted by mounting subversive activities . . ." began the infamous decree of December 13, 1968, which made permanent the complete suspension of civil liberties. "For twenty-five years," Alceu Valença told me, "everything in Brazil stopped. There was the phantom of communism and the cold war, there was the elite, backed by the military, sucking on the titties of the United States." Soon, Argentina and Chile would replicate the Brazilian prototype, with its many methods of suppression, including an unrelenting war against the popular arts. Caetano Veloso, the most publicized victim of that war, explained, "Often, the military took the wrong person. They were arrested by mistake. And there were times when I'd be walking in the exercise yard and certain of the young guards would whisper, 'I'm ashamed of doing this, I like your music.' They would do it very quickly and I had to pretend I wasn't listening. 'Caetano, I'm sorry for doing this. . . .' "

Thirty years later, none of the real culprits have been made to apologize. Some are still wearing medals and holding high office. In typical Brazilian fashion, the transition back to parliamentary politics—beginning with the *abertura* (opening) of 1979—was accomplished with immense patience and a marked lack of retribution. This is the country that went from monarchy to republic without firing a single shot. When he tripped at a fancy dress ball just weeks before being deposed, Emperor Dom Pedro II joked, "The empire stumbled, but it has not yet fallen!" And when Getúlio Vargas signed the decree ending his decades of dictatorship, he declared, "As there is nothing more to do, let's all go to bed!"

In politics anyway, most Brazilians don't see the point in spoiling for a fight. "Even the military folks eventually got fed up with the whole thing," was how Gilberto Gil put it. "Back in the early seventies, it was all repression, aggression, torture. The CIA, the Pentagon, they were training the people behind it. During this regime, we musicians were brought to realize that we had political work to do. It was frightening because, after all, we made music for individual pleasure, to be loved by people. But some of us had to become soldiers."

None could have been more unlikely than Geraldo Azevedo. This ultimate flower child couldn't hurt a fly, though I can see how he might have hurt a general. "Everything under the military was prohibited, all meetings, all discussions. You had to do everything clandestinely, even rehearsals. It was dangerous just knowing a leftist sympathizer or someone who had books on China! The first time, I was arrested in 'sixty-nine by the Navy and they took me to a prison in the middle of Guanabara Bay. I was there for forty days, twenty in solitary. Being a musician was bad enough. But I had worked in a group with Geraldo Vandré."

Vandré had written the unofficial anthem of opposition to military rule, "P'ra Não Dizer Que Não Falei das Flores." Of course, this song about "not speaking of flowers" had been censored in 1968, along with many other flowery ballads. With every recorded song having to be cleared by the government, Brazilian lyricists learned to stretch the boundaries of innuendo. Chico Buarque, who would flee to Italy, appealed to the government in the guise of a jilted lover. "In spite of you, tomorrow will be another day," went the refrain which somehow made its subversive way onto vinyl. "You who invented sadness, please be polite and disinvent that! You who invented sin should also invent forgiveness. . . ."

"The military censors had the mentality of schizophrenics," Alceu Valença recounted. "They were always looking for double meanings in the words. I couldn't sing 'Joāna, vamos viajar!' "— Joanna, let's go!—"because they thought I meant marijuana. Once or twice, I had to remove certain phrases just because they sounded accidentally like the family names of certain large land-holders." And Djavan, now one of Brazil's top moneymakers, was banned from performing Beatles songs—"I sang the Paul McCartney part"—because his teenage group was called LSD.

But Geraldo Vandré never performed again. Exiled to London, he eventually suffered a nervous breakdown. In São Paulo, I was told that I could find him wandering in and out of rehearsals of the symphony orchestra. Now Azevedo assures me that Vandré is recuperating here, in his hometown of João Pessoa. Like so many former colleagues, his old friend cautions me that it would be "useless to try and speak with him." Vandré is legend—everywhere and nowhere. "Vandré once sang, 'Our King Arthur is badly crowned.' I think that's why our government is doing so much damage to the cultural sector, cutting the funds everywhere. I think the government is still taking revenge for the role singers and artists have played."

But Azevedo still hasn't told me about the revenge inflicted on him. "By my second arrest in 1975, I was becoming well known. My songs won prizes at festivals and I recorded albums with Alceu Valença. So that second time, under the government of Geisel, was much harsher and more cruel. I had been informed on by a friend. Later, I heard that when Brazil got the contract for a nuclear power plant from Germany, President Geisel presented the German government with two official gifts. One was a record of Villa-Lobos, the other an album of mine. And at the time, I was in prison being tortured."

I don't know whether to press for details or stare down at my program. "They tried many things," Geraldo Azevedo continues in an even tone. "I remember they covered my face for ten days and left me in a freezer, without any clothes. They rang loud sirens next to my cell for days at a time. And then they applied electric shock. I used to pretend I had fainted. It was the only way to get them to stop. I received many shocks to the penis. But I left that place spiritually strengthened, determined to give all my energies to music."

João Pessoa's civic auditorium is spilling over with a crowd squatting in the aisles, sprawled in the space between stage and front row. Geraldo Azevedo captivates a full house with soaring melodies and flamencolike solos. Couples pinch each others' arms in excitement at seeing one of their idols in the flesh. They respond to the love songs by leaning on each others' shoulders and making goo-goo eyes. A North American audience would be embarrassed to show such public tenderness toward one another or a performer. Yet from the ranks of these gentle concertgoers come the death-squad vigilantes, the shakedown artists, the street-corner punks, the cocky torturers. The vast majority of this populace can hardly be accused of being "good Germans." But have they yet mastered how to be good Brazilians?

Tonight, music saves them from barbarism the same way it saved Geraldo Azevedo. Maybe music will always be Brazil's saving grace. Even in this provincial crowd, everybody seems to know all the words to the songs. I just wonder if they know the whole story. "When I was suffering my worst moment," Geraldo Azevedo told me, "the soldiers turned on a television program. A popular *telenovela* [soap opera] was being aired and the opening theme was one of my songs. The torturers recognized my voice. They covered the sound of my screaming with my own song. 'Now,' the soldiers said, 'we are really going to make you sing.' " These days, he is the one making others sing.

Music to Read By

PERSONALIDADE—Geraldo Azevedo (Philips)
CANTORIAS, 1 & 2—Geraldo Azevedo and Others (Philips)
XANGAI—Xangai (Auvidis)
VAI PASSAR—Chico Buarque (Polygram)

BIRDS MAKING LOVE

To die of thirst in front of the sea! Romantic balladeer Djavan's refrain refers to love unrequited. But this native of the Northeast could just as well have been singing about the heartache of the *sertão*. Thirty miles from the Atlantic at nearly any point, and you are already in the realm of perennial parch. In this scrub-brush landscape which the indigenous inhabitants called *caatinga* (the white forest), serious droughts occur every seven years. Geologists have determined that Brazil's interior wasteland is a climatological breakaway of Saharan Africa. The two are sadly similar in rainfall levels and searing light—if only Brazil's backwoods survivalists could be camels! Shaken out of my sleep after an all-night ride from the coast, I know I've arrived when the bus station's lone *taxista* takes note of a spotty, predawn sprinkle. "Yes, we're getting *um bem molhado*," he declares with unaffected fervency. "A good wetting. Thanks be to God!"

Piety and moisture—these are the hallmarks of Juazeiro do Norte, the "oasis" of the *sertão*. Though the landscape is not so much green as a cool, chalky gray, there are seventy-four natural springs in the surrounding Valley of Cariri. But holy waters are not what makes this market town in the poor state of Ceará positively biblical—and atypically prosperous. Both are due to Padre Cicero Romão Batista. Back in 1889, this local priest began attracting believers from all over the region when the host wafers which he offered at communion supposedly turned to blood. Various "miraculous" healings followed, causing Padre Cicero's followers to petition the Vatican for sainthood. Instead, the renegade priest was excommunicated within five years of making his claim—but continued to reign over Juazeiro and much of surrounding Ceará as a combination Billy Graham and Al Capone.

With the aid of a mercenary army, Padre Cicero asserted *sertanejo* nationalism. He took his place in the Northeastern tradition of *cangaçeiros:* processionist bandits like the spectacled Lampião, branded Brazil's "Robin Hood"; the much-serenaded Maria Bonita, Bonnie to Lampião's Clyde; and Antonio Conselheiro, another self-proclaimed messiah who refused to take baths or recognize any central government. In 1911, Padre Cicero's power was consolidated when his forces repulsed an attack by federal Brazilian troops. In one incident, his followers marched on Fortaleza, seven hundred kilometers north, to remove the provincial governor. Fervent processionals and ceremonies of flagellation offered relief for the poor. Long after Padre Cicero's death in 1934, his devout devotees known as Romeiros deluge Juazeiro during two annual pilgrimage periods. Many believe their savior will one day return to the *sertão*.

Dotted amid the yellow string hammocks for sale along Juazeiro's dead-straight main drag, on every counter of every hardware store, feed supply, and pharmacy, sits an unusual crockery figure. It's not a piggy bank for collecting tips or charity; it's the graven image of the good father, his white hair painted in beneath a wide-brimmed hat, his brown priest's cassock reaching all the way to his feet. It's as though a dashboard Jesus had been placed all over town. The only competition in moral influence comes from Charlito, as Charlie Chaplin is known. On my first stroll through Juazeiro, I can plainly see that the tramp in derby hat is more than a clown to these folks. They've posted his sauntering icon in bars, bakeries, and the café where it takes fifteen minutes to fetch milk for my coffee. He's everyman, the underdog of underdogs, and everywhere in this open tent of true believers, I come across the Portuguese text of Chaplin's appeal for universal love in the last scene of *The Great Dictator*.

I don't get it. The *sertão* is reputed to be the place where Brazil gets most gruff and unshaven. Social relations here are considered semifeudal. But where are all the migrant sharecroppers, bounty hunters, macho *vaqueiros*? In this Latin American version of the Australian outback, adulterous wives are still routinely and legally shot. A stray tourist, so I've been led to believe, can be run out of town for one wrong look. Yet I glimpse no hotheaded cowhands or swaggering Lotharios, just the most humble and chivalrous folk. Juazeiro's cobbled streets are lined with doll-size houses, enlarged by sculpted *faux* second stories, painted in feminine shades. Rather than enlivened with gunshots, the back alleys are flooded with sun and silence. Is this cloak of anguished quiet merely the discretion of people who have learned to keep their own counsel? The streets of the *sertão* answer, "No comment."

Yet this backward part of Brazil should serve as a musical source book. Portuguese and German, African and Indian influences ought to be more clearly traceable and audible. I keep my ears perked for a stray drumming session or, at the very least, radios blaring the jumpy lilt of *forró*, the Northeast's most distinctive beat. The name is supposedly a Brazilian adaptation of the English words "for all"—which is how nineteenth-century British peace-keeping forces invited the locals onto their bases. *Forró* is part polka, part square dance, part oral history, played by a standard trio led by an accordionist. The singer punctuates his long-running narrative with gentle clangings on the triangle. A drummer keeps time on the basso and perfectly onomatopoetic *zabumba*. Except for a band playing for tips at a soft-drink stand outside João Pessoa, I've yet to see any evidence that *forró* really is for all. I soon learn that out here, such a call to music is saved for occasions that celebrate the reunion of far-flung friends. Besides, Padre Cícero must not have approved of dancing. There's not a ballroom, nor even a good raunchy bar, in his entire fiefdom. Unwittingly, I have come to the one town in Brazil where music is less than sacramental.

A storefront Casa de Cultura is little more than a combination gem shop and kitschy watercolor gallery. The town guardians of the arts are playing cards at a table set a step up from the sidewalk. One local painter, the side of his face disfigured with thick strands of brown scar tissue from a bad burn, volunteers to help me locate a *banda cabaçal*. I confess ignorance of such groups, named after a type of drum, but I'm assured that they are about all that Juazeiro can offer of the folkloric. By now, I know anything consigned to this category is already doomed. Traditions thus labeled, however valuable to the understanding of a region, have lost all connection to daily life. Folkloric means bottling the wellsprings, means being bored "for one's own good." To paraphrase Goebbels, when I hear the word "folkloric," I want to reach for my earplugs.

"But first," says the disfigured painter, "you must see Luis Fidelis." This musician lives just around the next corner. A simple knock gains me access to a morning practice session. Why do total strangers in Brazil always greet you as though you'd phoned ahead? Luis Fidelis bounds to the door like a big puppy. He is hardly the backcountry strummer, but an unkempt, aging long-hair. Even indoors, a straw hat covers his bald spot. His house seems to be a collection center for the region's bric-a-brac. Grand-father clocks, crockery, sprung pocket watches, family portraits, are everywhere. The lamp shades are fringed, the bed a four-poster. I'm not surprised to learn that the musician has inherited the place from less bohemian relatives. Yet somehow, this house, like all those I'll enter in the *sertão*, suggests an ease of living rather than mustiness. The tile roofs let in plenty of air—no worry about rain—and an orange-hued light. Bedroom walls reach only halfway to the ceiling, giving the appearance that floor plans could be scrambled at will. A hidden atrium, crammed with potted flowers and parrots is greenhouse and outhouse.

Luis Fidelis is both thrilled and chagrined to be caught *in situ*. "What is a musician doing in this place?" He can't exactly say what holds him in this square town, as stifling as it is quaint. "I'm stubborn. I'd like to try and save our regional culture. But it's dying so fast, everything in Brazil that's based on slow, natural growth is dying."

To make a living, Luis plays the dance halls of Fortaleza, ten hours away. "For someone like me, the only chance for real money is to win a songwriting contest or compose a theme for one of the soap operas. In the meantime, I'm just another flathead." This peculiar bit of self-effacement turns out to be a general term for those who remain in the *sertão*. "We call ourselves flatheads because of this joke about how the dumb ones get flat heads from having their fathers pat them on their noggins and say, 'Now you stay here, son!' The smart ones, those whose heads are able to stretch, they take off for São Paulo."

In many small towns of the Northeast, it's difficult to find transportation to the provincial capital—yet buses leave every day for the three-day ride to the job-rich South. Esperança (Hope) is the name of the company that's transported me. Some mayors actually pay the fare for their town's unemployed just to get them out of town. The *sertão* is the equivalent of the Italian south's *mezzogiorno*, that sleepy region mired in underdevelopment which any nation worth its salt uses as a pool of cheap, exploitable labor. And just as Milan was built by Sicilians, so Brazil's skyscrapers and industrial parks were built upon the backs of rugged *sertanejos*. "There are Northeastern people everywhere," said Luiz Gonzaga Junior, son of the region's greatest singer. "And these are the people who built up São Paulo, Rio Grande do Sul, the Amazon. I'll bet some of them are in New York City now, just working all year and eating chicken."

The mass flight is readily explained by an average income of under $200 a year, life expectancy as low as thirty-five for up to 80 percent of the population. In some areas, average daily caloric intake is no more than in German concentration camps. Years back, some Brazilian scientists even claimed that the chronic malnutrition had led to the development of a new species—a homo sapiens with brains shrunken by 40 percent. Could that be what Luis Fidelis means by "flathead"? In such circumstances, people resort to blind faith.

"There's a tradition of extreme religiosity here that goes back to the native Cariri tribe," Luis explains. "Padre Cicero was just taking advantage of the tendencies latent in the people." Yet the first thing he wants to show me is the seventy-five-foot-high statue of the prophetic pretender still dominating the town from a crest at one end of the valley. In Juazeiro do Norte, Big Padre is watching you! The musician's made-in-Brazil VW bug strains to make it up the winding climb to the monument. The single-lane road is lined with the most feeble, daub-and-wattle excuses for housing I've seen. Most of the outer walls have chipped away to expose chicken wire and mud. Mothers sit on the front steps holding naked babies, just the way they do in north India. At least, in the urban *favelas*, there is always another hustle, some scheme that suggests a quick way out. Here the people appear to have no idea what to do beyond scraping together the next pot of beans.

Around the hilltop parking lot, vendors hawk pennants, rosaries, the ubiquitous statuettes, and even some of those two-eyed plastic viewers which show Padre Cicero in 3-D. It's the slow time of year in the large mission house. Barefoot lady attendants snooze in hammocks, ostensibly guarding several shrines which attest to a small portion of the Padre's drawing power. All four stucco walls are filled from floor to ceiling with formal black-and-white head shots of penitents seeking the Padre's healing powers. A larger storeroom contains an unsorted pile of *milagres*, tin representations in miniature of wounded body parts, knees and hearts and unidentified inner organs, mixed together with abandoned wooden legs and dentures. All that's missing from this testament to the sorrows of the flesh is an actual bone or two. I don't see how the staff can do their chores before such a mountain of aches. "Everybody in these parts believes in miracles," says Luis. "They practically emanate from this dry ground."

At this time of year, we're the only ones headed for the summit. That doesn't deter the site's beggars. One is an archetypal hayseed: red hair, freckles, and missing front teeth, a frayed pair of blue jeans three sizes too short, bare feet. This living scarecrow looks so cornfield wholesome that I'm shocked when he, too, thrusts out his open palm. I escape by climbing up the stairs built into the Padre's white plaster fifty-foot frock. A sign calls this oversized figurine the Third Largest Statue in the World. It's an earnest, if uncorroborated bit of hyperbole, since only two other public symbols exist in the Brazilian imagination: Rio's Corcovado Christ and the Statue of Liberty. I dare not shatter my proud host's illusions with firsthand accounts of far loftier representations of Ferdinand Marcos or Chairman Mao. With Juazeiro do Norte swollen by religious revenues to claim half the broad valley below, I can see why Padre Cicero is a big man. When I ask if he is a believer, Luis Fidelis winks and answers, "The greatest miracle Padre Cicero ever performed was this town."

The singer's search for signs of cultural life takes us to a clumsy new civic gymnasium, a gray Mayan pyramid turned on its head. In the brown dirt parking lot, a crew is just rigging up a white-and-orange striped circus tent. The sign over the big top reads MIAMI 2001. Inside the insufferably hot office of municipal planning we find all two of Juazeiro's other professional musicians. They are listening politely to a pitch from an energetic woman who's just moved to town. This do-gooder, hired to teach at a junior college, is determined to turn sleepy Juazeiro on its ear. She wants to enlist the local musical community in a "concert for domestic peace" as a statement against violence toward women. Now this is definitely not the chastity-belt *sertão* I'd heard about! Local authenticity is lent by the number of flies flitting about her black locks, even resting on her lips between exhortations. "It's because of that damn circus," one musician cusses. The elephants and the monkeys have apparently imported this swarm. What is it about Brazil that bends all experience toward a scattershot surreality? A wayward feminist trying to sweep away horseflies from the circus! I must be in some Buñuel frame, not the parish of the good Padre.

With no live music to be found for a two-hundred-mile radius, there's nothing left for me to do but sample the big top. My front-row seat costs less than fifty cents. A gang of scruffy kids hovers by the box office in hopes of a stray admission. Who can resist the instant moral rectitude obtained by treating a homeless orphan to his first circus? I treat not one but three unattended waifs so encrusted with dust that it's difficult to tell their complexion beneath dirty blond locks. They look more dazed than delighted by my sudden donation. The gleam in their eyes has been filmed over with *sertão* resignation. I fear that they'll resell the tickets as soon as I've taken my seat. But my treats shyly take their places in the back row of the big tent. Like the rest of the "flathead" crowd, they are quickly entranced by the antics of a clown named—what else?—Lambada.

MIAMI 2001 features one trained monkey and two grumpy old lions—hardly enough livestock to be responsible for all those flies. A dashing ringmaster offers a nonstop narration in the over-dramatized tremolo delivery favored by radio deejays. Every act is prefaced with the expletives "Fantastico! Espetacular!" A quartet of local girls in leotards provides the obligatory brace of buttocks. One of the trapeze artists is just making his grand entrance, chin high, when a wire stretched too low nearly takes off his head. The real thrill of the evening is provided on the crowded bus that takes the audience back to the center of Juazeiro. A tussle develops next to the driver, and, in an instant, two large men in brown suits rush forward, surround and disarm a local hooligan. They pluck a foot-long kitchen knife from his inside jacket pocket quicker than hunters skin a rabbit.

Next evening, I brave another bus to call upon a musical source recommended only as Alembergue. Somehow, this portentous name conjures up visions of cummberbunds and mustache wax. But the fellow turns out to be barely more than a teenager with bangs falling in his eyes. He sports nothing but a pair of shorts and rubber flip-flops. His hands are covered with dark soil from working in his courtyard garden and he speaks with a moderate lisp which filters his s's through a pool of saliva. "My mother named me after her favorite character in a soap opera. The Count of Alembergue!"

I'm let inside by a barefoot young girl with waist-long hair. I figure that this is the maid until I see her face plastered up on a wall full of publicity for club appearances and regional song competitions. She is Rosiane, Alembergue's accompanist, research assistant, and wife. He and the girl are so perfectly matched that they could be twins: both dark-haired, intense, and utterly unaffected. But Count and Countess Alembergue turn out to be far more than your average folksinging couple. Their house has the feel of a university anthro department. Aside from a dining table, there's no furniture—only tom-toms, banks of cymbals and bells, homemade vibraphones, and other strange configurations of bone and bark. The posters share wall space with detailed topographic maps stuck with red and white pins. Led to sit cross-legged on the cleared space of an Indian rug, I soon get the lowdown on the couple's personal crusade to resurrect the region's indigenous culture.

"In four years, I've only written four songs," Alembergue confesses in a conspiratorial whisper. "That's because I want everything I do to be loyal to the spirit and feeling of the Cariri tribe and other native peoples." Every chance they get, this young couple heads into the hills and canyons most remote from Juazeiro and other settlements of the white man. "People don't understand the rich spirituality of this place. Before the conquest, this was a very populated area. And before that, it was all under the sea. So there are lots of fossils and artifacts. And there are old-timers in all the villages with plenty of tales to tell." Alembergue shows me badly focused snapshots of surviving holy men with distinctively Asiatic features, entrances to caves and blurred paintings inside, runways of boulders which give the appearance of being placed in a pattern by earth-moving divinities.

He emerges from his storeroom with enough fossils, Stone Age arrowheads, and other tools to fill a provincial museum. He also brings out some spooky wooden masks with hollowed-out eyes, festooned with crops of horsehair. Ceylonese devil worshipers would do just fine with these totems. According to the testimony of the old *caboclos bravos,* as he calls the Indian braves, a spiritual guide with white skin and bright red hair once roamed these parts, leading the tribes through secret passageways in the rock to a *lago encantado,* some now-dry enchanted lake. And beyond, so Alembergue claims, to the Amazon through underground tunnels hundreds of miles long. This red-haired sage from the bottom of the earth also taught the locals the basic skills of agriculture. Alembergue swears that he's seen Egyptian inscriptions in caves.

It is happening again. Just when I think I'm actually following some train of thought, another Brazilian strays into some nether region of vague mysticism. I'm preparing myself for talk of spaceships and extraterrestrial landings when Alembergue gets sidetracked into showing off his one-of-a-kind instruments. As in the case of the more sophisticated music machines created by Uakti, there is a deep urge among Brazilians to expand their range of sound. Rosiane is the percussionist, moving deftly from strings of seashells to cowbells to gourds. Alembergue sticks to the more traditional guitar and vocals. He's not much of a picker, but the couple's repertoire is oddly moving. I can't categorize their music as Indian or Brazilian, *bolero* or *samba canção.* The lyrics are in the reconstructed language of their reimagined tribe. Alembergue uses Portuguese only to tell about the methods of the first Catholic missionaries in "civilizing" the natives: " 'It is wrong to worship wood, stone, or clay,' the priests told them. 'Now you must worship *images* made of wood, stone, and clay.' "

If I hadn't already seen similar instances of dedication to Brazil's musical roots, I would think of Alembergue as some eccentric genius. He's merely displaying the same zeal, inventiveness, and striving for elemental explanations shared by Hermeto Paschoal or Bahia's Carlinhos Brown. It's an instinctive curiosity, the intuition to go forward by going back, that renews the nation's musical sources. I never quite determine whether music is just a tool in Alembergue's search or whether the search is aimed at serving his music. With a wry laugh, he admits that his mother and father are horrified by his talk of lost tribes. "Though nobody in my family will admit it, I think I must be a Cariri myself." Funny, he doesn't look Indian.

And what are two nice hippie kids doing mixed up in basic archeology? I join the couple for a perfectly mundane supper of hot milk, salty cheese, and hunks of fresh bread. Alembergue even flips on the family television. TV Globo is carrying the Grammy Award ceremonies, live from Hollywood. In a major coup that will make headlines in all the local newspapers, a *forró* group from Recife gets honored for Best Foreign Pop or some such category. The telecast's long-haired rockers decked out in tuxedoes, the country crooners thanking the recording industry's "R and D" men, are not just thousands of miles from where I am, but eons removed from the primal urge to make music—for pleasure, intoxication or, in Alembergue's case, as a crusade.

"Come on," the Count of Alembergue insists after supper. I fear that he's leading me off on some trek to an enchanted gremlin's lair. But he just wants me to meet another musician. We trek up the soft gravel roads that climb the side of the Cariri Valley. Here, as in Rio, the poor build their shacks at altitudes government regulations can't reach. From the smell, raw sewage is trickling under our feet. This whole neighborhood is without electric power. But Alembergue knows just where to go. Around the back of one relatively permanent structure, we find a thatched hut raised on stilts. It is only just after supper but we're calling on a clan that's already bedded down on the mud floor. No video games, no soft stereo reveries, when you don't have the juice.

Call this my *samba* of the "Turd World." Here's what it is, and what it's not: on this planet, power comes down to rot. A question of mass toilet training—who remembers to wipe and who's refraining. A pile of leaves left outside the front door. Who knows how it got there for sure? A foul thing, growing ever higher, a ready-made funeral pyre. And someone's absconded with the idea of responsibility until the rot attains respectability. They dance dances to the garbage! Pray to the gods of the sewage! Yet lives made more earthy are lives less trustworthy. But the funny thing is: where filth is prevalent, poetry is more relevant. While back in the First, everything is reversed. The cleanup is going full-time, but they've lost the rhyme. Chaos nobody will tolerate, washing away the good with the great. For all the wrong reasons, everything turns out right. Sanity triumphs, but wisdom is swept out of sight. So there you have it. The North-South split. A matter of hygienic habit.

Candles are lit in response to Alembergue's greeting. In a moment, three near-naked black children—no, seven, the younger ones with tell-tale distended bellies, the older ones brawny from field work—have roused themselves and moved outside onto the bamboo landing. Setting out their one chair, they quietly await the arrival of a respected elder. Everyone sits at the knees of the frail father Alembergue calls Mestre Antonio. He is the chief musician and teacher of the region's oldest *banda cabaçal*. And he belongs to the ethnic category known as *caboclo*, connoting an assimilated Indian whose genetic strains have mixed with white or black. Mestre Antonio looks awfully African to me, but he insists that his music is "all Cariri." His father, and his father before him, have been the chiefs of their musical tribe for a continuous 160 years.

"I only flew in an airplane once," the old man says proudly. "That's when I knew there was no heaven because I didn't find my brother up there." His brother must have been quite a charmer. "He had thirty children and killed off three wives doing it. Then he died, aged ninety, in the middle of dancing." The *cabaçal* bands are known for their fierce dances, duels with long sharpened knives meant as exorcisms. "Our music is for healing, not for money," says the Master. "If we fight in our dancing, then we won't fight for real."

Mestre Antonio makes me a gift of a newly carved wooden flute—the other main instrument of the *cabaçal*. I can't get a sound out of mine, making the children laugh. The Master toots away like Jean-Pierre Rampal. We hardly have to coax him into a sprightly tune which wafts down toward the parks and plazas. Working in the field, he says, is the source of all his inspiration. In a day, he comes up with enough new melodies to try for a month. Of his technique, he says, "I imitate the sound of birds making love."

I think back to the Grammy telecast. Could this band leader really share the same art form, the same planet, with Led Zeppelin or Lawrence Welk? And is the wealth of artistic corruption back home the reason why my search for pure music must take me so far? In this musical manger, this primal place of conception, I try once more to get an answer to my obligatory question about what makes Brazilians so musical. Mestre Antonio stumbles, never having been required to get so analytical. "It must be because we live in a place of so much happiness."

That's not exactly how I would describe this hut with the scent of piss seeping up through the floorboards, this valley of red dirt and horseflies. Either everybody around me is lying or I have to change, fundamentally, my concept of happiness. With the Count of Alembergue nodding encouragement, I spin a vision of a life spent in unceasing shifts of toil and music, living under the stars, without light bulbs or television to outshine them. As one popular song goes, "Oh, the nights of my *sertão*!"

"Yes, our happiness is boundless," the old man keeps repeating, more and more firmly. In the most desperate places, I get the most poetic paeans. In Brazil, you can never be accused of idealizing poverty. That's because the poor beat you to it. "We can't help but celebrate this happy place."

Music to Read By

BRAZIL: FORRÓ, MUSIC FOR MAIDS AND TAXI DRIVERS—Compilation (Rounder)
FORRÓ, ETC: BRAZIL CLASSICS 3—Compilation (Luaka Bop/Warners)

IF PELE COULD SING

Seven hundred kilometers from nowhere." That's how Luiz Gonzaga Junior described his father's birthplace. Backstage at a concert hall in a Rio suburb, the citified son of Brazil's greatest country singer made his ancestral home sound like the far side of the moon. "Seven hundred kilometers inland from Recife, seven hundred from Salvador, seven hundred from Fortaleza. The town is called Exu, that's an Indian name for a honeybee. A very dangerous bee. If you want to know something about music that comes out of dust and poverty, you must go there. Then you'll understand why the songs of Luiz Gonzaga will never die. My father is forever."

Who could blame Gonzaguinha, or "Little Gonzaga" as he is popularly known, for getting grandiloquent about "Gonzagão"? While there are very many characters in Brazil whose dearth of accomplishments is further diminished by the diminutive *inho*, few are big enough to earn the ending *ão*. It is hard to quantify Luiz Gonzaga's importance in Brazilian music. He could be compared to some groundbreaking hillbilly star like Hank Williams. He could just as easily be thought of as a counterpart of Woody Guthrie, with a bit of Louis Armstrong thrown in.

Though no great instrumentalist, he reigned until his death in 1988 as the undisputed King of the *Baião*—a variant of *forró* which became nearly his personal signature. As a great star of Brazil's radio era and the early days of mass recording, Gonzaga's evocations of daily life in the *sertão*, his smooth delivery and accordion, his outfit of leather cowhand cap and tasseled vest, gave Brazil's rural poor a sweetly dignified presence on the national bandstand.

Where Gonzaga Senior was jolly, rotund, and unthreatening, Junior looked scrawny, bushy-haired, wild-eyed. He had the bony cheeks and terrorist goatee of what Brazilians call "a face dying of hunger." Despite winning recognition in his own right as a modern balladeer and songwriter, Gonzaguinha still spoke like the illegitimate product of a youthful liaison—hungering for a father's acceptance. "I was raised in Rio, far away from him, but I've been doing my father's work since I was young. Maybe my father didn't have much chance to see me, but I know he was very proud of my being a musician. I know that he had confidence in me." With a loyalty that could only be born of abandonment, he asked, "My father was famous, so why do I need to be famous?" For Luiz Gonzaga's son, the trappings of stardom included being hip enough to disdain stardom. "I like to be able to walk in the street, to talk with the people, to drink with the people. I'm just another worker. A worker in beauty."

Perhaps that's why I'd caught up to him in a plain changing room at the back of a grimy auditorium next to a bus depot. "I don't play for money," Gonzaguinha assured me. "You don't have enough money to compensate me for the pleasure I get when I play. Unfortunately, here in Brazil we are developing your 'star system.' But that has nothing to do with music." As though to underline his point, this famed singer's dinged-up, brown Ford station wagon wouldn't start. His percussionist and I had to give him a push. Leaning my weight into each heave, I came face to face with the proud heir's bumper sticker. I LOVE GONZAGÃO.

Fortunately, I have not had to push my way to Big Daddy's hometown. To complete the pilgrimage, I hire a car for the last fifty-mile stretch from Juazeiro do Norte through the no-man's-land between the extreme western corners of the states of Ceará and Pernambuco. My driver hardly needs to be told where to go. The tiny town named for the honeybee is his most-requested excursion. "Aside from the bandit Lampião," the young cabby in a Lacoste polo shirt tells me in complete earnestness, "the two greatest men of the Northeast are Padre Cicero and Luiz Gonzaga."

On our way to the hometown of the latter late great, we pass Crato, birthplace of the former. This other side of the Cariri Valley is clearly the other side of the tracks. Advertised in red lettering, a "SWING MOTEL" marks the outer city limits. Crato is not exactly Sin City but there are a few bars and pool halls around the main square. The whole place appears more green and relaxed, out from under the good Padre's rectitude. Indeed, as a young priest, Cicero Romão Batista moved his congregation out of Crato because the people here were more skeptical of their native son's miracle working.

I make a quick stop to search for a local deejay and find him broadcasting from a glassed-in studio inside a convent. After forty years of spinning *forró* music, Eloi Teles de Moraes has been forced by local record merchants off commercial stations. "They would no longer buy advertising because I refused to play today's *forró* hits. They are played by city people, full of sexual innuendo and coarse imagery." This purist with a pencil mustache is unimpressed by the local paper's headlines about the Grammy Award just won by the U.S. *forró* release titled *Music for Maids and Taxi Drivers*—referring to the maids and taxi drivers of Brazil's big cities who began life out here as farmhands. "In the old days," moans the deejay while a record is playing, "the music respected country folk and celebrated the natural cycle of their lives. Planting, harvesting, marriage, birth, death—this is when the people must have their *forró*!" He punctuates his music hour with announcements of tractor sales, auctions, baptisms. Grandiloquently trilling his r's, screeching like a soccer announcer after a goal, Senhor Eloi offers his listeners more "Forrózinho, bem grande! Bom demais!"—"A bit of *forró*, well done, couldn't be better!" Off-air, he concedes, "True *forró* is going to disappear along with the differences between city and country. The new technology is stripping the people of their true clothes. It's not like the days of Luiz Gonzaga."

Luiz Gonzaga was an old-fashioned believer. He often mentioned Padre Cicero, sometimes in the form of shouted punctuations to accordion riffs. At his death, Gonzaga's body was flown back to Juazeiro and lay in state at the cathedral where Padre Cicero preached. A major controversy, still discussed in these parts, ensued when the skeptical Gonzaguinha tried to block this portion of his father's wishes from being carried out. Before a compromise was struck, an actual tussle between priest and singer broke out on the church steps. Even without such shenanigans, the funeral was one of the great events in the history of the region. A massive cortege, crowded with musicians and politicians, had followed this same road, up along a surprisingly forested ridge, back to Exu. The procession was bracketed by the red fire trucks of the local *bombeiros*.

Across the border with Pernambuco, the hills are drier, the vegetation more scraggly. Nothing I see in the *sertão* approaches scorched-earth desolation, just a blue-tinged high desert which would compete well in boulder-strewn barrenness with portions of New Mexico. Things do grow here, just not useful things. No fauna is tall enough to block my view of another huge valley into which we descend in one cascading switchback. The single clump of houses below is Exu, from *inxu*, indeed a Carifi word for "honeybee." Aside from music, the town's other claim to fame is murder. A long-held family feud over water and women has led to dozens of shootings and poisonings, including the sudden demise of distant relatives living thousands of miles from Exu. The highway through town hardly reveals a setting for mayhem: a single gas station and three or four roadhouses.

I make brief stops in the Gonzagāo Restaurante, the Bar Gonzaga, and the Asa Branca (White Wing). This was Gonzaga's signature tune, a stirring, up-tempo anthem which describes the plight of a peasant driven off his land by drought, "not a plant in my fields . . . my horse died of thirst," and his wait for the rains to fall again so he can "return to my *sertão.*" Nobody is eating at the yellow Formica tables, skating rinks for flies. Beer and barbecue constitute the menu. The waitresses are outnumbered by portraits of "the King" at various stages of his career, whole walls mounted with Gonazaga album covers. I wonder how much of this affection is genuine, how much mercenary. AI QUANTA TRISTEZA . . . FAZER BAIÃO SEM TU! goes the banner hand painted on the wall inside the Asa Branca. "Oh, how much sadness . . . to do the *baião* without you!"

A quarter mile down, just before the road leaves town, there is a symmetrical compound facing a swampy watering hole. The front gate is open but the building is closed. We will have to return after lunch, but I don't expect the unlocked shrine to look any less desolate. This could be some sort of military outpost except that the boxcar in the middle bears the oversized lettering MUSEU DO GONZAGÃO. Despite earning enough to lead the high life in the big city, Luiz Gonzaga always returned to his boyhood home, enlarged by several white barracks bedecked with baby-blue shutters. To the left, duly labeled in matching blue letters, is the former home of Januario, Gonzaga's musician father. To the right is the motel-style housing which Gonzaga built for the many musical cohorts who accompanied him here. What could all those luminaries have possibly done except pose for pictures or jam with the master?

Staggering through the heat back toward town, I come upon the communal washing post. Against concrete pillars built beside a covered trough of water, giggling housewives beat their clothing to submission. At the sight of me, they stoop further toward their task. These housewives are most un-Brazilian in their modesty, covered with kerchiefs, T-shirts, and ankle-length skirts. Their skin color is no darker than sunburn, yet something about this ritualistic scrubbing underlines the *sertão*'s connection with Africa. A second visual clue, more telling than a whole set of meteorological tables, is the way all the women carry jugs of water or square tins of cooking oil balanced on their heads.

A square grid of wide streets has been built to one side of the highway, lined with stucco fly traps lost in a permanent glare. I'm relieved to find humans in this warren of unstinting Casbah white. It's high noon on the prairie, but a group of stubbly-faced drunks have gathered in wicker seats on the sidewalk before a corner tavern. They've got a good start on the day's stupor. These men wallow in a luxuriant indolence suggesting they've been unemployed since prenatal days. With a wink, they insist that they are hard at work on "an important project." The project's goal is made obvious when they offer me a swig of home-brewed *juiabo*—there being more variant nicknames for sugarcane liquor in Brazil than there are for favorite musicians. A round holder for bottles is mounted on a tree trunk near the corner, complete with a sign asking patrons to "cooperate" by always keeping the metal coil filled. I expect cynicism from these men concerning Exu's single claim to fame and tourist lure. But the "project manager" quickly volunteers, "Gonzaga is our myth." Another *cachaça* hound, eyes a horrible shade of bloodshot, elaborates, "We have only two kings here. That's Luiz Gonzaga and Roberto Carlos." Carlos is the former folksinger turned commercial crooner, a Brazilian cross between Julio Iglesias and Perry Como. "And we'd have three kings," he adds, showing me that even out here, soccer is not forgotten, "if Pele could sing."

"The King Comes Home" is the name of the radio program that blares from an old loudspeaker mounted above the saloon doors. An hour of Gonzaga hits are spun every day at this hour by the town's fledgling Asa Branca FM. Before I know it, one of the younger imbibers is leading me around the corner. He is the proud founder of the station and one of only two disc jockeys. To get to the attic studio, I have to climb upstairs through a trapdoor. A single turntable and transmitter sends the music to a ten-mile radius. The station isn't licensed to accept advertising yet. But my brash host João has already taken the show biz handle of "Jota Grandão" ("Big J"). Before I know it, he sticks the microphone in my face and asks why I've come to the Gonzaga Museum, whether my book will feature Exu or the music of "the King." By the time I'm done, a group of neighborhood kids has gathered downstairs for my autograph. This is the first interview in English on Asa Branca FM.

I get VIP treatment back at the museum. My guide is the daughter of an orphaned Exu girl who was taken in by Gonzaga and served as his lifelong housekeeper. Understandably, this god-daughter has only hushed adoration for her mother's benefactor. She shows me photos of the pudgy, dimpled singer taken shortly after his *nascimento* as Luiz Gonzaga do Nascimento in 1912. Under glass is his first contract with RCA in 1941, for the princely sum of 150 *reis*. I wonder how much that is in *cruzados, cruzeiros,* or *cruzados novos*. Or how many times the singer received less than his just royalties, considering the display of Gonzaga's prodigious output has reached 241 LPs at last count. I get to watch videos of memorable television specials and a bit of the funeral controversy back in Juazeiro. My guide makes me rest on the single outdoor bench in the middle of a Parque Asa Branca that consists of concrete squares chiseled with the most memorable Gonzaga song titles. There are thousands of trophies, awards, keys to cities, and photos of various band members, including the midget drummer Gonzaga nicknamed "Minimum Salary."

More impressive is the most renowned instrument in Brazil: the first of Gonzagão's ivory *sanfonas* (accordions), engraved in mother-of-pearl, E de Povo (Of the People), a neat summation of Gonzaga himself. I remember Gonzaguinha telling me, "Everyone who knew my father would tell you that he was very humble.

He wasn't interested in anything that was far from the people." When I sign a guest register, I notice that the column under occupation is most commonly filled with the words *domestica* and *camioneiro*. Those maids and drivers really do love this music. And they are not ashamed to show their love or list their humble professions.

That's when I notice a hastily added alcove which documents the star's relationship to his son. One photo shows a teenage Gonzaga Junior bashfully strumming the guitar for his father while both stretch in hammocks. "Gonzaguinha supervises everything here," says the goddaughter. "He is most kind to all of us." Now I know why Gonzaga Junior, a child of Rio, had told me, "The Nordestino is very primitive and very direct. The life is so tough, you've got to be that way. But music is the thing which opens all the doors: to good and the devil, to *saudade, sol, praia, miséria, floresta.*" Longing, sun, beach, misery, forest.

"My father came from a dusty, crumbling place, but people are happy there and they show it. That's because—can you say this in English?—there is no relationship between poverty and poetry. That's why Brazil is pure music."

When word reaches me six months later that Gonzaga Junior has been killed in an auto accident—another victim of the Brazilians' fatalistic flirtation with speed—I can't help thinking about how Exu's faithful goddaughters and drinkers will get along without their "worker in beauty." I can't help wondering if he died in the same jalopy which I had helped push down the road. But none of that matters now. Brazil *is* pure music. And, like his father, Gonzaguinha is forever.

Music to Read By

PERFORMANCE—Gonzaguinha (Capitol)
ASA BRANCA—Luiz Gonzaga (Sigla)
ASA BRANCA—Compilation (Rykodisc)

MEET ME IN SÃO LUIS

Everywhere I go, the natives ask me about the progress of my *pesquisa*, Portuguese for research. But they don't understand. The duty of a researcher is to stay put. The duty of a traveler is to move.

There is no reason for stopping in Piauí, a province for penitents condemned to wander the scrub brush. When the military regime banished Caetano and Gil to England, Chico Buarque to Italy, one João do Vale, a legendary country singer known for spending every cent of record royalties on *cachaça*, flattered himself by thinking that he, too, was in danger. As the joke goes, he hitchhiked to Piauí. The poor man's exile! Teresina, where I change buses, is so hot that it's said the vultures fly with one wing and fan themselves with the other. Rest stops along this route provide nothing but exhaustion. A boy with a bad limp totes plates full of beans to the drivers while the passengers wait outside with the town mule. "Tchau!"—the transplanted Italian *ciao*— cry the kids who surround our coach holding out oranges as round as their imploring eyes.

Two more full days on the road take me further north from Juazeiro do Norte, through the poorest part of the backlands and back to the coast. Madcap drivers chew up the frontier one-laners at speeds nastier than I like to watch. The reading lamps are busted, the seats assigned, so there's no way to escape the slurpy smooches of the amorous couple in the row before me. In the midst of the void, my shortwave picks up the BBC's signature beacon of historical certitude, "This is London." But what this is this? From here to there, I discover nowhere. A nothingness nothing like any other. The distance between two points has become quite pointless. Obsolete, not a treat. And "nothing could be finer than to be in Petrolina in the morning. . . ." Now I'm singing a transportation *samba*. "Meet me in Saint Louie, Louie!"

Brazil's version—São Luis—is no gateway to the Mississippi, but capital of the mucky state of Maranhão, considered a transitional terrain between rainless desert and Amazon rain forest. How welcome, after so much time on the dusty trail, is the profusion of *babaçu* palms, their fanlike fronds betokening a biblical oasis. Most isolated of Brazil's colonial ports, São Luis claims as its single remaining distinction the *bumba-meu-boi*, a dance and beat associated with June's Feast of São João. Though I'm not expecting to see any samples of this agricultural pageant so soon after Carnival, I've come to find out just what's connoted by the verb *bumba*. The *boi*, in this case, means cow. That much I know. As the saying goes, "Anyone in Maranhão who doesn't dance the *boi* already has horns."

According to my road atlas, São Luis is inhabited by six hundred thousand souls, excluding cattle. But you don't have to travel long in the so-called developing world—is it one giant darkroom?—before you learn that mere population does not a city make. It's the merciless concentration of capital that keeps streetlights lit. And São Luis attracts little more than spare cargo. I'm lucky that a fellow bus rider offers me a lift from the station to town in the bed of his Ford pickup. Though it's only just past dark, we're practically the only vehicle on the road. The impressive provincial government offices are pointed out to me as the setting of frequent food riots. The only people circulating around the main *praça* are a perfunctory contingent of whores. Later, they're joined by a tattooed glandular case who comes to practice karate kicks against the wrapped trucks of the square's palms. The single hotel offers a room with freshly laid cockroach eggs positioned daintily on my pillow like good-night chocolates.

Patrolling the better-lit side streets in search of *movimento*, that much-abused Brazilian term for night action, I'm invited to share an "x-burger"—as the Brazilians write "cheese"—and a beer by the sort of drunken roué you find in every Third World backwater. As always, he is eager to practice his English, fancies himself more sophisticated than his brethren, rambles on about the meaning of life and the Latin love of the *siesta*. Predictably, he soon descends from wistful heights to beg for a favorable exchange of currency, a handout of a book or magazine. Worse still, he demands your company on some interminable tour of the town. It's remarkable how often the traveler's worst enemy is hospitality. Fortunately, the unshaven Socrates of São Luis has his attention diverted by a port prostitute. This brown-skinned *piranha*, as such girls are aptly called, can't be more than fifteen. She's wearing braces. But there's nothing undeveloped about a chest showcased in nothing more than a black bra. This crowd can't afford her—the *piranha* yearns to become the exclusive property of a Dutch sailor—but she doesn't mind sitting in the professor's lap anyway. He complains that Paulistas and other interlopers from the South are ruining São Luis. "Things used to be so *tranquilo*." I can't imagine how there could be any less *movimento*.

I've been warned that the colonial core of São Luis, like Salvador's Pelourinho, is in an advanced state of crumble. Why isn't there a contest for all of these formerly opulent trading posts, a race to oblivion where first prize is judged by the most gutted granaries, the highest trash heaps, the greatest number of doorless doors and windowless windows? By daylight, I find more proof of the unreliability of advance information in Brazil. Descending the elegant marble steps toward the old waterfront, I am in a whitewashed, sandblasted, refitted Casbah. With much civic elbow grease, somebody has restored the abundance of Portuguese *azulejos*—blue tile facades in geometric, Islamic patterns. Many of the buildings are so newly remodeled that the panes of fresh glass are protected by taped X's. In all directions of the central market, self-consciously folkloric restaurants and gift shops have moved into the high-ceilinged stalls. Inside, the cafés are commingled with a fresh catch of shrimps offered in straw baskets pinched up at the ends like Chinese dumplings. The teeming life of the port has been replaced with some middle-class version of quaintness. The problem is that there isn't enough of a middle class here to animate such an impressive endeavor. São Luis, left to its own devices, disintegrates before one's eyes. São Luis, retiled and refitted, resembles one of those dreamscapes by de Chirico. Scrubbed clean of memory, a perfect balancing of spatial proportions, staircases, sharp corners, and wrought-iron lamp posts leads the eye everywhere and the mind nowhere. The boutiquing of history.

How has all this urban renewal been accomplished at a time in Brazil when there's so little resolve or funding? Dazed and disoriented, I actually believe for a few foolhardy moments that a full-block eighteenth-century palace, just repainted a Mandarin red and surrounded by freshly graveled lots, is the place my guidebook map identifies as the Museum of the Negro. I should know enough about Brazilian priorities to realize that would be the case only if the local government were taken over by the modern-day equivalent of a slave revolt. When I peek inside the courtyard, two eager librarian types whisk me away for a VIP tour of what was once the largest convent in São Luis. They've got the keys to the marble-floored archives, conference center, research library. It's not until we enter a room stacked with framed portraits, collected memorabilia, and newspaper caricatures that I realize just for what—and whom—this space is being prepared. Every picture, including several self-portraits in oil, displays the suave countenance, graced with trademark handlebar mustache, of José Sarney, Brazil's most recent ex-president.

A conservative governor of Maranhão, Sarney was chosen—probably to reassure the military—as the 1985 running mate of the savvy, popular governor of Minas Gerais, Tancredo Neves. In one of those modern-day Sophoclean tragedies that Latin America stages with regularity, the elderly Neves became ill on the eve of his scheduled inauguration as the first freely chosen leader of Brazil in over two decades. A month later, without ever taking office, Neves died of an internal infection most likely caused by the presence of too many attending doctors. Some still suspect poison. Thrust into power, Sarney's four-year tenure was marked by inaction, inflation, and flagrant corruption—of which this grand edifice seems the last vestige. Quite mistakenly, I have wandered into Sarney's Presidential Library, constructed under the guise of Brazil's first Monument to the Presidents of the Republic. It's as though I have shown up at the Nixon Library in Yorba Linda and, without even showing credentials, been treated as an honored guest. But Nixon's library houses something of interest—transcripts of bugged phone calls, at least. Here, there is only the formal vacuousness of Latin America's public sector, a big show that does a poor job of hiding the fact that power resides entirely elsewhere. On a wall-size tablet listing all the country's leaders since the downfall of Emperor Dom Pedro II, they have made the unfortunate decision to list professions. Beside two-thirds of the *presidentes* is the word *militar*.

Suddenly, the resurrection of São Luis makes perfect sense. A single hand waved a magic wand. President Sarney left these parting gifts to his native city. Too bad they can't rotate the presidency annually. Thanks to favoritism, most of Brazil's cities would be refurbished. Later, I hear that Sarney's son owns most of the radio stations in Maranhão. He opened a nightclub in town just so he'd have a place to practice becoming a musician. But Sarney Senior's largesse does not extend even as far as the nearby side streets where the cavalcade of limousines will soon pass on their way to the dedication ceremony. Barefoot beggars and scrawny dogs seek shade in collapsed vestibules. Burned-out shells of seventeenth-century mansions are sprayed with graffiti that read VIVA MARX.

Nor has there been any matching grant for the Museum of the Negro, directly across from the convent in a private house so unimposing that I walk right past it two or three times. The exhibit here is just an advertisement for the local houses of *candomblé*, known in São Luis as *minas de criollas*. Glass cases hold a couple of ceremonial *conga* drums—jam sessions here are called *tambores de criollas*, "creole" attesting to the Caribbean's proximity—along with several frilly dresses used by the city's outstanding *mães de santos*. These matriarchal priestesses have obviously provided more service to the black community than any politicians.

The search for a local music expert named Zé Pereira takes me into the basement lunchroom of São Luis Bell, where two or three other employees of the phone company also qualify as players. Are Brazil's airline pilots, its heart surgeons and nuclear engineers, even its economists, just musicians between gigs? Zé is the popular diminutive of José, and looking for a Zé Pereira here is like looking for Joe Smith in Iowa. (One Zé Pereira was the founder of Rio's first Carnival club.) In Brazil, however, you nearly always find what you're looking for, even if you never find *who* you're looking for. Further recommendations lead me to Carlos Lima, an elderly gent who has spent his life as the leading amateur historian of the *bumba-meu-boi*. Lima is a henpecked soul whose sprawling house is full of humorless, disapproving children. They are outnumbered by pet turtles who crawl through the house, as unregulated and plodding as my host's curiosity. Lima boasts the largest private collection of *amos*, the symbolic cow torsos, made of black velvet lovingly inlaid with sequins and stones, under which the lead *bumba-meu-boi* dancer prances.

While ripened mangoes fall like cluster bombs off backyard branches, Professor Lima runs through the basic plot of the *boi*. As reenacted by dozens of traveling groups and street bands, Pai Francisco, an old black slave, marries Mae Caterina. While pregnant, she gets the strange craving to nourish her offspring by eating the tongue of their *padrinho*'s best cow. The irate plantation owner hires the local Indians to recover the livestock expropriated and slaughtered by his slave. Thanks to their magical powers and solidarity with the blacks, these indigenous detectives manage to find and bring the cow back to life. All classes and races celebrate the bovine resurrection.

According to Lima's research, the ritual was originated by *gauchos* on long cattle runs up from Minas, Goiás, and Bahia. Is there anything in Brazil that didn't begin in Bahia? These cow-pokes swapped campfire mythology the way the Northeast's *cordel*, or "shoestring" poets, spun their oral epics. The first mock bulls were probably made of straw and used as toys by children. The first public reference to *bumba-meu-boi* came as early as 1848, when a local priest wrote a letter to a newspaper editor complaining about—what else?—pagan revelry. With everyone searching for their cultural roots, such pagan revelry has come back into fashion. Folklore is dynamic, says Lima, noting that the citizens of São Luis have incorporated into the *boi* such items as Nazis with bows and arrows. Neil Armstrong landing on the moon. During the period of São João, more than a dozen *boi* groups tour the city, performing from house to house or at private parties and balls. Suddenly, says Lima, "We have a *boi* of the elite to go with the *boi encantada*." Oh sure, the enchanted cow, my favorite. When it comes to the vestiges of pagan cow worship, I'm having trouble distinguishing truth from bull.

In the meantime, I carry on a nightly search for music. Around the waterfront cafés, musicians sing for tips to amuse the sparse dinner crowd. I've begun to recognize the same tired classics of Caetano, Chico and Roberto Carlos, reinterpreted through too much amplified tremolo by a thousand fledgling troubadours. With the largest concentration of blacks outside Bahia and a location far closer to the Caribbean, São Luis has become known as "the Jamaica of Brazil." But the *reggae* clubs here are open only one night a week and offer taped music. São Luis is still enough a part of the Northeast to have its own Forrodrómo. I never get inside this dance hall disguised as a skating rink. Some taxi drivers say it is shut down permanently, due to the state of the local economy. It seems that I may have come to the one spot in Brazil which cannot support its own sounds.

There's little that passes for the local along hideous, neon-bathed satellite sectors between downtown and wild, unexploited beaches. Has anything beautiful been constructed anywhere in the world since 1950? Or is it that our concept of beauty hasn't caught up to contemporary building materials? Frustration forces me to try the tourist excursion to Alcântara, another early capital of Brazil gone to seed. The place is accessible only by a three-hour junket across the harbor on a daily ferry. And my sailing is three hours late, as it must be every morning at this time of year. Each low tide renders useless a dock set too far inside the bay. I wonder why no one has thought of moving the location of the dock. Eventually, more people than I've seen wandering about ghostly São Luis pack onto the ferry.

Signs at the ticket office warn against just such overcrowding. "Get on this boat and it may be your last ride!" The cartoon death ship pictured is a scummy, patched-together double-decker with people dropping off one heavily listing side. High waves wait to devour this man-made disaster-in-the-making. Death, in Halloween black cape and reaper's scythe, scans the scene with pleasure. The scary thing is that the boat in the posted drawing looks exactly like the ferry to Alcântara. The hazard could have been sketched from life. But nobody pays any heed. Such is the weird stage which Brazil has reached. In other parts of the Third World, they simply wouldn't bother to post notices about overcrowded vessels, polluted beaches, or collapsed highways. Here, they may not be able to repair or correct the danger, but the authorities are organized enough to print signs. "Do not board an overcrowded ferry" is the one I can barely read through the standing-room-only overload in the cargo hold. Brazil knows better. It just can't afford better.

My guidebook errs in the opposite direction, offering a single tellingly succinct sentence about how the crossing can sometimes get "a bit choppy." In twenty minutes, our deluged life raft is out in open sea, a deep green sea with very white whitecaps and loads of Utamaro waves cresting and crashing and blotting out all horizons or hope of arrival. Half the locals are heaving it over the back, while the other half chomp stolidly on apples and Popsicles. Most have to bear the risk and the seasickness in order to get home to some outlying village. But I have no excuse. At least, the *conquistadores* set sail to these treacherous lands in search of loot, land, and poontang. But what are we tourists looking for? A fleeting encounter with a barefoot innocent, a few snapshots of a stately world long since disfigured, shreds of clues as to what it must have once felt like to be rooted in a whole culture or epoch? Is it worth drowning just for another half-day "experience"? We modern-day wanderers are more foolhardy than olden times' explorers because we aren't setting out blind. We've got documentaries to warn us, headlines of crashes to temper us. We know the odds perfectly well, can calculate the ratio of danger to reward, and still we set out. We deserve every dose of malaria we get, every emergency landing, every roll of film sunflashed.

After ninety minutes, I disembark and stagger toward the nearest bottle of *agua mineral*. A free-lance navigator accosts all those with a green look around the gills. He wants to convince me to return on his spiffy catamaran. He is probably offering a much safer ride back, but he doesn't know anything about salesmanship or image. I might trust this small wall-eyed man with a two-day beard if he wore a striped shirt and a braided captain's cap! But why trade dangers known for unknown? In my two hours ashore, Alcântara lives up to its billing as a most ruinous ruin. Oxen graze in the shadow of the town chapel's single standing wall. There are plenty of vine-covered underpinnings to buildings long pillaged, a pillory post where criminals were once whipped. At a most unique historical museum, a number of rifles and handguns have been checked at the door. Viewed strictly in terms of sights worth seeing, there are very few places in the world worth more than a detour of two hours. Paris, perhaps. Rome, I'll grant you. And yet is there any human community, down to the meanest, rat-infested outpost, which is not worthy of being lived in with fascination for at least a hundred years?

I survive the return trip to Maranhão's town without music— worse than a town without pity. My prior inquiries succeed in flushing out Zé Pereira, who fetches me for a Saturday-night fling. An employee of the Banco do Brazil, he is no more the model bank teller than Franz Kafka was your basic insurance agent. Zé is wan enough for office work, but he's got a curly mass of hair going in all directions and a zealot's light in his eyes. By now I know that Brazilians reserve such zealotry for music. Our first stop is the rehearsal space of a dance troupe run by Zé. The group attempts to give modern instrumentation and interpretations to the *bumba-meu-boi*—or the *boizinha*, as he calls it. Is there any noun which Brazilians can't make smaller and more familiar? Pereira proudly displays costumes and masks which are stunning, sparkling, incantatory.

At his surprisingly plush two-story bungalow, set in the all-black district of Madre de Deus, he shows me videos of the troupe's last performance. It doesn't matter if Zé is as fair and freckled as anyone can look in Brazil. This self-taught musicologist is no honky straining to become one of "the brothers." He is completely natural exchanging greetings with black friends and neighbors. Unlike North America, race isn't a simple matter of "either/or." Here, Zé Pereira can be as black as he wants to be because nobody is checking. It is no different with the millions of *samba* and *candomblé* devotees who are "white," at least in appearance. So long as it's done with sincerity, being Brazilian is enough to gain entree into any Brazilian identity. Zé is another in a long line of Brazil's half-crazed conservators. In their collective care, it seems that the music will be safe for at least one more generation. "But the culture is losing strength," he recounts the usual sad story, "because there is so little money or organization. The best people in music either become professional or give up. They see others making money off the Carnival, off their energy, when they're only paid in beer and transportation. Because Maranhão is not just poor, but *super-pobre*. It's the end of the world. O fim do mundo."

It's already past midnight, but Zé Pereira takes up the challenge of digging up some indigenous São Luis sounds. Just as we're leaving his house, a number of Zé's neighbors are miraculously and spontaneously shaking the streets with a pre-June practice *bumba*. A core group of ten dancers pick up followers and we sprint alongside. At the center of the swirling action, a young man hoists the *boizinha* and makes this velvet cow twist and buck. The other dancers twirl in full circles but keep moving at a remarkable speed, urged on by silver *maracas*, bells, small *congas*, and, most distinctively, two narrow blocks of wood known as the *matracas*. This urgent sandpaper rubbing is the unique ingredient which animates the whole parade. Groups of women are spinning one another around, arms upraised joyously in a gesture familiar to me from news reports of an African National Congress rally, a celebration of independence in Zimbabwe. Like nothing else I've seen in Brazil, the *bumba-meu-boi* is purely African. And that means it is purely elemental, appealing to the most natural urges of a whole, impure planet. No wonder African culture is like a virus that devours every host body where it is implanted! "African," after all, is just a code word for a delight in motion, the senses, sun and stars, of everything that's inherent to us, including our high-stepping parade toward death.

I can't help hurtling along in stutter step, giving into the dream even though its rural references are hazy to me. This session, Zé Pereira declares with undisguised rapture, is *quentisimo!* The hottest. For hours afterward, my musical guide carries on a vain search of underlit, unpaved humps of ghettoes where all the real cultural ferment of São Luis takes place. We stop at several cavernous garages where *reggae* is blasting, but all of the dancers have gone home. Every bouncer and bartender greets Zé like he's a long-lost mate. Forget President Sarney's restoration and the pretty blue tiles. I have the feeling I'm on the outskirts of Lagos or Capetown. On our way out to some beachside roadhouse, a total electrical blackout hits. With the streetlights gone dead, candles start to flicker in all the upstairs bedrooms. Now the brightest item around is the ocean by moonlight. Wild breakers erode the city's dubious hold on the promontory. It's just another

Saturday night in São Luis, where civilization as we know it is a flickering sort of light. Zé Pereira keeps right on driving, trying to find music at the end of the world.

Music to Read By

OH!—Bicho Terra/Zé Pereira (Guizos/BMG)

THE RIVER OF BAD TASTE

I am but a jaguar's leap from the Amazon—ready to follow my premise to follow the music to the bitter end. I have come to the eastern edge of the rain forest not as Mister Kurtz pursuing a private fiefdom or Jacques Cousteau after some rare species of minnow or Claude Lévi-Strauss in search of the last Yanomami to be given a boom box. My expedition isn't for tracing the source of endangered waters but tracking the disputed origins of a deceased dance craze.

After an overnight ride to Belém, I feel like I've gone over every speed bump in Brazil. Whose bright idea were these paved humps which offer premature ruin to human and mechanical shocks? At least, there are signs to warn the driver of each approaching *lombada*. Could this be the derivation of that sinuous, up-and-down dance? The first germ of what jazzman Hermeto Paschoal jokingly called "the AIDS of music"? Or did the "safe sex" of the nineties really originate in the thirties, when it was banned by dictator Getúlio Vargas as "the forbidden dance"? A few Brazilian newspapers state the fact unequivocally, but I get no independent corroboration. According to singer Marcia Ferreira, "The name came from a deejay in Belém who didn't know what to call all the new rhythms filtering in from Colombia, Peru, and the Guyanas." Perhaps he's the very one who's now screeching through my taxi's back speakers, "Belém, here is your music!" A bouncy, nautical music it is, with twangy guitar and the thump of tom-toms at a breakneck pace. It's the sound of the Caribbean translated into Portuguese. Though French promoters have already appropriated this music for all it is worth, this doesn't stop the voice on the radio from crying, "Belém, don't let anyone take your *lambada!*"

To the banal, cling the most mysteries. At four in the morning, I'm more concerned with finding a hotel. Mistakenly, I ask to be taken someplace with a river view. I'd always pictured this urban chancre at the river's gaping mouth as one sleazy, waterfront juke joint. Why, when it comes to geography, do I have such a dirty mind? Instead of a flophouse on stilts, I get a fifteen-story commuter hotel. At noon, I wake to find I'm facing Belém's Praça República—main square of this rubber boomtown that has long made a strained attempt at European civility—dotted with the best art nouveau kiosks this side of Paris, open-air cafés with wrought-iron tables, statues of sprightly nymphs at play around lolling fountains. In the environs, there are more than a smattering of *sushi* bars. The Teatro de Paz, built in 1874 as a municipal opera house, sits in stodgy splendor, painted a baby-bottle pink. More impressive than its counterpart in Manaus, the edifice is an incongruous stab at high culture amid the primordial. There is no opera company in Belém. According to a single hand-scrawled announcement, Paulo Moura and Wagner Tiso are coming next month to fill the place with Brazilian jazz fusion.

This city of one million has been coasting on its laurels ever since a British botanist broke the rubber monopoly by sneaking 70,000 seeds of *hevea brasiliensis* past Belém customs and onto Malaya. Brazilian customs! That's an oxymoron where nobody is too vigilant, nothing very customary. In the late 1700s, Belém's population had dwindled to the point where the Portuguese authorities coaxed white men into marrying Indians with an offer of "one axe, two scissors, some clothes, two cows, and two bushels of seed." The 1835 Cabanagem Rebellion killed off 30,000 disgruntled settlers. Today, the only sign that this transplanted Bethlehem is built upon wilderness is a citified rectangle of genuine jungle preserved by a Swiss naturalist, Emilio Goeldi. His institute is Belém's best spot for viewing Day-Glo orange parrots, slinking *caipibaras*, the gargantuan *Victoria regia* lilies that could serve as floating billiard tables.

So far, I can't even find my way to the water. Only the subtle downgrade to the Avenida Presidente Vargas tells me that I must be strolling toward the great "river sea." On the sidewalk before state office towers of little distinction, there are more deformed beggars per square block than anywhere this side of Benares. Are people coming to the river to die, as they do India? Or could that fellow who is just a torso propping up a cardboard sign, this woman with flaps for arms, be victims of esoteric diseases raging out in the bush? Souvenir shops provide the other compelling evidence that I've entered a unique habitat stretching west for a distance equivalent to the continental U.S. You can bring Grandpa a bamboo blow gun, a toucan carved from Brazil wood, or a case of pure *guarana*, the main ingredient in Brazil's most popular and supposedly aphrodisiac soft drink. Between block-long warehouses, I catch my first glimpse of a tepid pewter pan mirroring a threatening sky. Smack on the Equator, Belém's forecast is always for rain. And the Amazon is no fount of tears but the source of all wealth, far too utilitarian to be scenic.

The quickest way to feel that you are in Amazonia is a visit to the fish market. Ver-o-Peso (See the Weight) has been Belém's town landmark ever since the first trader noticed something was fishy about both kinds of scales. Considering it houses the whole bounty of the Amazon, this venerable clearinghouse, marked with four pointed turrets, is shockingly small. Only the marine species come in extra large sizes: gleaming sides of *dourado* as well as various primordial serpents are hacked up with machetes into cross-section slices that make for a week's seafood. Each hunk of sea monster comes in the organic Saran Wrap of banana leaves. Outside, narrow rows of lunch counters and wooden stalls offer home-bottled *tucupí*, a cooking sauce made from fermented manioc, that works like novocaine and looks like milk glowing yellow with irradiation. The leafy tops of strange roots are shoved through grinders to make a bitter *pesto*. I've been served puppy dog in Korea. I've been feted with steamed tortoise and deep-fried baby sparrows in Beijing. I choked down bear paw *sushi* in Tohoku. And I sampled the gallbladder carved out of a live snake at my table in Canton. But if a world be judged by what it eats, this one is as far from mine as I've ever been.

In the medicinal section, old ladies with skin puckered like something that's been soaking too long use sign language to show me which plants purport to cure what organ. The native herbs are unrecognizable to me, but not so the Indian imprint on the faces of these streetwise druggists. Perfume essences squeezed from Amazonian flowers—their liquid so intense an amber that they make the eyes tremble—are sold for pennies in vials like surplus contact-lens containers. These hang in stringed braids, clinking like wind chimes. Plenty of local merchants have learned that there is a living to be made off T-shirts that call for the preservation of jungle fauna and animals. Yet they sit beside stalls offering rare jaguar pelts, rolls of cobra skins, whole alligator heads, *jacaré* teeth—a who's who of the endangered. Every sort of soap, cream, or container that can possibly be made from a turtle—the poor household *tartaruga*, once so plentiful that every patch of Amazon beach was clogged with them—is openly on sale. Why should the poor of Belém bear the brunt of conservation? So far, none of the local poachers have even learned to evince mock shame.

Past the Ver-o-Peso is an anchorage for hundreds of commercial tugs. Their prows most often christened *Maria* in flowing shadow script, they look underpowered for their daily challenge to the world's largest natural spigot. Sitting by the wharves, puffing on their pipes are fishermen whose *indio* brooding is outdone by the perpetually furrowed sky. Raising my Nikon in homage to the river god, unable to resist another still life of blue netting and pink plastic pails, I feel a tug at my left pocket. By the time I lower the viewfinder, a boy is walking off with some paper bills held in his clenched fist like the tail of a rodent wriggling in an eagle's claw. They are my bills, of course. The element of suprise, in this case, is that the theft has been accomplished so artlessly. I appeal to a couple of the shrunken, doll-like perfume vendors. They start to cackle. There's no point in blowing the whistle I've kept around my neck. I give a shrug that shows I've spent my alarm tooting along to too many *sambas*. "It happens," as my pal Lobão would say. This is the way of the world, and even down by the riverside, the surest way to enter the world is to run into something bad.

On my first foray into Belém's raunchy night life, I opt for a concierge's recommendation for authentic music—and find a typically Brazilian strip show where the "full frontal nudity" is heavy on the rear view of things. This gives me a chance to check out this club's real claim to fame. It's really there, just like my guidebook said it would be. Why are guidebooks always right about banalities, dead wrong when it comes to generalities? Three rooms of rest are provided, marked "Homens," "Mulheres," and "Gay." In Brazil, the musical labels also change every fifty miles or so in any direction. Can you imagine if every city across the Midwest claimed its own rhythmic tradition, a special sound to celebrate the unique ambience and rites of Des Moines or Omaha? Packaged these days as a mere *lambada*esque forerunner, Belém's traditional rhythm is known as *carimbó*. At a well-touristed establishment called Sabor da Terra, I learn that the name is derived from a drum made out of a hollowed tree trunk. I also get so much *carimbó* that I wish I'd never asked.

The native rhythms come as watered down as the minimum two cocktails served in scooped-out pineapples impaled with plastic umbrellas. A bunch of *conga* players sit to one side of the stage, wearing frozen grins and quaint native garb approximated by the generic straw hat, white tunic, clam diggers with frayed cuffs and bare feet. The lead vocalist offers a lengthy introduction to each number in the major romance languages, ending with the cry, "And now, gentlemans and ladies, our treasure of *carimbó!*" Whether we're supposed to be witnessing a wedding dance, funeral or Feast of São João, the soft, Caribbean-influenced flute and tom-toms sound identical.

From Bora-Bora to Bangkok, these tourist shows could be staged by the same road company. There is always a painted backdrop showing the locale as it looked in some idyllic, often specious past. In this case, the Ver-o-Peso fish market is depicted without any of its contraband air, amid sparkling churches and a few Indian huts. The dancers are invariably wholesome kids recruited from the local Dominican college, the boys tanned and strapping, the girls tanned and buxom. Their teeth are Ultra-Bright white, manes black, skin brown and ample. Soft ankles model seashell amulets, a twirl of grass skirts reveals a flash of hip and thigh, just enough *National Geographic* titillation to keep the guests awake during innumerable renditions of the hula, the limbo, the Philippine stick dance.

At least, these Belém kids actually look to be having fun—in contrast to the glum crowd of Germans and Japanese fiddling with their swizzle sticks. Paid escorts clap along to the music, trying to stir some life into their comatose mates. The most Aryan intruder invariably sits with his arm around the most dark, the tallest with the most petite, the brutish with the most frail. This attraction of opposites is nearly as predictable as the floor show. Flashbulbs click, documenting the improbability of such fleeting liaisons. At the end of every Third World minstrel show, the prettiest dancers always fan out into the crowd. They reach out their warm hands and thrust their wide hips toward tonight's volunteer victims. The lure of a free feel coaxes every blushing Hans or Joe or Juki up on stage. To the great hilarity of their pals, the pale ones attempt to go native. The finale at Sabor da Terra involves making each customer claim his dancing partner by plucking a red kerchief off the stage with his teeth. One German splits his pants, another cheats by dropping to his knees. Each gets his complimentary bottle of *cachaça*. When the fun is over, half the town's beggars are waiting outside.

Still, I am determined to meet Belém's self-crowned "King of *Carimbó*." The title must have some substance. When it seems that I've copied the wrong address, my driver shouts, "Why didn't you tell me you wanted the great Pinduca?" I wait forever in a foyer entrance off a living room whose overstuffed furniture appears to have been covered for years with plastic and white plaster dust. Is this family just moving out or moving in? Eventually, I hear rumblings from the back hall—a prestidigitator's top hat out of which more and more surprises emerge. Sometimes, all Latin America feels like one magic hat. In regal order, the King himself is the first to grant an audience. He would be perfect as a duke or an earl, like Trinidad's "Lord Kitchener" and other chieftains of Caribbean pop's oral oligarchy. Pinduca has a face crumpled into a smiling ball. He is wiry, very black and elegant in spiffy, stay-at-home whites, Bermuda shorts, and matching leather loafers worn without socks. Self-confident without being self-important, he has been the benevolent ruler of family and band for thirty years.

"And I plan to play thirty more," boasts the fifty-eight-year-old Pinduca with an effervescence which proves his point. "My father is still making music at ninety-seven." In the beginning, Aurino Gonçalves performed in a wide-brimmed straw hat encrusted with lucky charms, beads, and shells on the brim which spelled out the dumb nickname "Pinduca"—and the name stuck. His heirs, however, have been titled according to their musical rank. Ambling in one by one, holding guitars yet wearing neckties, the sons are so respectful of their old man that they hardly make a move in their father's presence without muttering "Com licença," that humbling form of "Excuse me." They introduce themselves as Roosevelt, Douglas and Stanley Quinto, "Stanley the Fifth." I don't ask the name of his kingdom.

Pinduca came from a settlement up the Amazon and *carimbó*

has always been his first love. "But I invent a new rhythm on each of my albums," he claims. "My newest beat is called *surubá*," he tells us, cracking up his kids with this slang term for "orgy." He doesn't appear to have a record player, but he brings out a stack of albums: *Pinduca, Volumes One through Twenty*. And there are more. "I can write a song in half an hour," he assures me. "I go out in the street and look at the news of the day. If you want, I'll put a song about you on my next album. 'Senhor John visits the King of Carimbó.'" His sons, too, claim the band can play anything. Says Stanley, "We even throw in a little Nuyawk, Nuyawk!" I presume this is another regional rhythm I've never come across, until the entire Pinduca clan bellows out, "Start spreading the news . . . I want to be a part of it, Nuyawk, Nuyawk!"

Pinduca almost pulled off an American tour, until an unscrupulous São Paulo manager demanded "ten times more money than anyone could afford, besides wanting to take ten of his relatives with him." There's no disappointment in Pinduca's tone. He does everything with a twinkling sprightliness that could only be bestowed by a musical life. "Do you know why the Brazilian army has always stayed out of war?" Pinduca asks gleefully. In a brilliant pantomime that puts even his respectful sons into hysterics, he shows a Brazilian soldier heading into battle, rifle in hand. A bomb goes off to the left, a grenade to the right. His head cocks. The bombs begin to explode more rapidly overhead, going so fast that he has to move his hips in time. He throws down his weapon, engrossed in his steps. The soldier can't help doing the *samba*. Why not? In this society, every calamity has its resonance, each clear and present danger can be turned melodious. For the Brazilian, even war has a beat.

Predictably, Pinduca is not satisfied with his status as King of *Carimbó*. He also claims a patent on Brazil's latest and most dubious international cultural contribution. "Nobody used the term *lambada* before me! You see! Look here!" He points out the dread word in the title of a couple of tunes recorded as far back as the mid-seventies. He insists that the word was derived from a local slang term for a double shot of *cachaça*. "When you want this much, a full two fingers in the glass, you say, 'Give me a *lambada*.' And the music I made is the kind people want to hear after they've had a few *lambadas*. Fast and hard, that's how everyone likes it over on Marajo Island." Pinduca even backs up his claim by singing out a recent lyric, "Lambada p'ra ca, Lambada p'ra la, Lambada nasceu no estado do Pará . . ."

Lambada over here, *lambada* over there. *Lambada* was born in the state of Pará. Could that birthplace be Barcarena? This is the river settlement where I've been told that I can track down Joaquim Vieira, a local bandleader whose songs were released in France to bolster the *lambada* craze. "Vieira! That old fake! He's sad, very sad." The vehemence of Pinduca's derision, the harshness of laughter from the King's court, merely increases my resolve to make the excursion. "Yes, you should see his lousy little shack, those filthy streets. Go see for yourself where the great Brazilian musician lives!"

Next morning, I head into the wilderness on a modern, double-decker commuter ferry. Of course, *lambada* pours from the speakers at the stern. I've disdained a deeper plunge into Brazil's green subconscious because the music of the Amazonian peoples has little more than a symbolic influence on contemporary Brazilian sounds: MPB, *samba*, or *tropicalia*. Of course, there was a familiarly Brazilian bent toward rhythm and licentiousness among the five or so million inhabitants at the time Brazil got its name. It's probably the longest-running bit of white man's conceit that Indian maidens actually greeted the Portuguese shouting seductively, "Let's play the game of 'We have two backs'!" The tribes did—and still do—dance standing up for almost every sort of religious rite. Pre-Columbian instruments abound, with drums and reed pipes now readily categorized by musicological sleuths into "idiophones" and "membranophones." The first Carnival-style shaker may have been made from a human skull and bones. Before they became adept at

Catholic madrigals and the mass liturgy, the native Tupis composed paeans in imitation of jungle birds. Brazil's natural abundance inspired them as it does their modern-day descendants.

One researcher neatly summarizes the Indian influence on
Brazilian music as "a nasal tone," a "tendency to end a verse in
a lower note," and words which do not merely dwell on lost love,
thus encouraging the Portuguese to develop a "more complete
lyrical contemplation of life." While many of Brazil's current
lyricists, from Milton Nascimento to Caetano Veloso, invoke an
Indian heritage or the Indian cause, they are no more naturally
connected to Brazil's once-teeming indigenous life than the many
Carnival tribes I've seen. There is more than a little confession in
the widely repeated self-deprecation: "The only thing Brazilians
inherited from the Indians was our laziness."

My own laziness at the prospect of an Amazonian expedition
leaves me both disappointed and relieved. I can't say that I've ever
felt comfortable in any place that qualifies as primordial. After
all, I'm a native of that man-made hothouse, New York. It took
me ten years of living in California before I ever noticed foliage,
outdoors or in. And I believe camping out should be resorted to
only as an adjunct to homelessness. I don't trust myself to remain
psychologically intact unless I'm within a ten-mile radius of some
satellite dish bringing down the latest headlines, a decent bookstore or takeout chow mein. Where Chinese dare not go to set up
shop, I dare not tread either. Give me garish advertising, bad
government, crowded trains. Nothing terrifies me more than the
absence of everything I hate.

At this point, the jungle is not exactly Joseph Conrad material.
Still, after a few minutes' chugging upriver from Belém, it *is*
jungle on both banks of the mile-wide river's shallow trough.
Islets appear, emerald swarms of vine and pod clinging to clods of
breakaway soil. The horizon's silhouette is anarchic and ragged,
one set of fringes shooting up here, a palm trunk craning its neck
there, a million fronds in search of forgiveness from their creator.
The whole mussed-up mess could use a crew cut. Give that boy

a good trim! Brazil's poor environmental record may be attributable as much to the Brazilian weakness for shortcuts as to economics. But anyone who thinks the people who have tamed and burned down so much of the rain forest are just greedy or desperate must surely be denying their own quite human impulses to impose order on nature's incomprehensibility. The urge to destroy is an aesthetic urge.

On this gray morning, the mass of growth doesn't look particularly impenetrable or threatening. But whenever we skirt the shore, the treetops shoot up at least five times higher than our impudent little ferry. This vessel holds little romance, outfitted with a snack bar and radio on the loudspeakers, plastic bucket chairs instead of hammocks. A gently proud Amazonian advises me to be on the lookout for pink river dolphins. From the boat, the most startling vista is back toward Belém. Behind the rolling contours and Portuguese spires of the old city loom rows of housing towers like those you might find in the Bronx. Each balcony, just big enough for barbecuing, comes with a water view, a perspective on a river which extends farther than any man can imagine. From the aft deck, it's easy to imagine how wondrous all those concrete turrets must look to somebody who's been floating downstream for weeks. Urbanity is truly in the eyes of the beholder. Belém, from out here, has got to be the greatest city in the world. And what's often lost amid all the talk of wild savages and unlimited frontiers is that Brazilians are among the great city builders.

Disembarking at a rickety wharf in a clearing on the far side of the river, we could be a couple of provinces away from the city. An antique school bus waits to take everyone up the only road in sight: a straight bifurcating line of dirt firebreak. None of the passengers are surprised when the wheels get temporarily mired in this always damp highway. Is it audacity or stupidity, stubbornness or something unnamably ridiculous that brings mankind here? Perhaps the pioneer is no visionary, but someone who simply has no place else to go.

With no warning, the unpaved road turns into the main street of Barcarena. The place has probably been here fifty years, but it still has the look of a campsite established the day before yesterday. Tropical log cabins, pastel paint worn away, sit on stilts above the swarms of dogs, pigs and insects. Heat waves distort my view of naked children frolicking in mud lanes that crisscross each other with no evident purpose. The skyline is all coconuts and TV antennae. Is this the last American promised land?

Joaquim Vieira's house is supposed to be "catercorner to the Mayor's." But City Hall should be called City Hovel. And the dilapidated thing across the street reminds me of an abandoned Borneo tribal longhouse. This shack is turquoise, peaked roof and all, and sits on wobbly pilings in the shade of a single encroaching *ceiba* tree. I pace on a narrow porch lined with a crude railing. There's no front door to knock on, just a cutout in the walls of straw matting. My hellos are ignored by a young boy who's lying in bed not three feet from me. His open room doesn't appear to be graced by electric light, yet he's mesmerized by a television. I can see inside just well enough to notice that the entire front room is wall-papered, or should I say paneled, with record albums. Are they Vieira's? I've found my journey's ultimate destination, where music is literally a building material.

The man who finally emerges is a hulking carpenter who goes to fetch his boss with a grunt. Joaquim Vieira, who could be a prematurely age forty or a very youthful sixty, greets me in a floppy silk shirt, shorts and thongs. He's a tan *mestico*—though a Brazilian might use one of a number of labels which more subtly fix his Indo-Euro mix: *caboclo*, *cafuzo*, *mameluco*, or better yet, no word at all. He affects a sliver-thin mustache and his overgrown silver hair cascades back from his forehead in tight, equidistant waves. With a few social advantages, this Vieira might have been Cesar Romero. "I'm going to be moving soon," he explains, though I know by now what "soon" might entail. "I used to live in São Paulo, you know. I've toured the entire nation. I am, after all, the inventor of the *lambada*."

Somehow, I knew this was coming—but not so quickly. "Yes, my lawyers are trying to receive a settlement for that." Much too soon, I realize that the musician's halting speech and gait, his painful lack of social graces have long been overcome by an unblandished megalomania. "I am the musical maestro of Pará," Vieira states nonchalantly. This moves me to ask for some proof of his talents, a request which I instantly regret. My host calls the big carpenter to set up a stereo, piece by piece, on the porch. Nobody has used the cheesy, combination turntable-amplifier for months. The needle skips each time anyone adjusts their weight on the planks of the porch. The albums are chosen from a coverless stack which the carpenter treats like sheets of sandpaper. They sound like they were recorded inside an oil drum. The guitar picking is distinctly Hawaiian. The harmonies are so crude that they make Pinduca's *carimbó* sound like Villa-Lobos.

I'm not really interested in whether or not this is *lambada*, but in why people who live in slow, sleepy places like their music so fast. Could it be that these backwater types who seem to do so little have internal lives which run at hyperactive high speed? "I play what the people want," says Vieira. "If I play too slow a beat in Pará, the people all shout, 'What's the matter, did somebody die?'"

This is not the sort of town anyone would want to die in. "These days, the people like to hear *brega*. Yes, I'm doing mostly *brega* now, developing the *brega* sound." I'm mystified at the boastful use of this term, since back in the big cities of Brazil, *brega* connotes any sort of music that's done in bad taste. Is Vieira campaigning for the title "King of Kitsch," the Brazilian Lawrence Welk? At this point, our lesson in musicology is interrupted by a more powerful sound system set up on the porch across the road. Some cocky teenager, like cocky teenagers the world over, is determined to blast last year's top hit by Madonna. Vieira makes a vain attempt to turn up his volume, but he looks resigned to defeat in this round of dueling Victrolas. Rock is everywhere, shaking the roots of the rain forest.

The lumbering assistant has located one special album and hands it over to his boss as though he's done it a thousand times before. "You see what it says here? 'Lambada das Quebradas.' Right on my album! I was the first." Vieira doesn't shed any light, however, on the derivation of the word or why the beat should be *quebrada*, which means broken. "Nineteen seventy-eight, that's the copyright date," he explains, "but the record took four years to record, so I started playing this song in 'seventy-four." Why point this out unless he's aware that this would put him ahead of Pinduca in the *lambada* sweepstakes? Even if he really has hired a team of lawyers, I can't imagine what someone like Vieira would do with the money from the world rights. It's like a feud over the design for the Edsel. Vieira's grin gets wistful when he tells me, "You know, I once owned four American cars at a time."

Then what is he doing in this place? It's sure not Brasília. It might be Imbecília. And perhaps this "maestro of Pará" really is the pure source of the musical waters which I've been seeking. Only somebody close to the basics could be this full of impenetrable self-admiration. When I start to make excuses about getting back to Belém, Joaquim Vieira does not react. Folks move deliberately slowly out here, savoring each encounter, however futile. Apparently, he presumed that I was going to spend the night with him, in the shade of his porch, serenaded by pork products.

Grudgingly, the inventor of *lambada* guides me to the bus depot. He strolls down the mud boulevard like he owns it. I expect him to start waving as though we two are a motorless motorcade. He insists on showing me the river landing dressed up with a marble bench and several wrought-iron gaslights. The bar beside this pretty Amazon tributary is entirely empty in the late afternoon. O Sol Brasileiro is the establishment's name, proclaimed in patriotic green-and-yellow lettering. Does Vieira actually believe it when he declares that this squalid clearing in the bush is "tranquil, joyous, and God-fearing"?

One discovery of travel, perhaps best not made, is that most people in the world live in places redeemed solely by the fact that they live there. Yet they would never dare tell that to the traveler, let alone themselves. They don't want to see that they're stuck and I don't especially want to see it either. So, like this town, I'm left awash in rationalizations. Shall I venture farther like an expeditious Mister Stanley, inquiring of each passer-by, "Doctor Lambada, I presume?" Or trace the imitators of every bird call extant in the forest? More often than not, it turns out the inspirational items which first lured you into the field are precious flowers that grow out of a rough and overtilled soil. The great treasures—in this case, João Gilberto, Milton, classic *samba*—which you figure will lead you to greater loot turn out to be more rare than you had even thought. To go into anything that draws you, to follow a passion all the way, leads you deeper into mediocrity.

"Don't forget us!" Joaquim Vieira cries out while I board my bus. At the last second, his broad smile turns pained. As I hurry off in search of prettier climes and more formidable talents, the local legend's farewell offers the terrible admission that I am bound to forget. I can't help wondering if those who, at a great distance, idealize life in this befouled wilderness would really care to stay out here any longer than I have. Do they ever consider the plight of the disheartened settler to be on a par with that of the horn-billed toucan? For the thousands of educated types who cruise the cafés of urban Brazil in T-shirts proclaiming Ecologia or Amazonia SOS, as well as their counterparts in New York or Berlin, the rain forest is merely a reassuring abstraction. Whether twinkling before debt-ridden generals as a place of unlimited plunder, or standing coyly pristine as an unspoiled Eden, the Amazon gives palpable form to Brazil's mass delusion about being "the country of the future." It gives the world one last pretense to pretend that all is not lost.

Given the electronic clear-cutting of indigenous instrumentation, Brazil's most threatened species may be Brazilian music. Call this my endangered *samba*. To keep all this gentility, this insouciance, this necessary madness from vanishing, we need to create a harmonic refuge, a melodic preserve. A place where there's a ban on elevator music, canned laughter, imported heavy metal, deracinated rock. To save the music, a vast zone of silence.

I can't say I've come any closer to charting the primordial origins of this music—this "kiss of three longings"—than various expeditions have come to locating the Amazon's initial trickle. I only know that my exploration of Brazil's melodic hinterlands has to end here—not only because there aren't many more rhythms lurking beyond but because I'll soon be reduced to interviewing every campfire strummer, army marching band, local Michael Jackson impersonator. And suppose I discovered the inventor of *ginga*, the secret lair of the *candomblé* gods? What claim could I make? The truth is what Tom Jobim told me at the beginning back in Rio. Just because we call a woman Maria, that doesn't mean we understand Maria. As with the Amazon, what matters most isn't uncovering how the flow got started but where the torrent carries us and what techniques we must use to keep ourselves afloat. Like everything we learn to love, the music is just another excuse for going the next mile.

Music to Read By

LAMBADA (CARIMBÓ)—Nazaré Pereira (Playa Sound)
OS CRIADORES DO LAMBADA—Compilation (Atoll Music)
PINDUCA, NO EMBALO DO CARMIBÓ E SIRIMBÓ—Pinduca (Copacabana)
ATÉ O AMAZONIA—Quinteto Violado (Polygram)

THE SAMBA OF THE
UNIMPRESSED

They leave home the first chance they get, born travelers who recognize that home is but the first stop on a cheap package deal. Instead of a birth certificate, their birthright is an open-return ticket. Every man a king, at least of his itinerary! Everybody free—to be elsewhere! Their inheritance is a passport whose pages can never be filled.

So they begin to comb the earth, comparing postcards to the blue sky. The Grand Canyon may have been grand to some prospector on a donkey, but not to them. The Greater Antilles could pass for the Lesser. Compared to their moods, the black hole of Calcutta doesn't seem all that black. China looks downright underpopulated and they are disappointed that the Hindu unwashed don't display more sores. Paris just isn't as rueful in color as in black-and-white. They wonder about the Seven Wonders.

Viewing themselves as truly sophisticated, they become addicts of the stupendous, occasionally falling prey to the cheapest sorts of fraud. They arrange to be thrown from camels, they prefer their meals fly-infested. They pay for the privilege of being exposed to incurable diseases. They beg to be turned into beggars, dare disaster to sneak up on them! What better means to break the shackles of superiority than stumbling toward the next blind alley, oohing and aahing all the way? If only their inner compasses could lose track of longitude and latitude!

For the moment, they have outgrown this pipsqueak planet—and outer space strikes them as a joke without a punchline. Worst of all, they actually believe that they are the first ones who have not been given the universe they deserve. Now countries are boroughs,

*principalities monorail stops, mountain ranges mere parks, with
reserved picnic sites atop each peak. Southeast Asia is a red-light
district, all Latin America one barrio, Germany an industrial park.
Every corner grocer provides couscous, corned beef, kim chee,
satáy, salsa, camembert. There are no undiscovered places left,
they conclude, only scenic spots in the mind. Which makes them
suspect that even in their minds, those places are best left unvis-
ited. Utterly undistinguished, without charm. Not worth a detour.*

*They conclude that there must have been some kind of mis-
take. They exist in a world where nothing is as it once was, such
a short time before. They concede that the trouble may rest with
eyes grown too big for their feet. Why, they ask themselves re-
peatedly, can't they be content with smaller surprises: a forgotten
note discovered in a pocket, the sensation of a bloody nose! But
no wrecker's ball can bring down their expectations. The tallest
skyscrapers hardly scrape their metaphorical armpits. The Hima-
layan peaks barely reach the heights of their unfulfilled desires. It
is their dissatisfaction which is epic. Their disappointment would
break all records if it could be measured like a jungle waterfall's
vertical drop.*

*In the epoch of the unimpressed, the only regions worth any-
thing are the ones where they have yet not been. And once they are
there, they are nowhere. The only thrill is in finding a place where
they do not belong. But they do not belong anywhere, not even at
home. The only point in becoming familiar with foreign places is
how they make familiar places feel foreign. The farther they go, the
less they want to know! The more cuisines tasted, the more currency wasted! The known world is shrunk-to-fit, and a T-shirt is all
they've got to show for it. So sing a shrinking world samba, a blues
for the last Guide Bleu! Down with helpful phrasebooks! Hotel
clerks' dirty looks! Once they've found "the real China," nothing's
left but Carolina! Fell for a maiden in Bali, now the surf is no
longer jolly! In the realm of desire, it's not so hot to be a frequent
flyer. And the landings are as bumpy as they are enlightening. Just
who was it that told them travel is broadening?*

▲▲▲

The World (*O Mundo*)

Ladies and gentlemen,
Haven't you heard?
It seems that there is a place—
I believe in Brazil—
One happy man exists.

—Vladimir Mayakovsky

△▽△▽△▽△▽△

SUGARY SONS

It's easy these days to go around the world discovering that the world isn't what it used to be. Arriving back in Rio, only to have my record-stuffed duffel tossed unceremoniously onto the curb by a cussing cabby, I can't help wishing that this window on Brazil still shared the rest of the country's sweetness. Rio, that scoundrel city! Has Rio always been a place that dares you to hate it, knowing that in the end you won't be able to resist its waters, electric hills, smoky turnabouts, night action? Even in its colonial days, the town was known for its extravagant cruelty, foul odors, and epidemics. Rio is bad on your morals and hard on your kidneys. Rio, corrupted and befouled, still cuts its deals, takes its cut, shows no quarter. Rio tries to get away with murder and usually does.

This is one of those places I would have liked to have seen in another era, almost any other era when the locals could still boast straight-faced of their *civilação cordial*. So I spend my last days looking for scraps of cordiality past. A return to the forties will suffice, for even in that recent period, Copacabana defined elegance and spunky chanteuses like Carmen Miranda presided over a *joie de vivre* not yet merchandised. I don't find it, however, at the Carmen Miranda Museum—more proof, should any be needed, that this is the most music-minded society on earth. Unfortunately, this circular crypt is much more somber than its subject—filled with a static exhibit of the singer's outlandish haberdashery creations, plus numerous awards and plaques. Nearly forty years after her premature death, the Portuguese-born singer remains an object of sincere, if ambivalent, reverence. The "Pequena Notavel," or "Little Notable" as she's called here, is a source of national pride for having made it as a Hollywood star. She is also a source of embarrassment for carving her career out of playing to a stereotypical vision of all that is "Latin." In that light, she is the target of many critical *sambas*. At the same time, an unofficial, all-male Carmen Miranda *samba* school dresses up by the hundreds as their campy heroine. But few realize that her younger sister, Aurora, can be found in a posh Leblon condo—all too eager to pull out her tidy scrapbooks and show-biz mementos.

"All Brazilians can sing, but Carmen was special," says Aurora, who resembles her sibling with a natural brightness that makes her look remarkably young for her age. "It wasn't easy for the family to have come from Portugal. We were daughters of a barber, you know. She was one of the first women to make it onto the radio. But she had what we call 'artistic veins.' From the beginning, she was always designing hats and dresses. Carmen never ran out of ideas." Aurora clearly had some of those veins herself, because she teamed with her sister in an act that toured South America as Las Hermanas Miranda. When Carmen brought Aurora to Hollywood for her honeymoon in 1947, Aurora sang at El Cairo and did some of the voices for Walt Disney's cartoon *Joe Carioca*. She was even the first singer to record such a time-honored Brazilian standard that I could hardly imagine there ever having been an original, Rio's anthem "Cidade Maravilhosa." Now Aurora rarely ventures out into the Marvelous City. She sits amid antique furniture in a dehumidified condo, hermetically sealed off from the beach orgy below.

The true Carioca spirit—more rueful than hedonist, more natural than savvy—survives only at the higher altitudes. Quite by accident, I find that spirit in an outdoor *botequim* at the top of a steep cul-de-sac above Lagoa, the fashionable district which rings Rio's inland lagoon. The bar's floor is just one square slab, its roof coconut leaves, its view of the ocean blocked by surrounding high rises. But I soon learn the tavern has become a symbol. It's name is the Sacopá, as is the street and the proprietor. He also turns out—surprise—to be a musician. While I've been told this is a good spot for *chôrinho*, Luis Sacopá leads a band of friends, seated around a table laden with beers, in an endless round of *samba*. Behind the canteen's kitchen, in several concrete-block cabins spread along this still lush slope of Atlantic forest, he and his family have been living since long before the Lagoa's developers.

"This street was named after my grandfather. He was a musician, too, as was my mother. She's ninety-three now but still composes *chôros*. She even wrote one about the Americans taking a rock off the moon!" With six of his eleven brothers, he is refusing to be driven off his patch of the planet. Now he proudly points toward a back wall covered with the clippings of newspaper stories about his valiant stand. "I've been shot at, I've had marijuana planted by the police. I've been sued by politicians. I was even offered a fancy apartment in Ipanema. But why should I leave? I couldn't take my chickens or pigs. I wouldn't be able to grow bananas or papayas. And I couldn't see the stars at night—or listen to the birds instead of traffic. You see there!" Luis points to a massive block of condos blotting out all sun from farther up the hill. "That was built by a senator who accused me of disturbing nature!" Nothing is left now that is indigenous to this place but Luis Sacopá and his music. "Rio was better fifty years ago. Now you have to bribe someone to play your songs on the radio. The chain is broken. The natural way is destroyed."

So what else is new? By now, I've heard enough about Brazil's decay. But on my last Sunday, I drag myself to meet one last musician. A devoted member of the Miranda *samba* school has arranged for me to meet Sinval Silva, the storied composer of some of Carmen's earliest romantic ballads. I find him at the bottom of the Tijuca slum called Morro da Formiga (the Ant Hill). As my breathless escort tells me, Sinval epitomizes the classic *sambista*—who "lives on the hill and hangs out in a bar." Though I'm nearly an hour late on a muggy afternoon threatening to storm, this dapper octogenarian has waited patiently in a corner cooled only by a single ceiling fan. Though he has to be helped from his chair, Sinval is meticulously outfitted in a fresh white shirt and black suit coat. A trimmed gray mustache graces his tan face and taut light-bulb skull. He doesn't complain, worrying instead about my safety "as a foreigner in a dangerous place."

As soon as the driver finishes "a big coffee" that "takes half a century," Silva leads me to a packed VW van which is the only means of transport up the steep slopes to Rio's "upper depths." By now, I am no longer shocked by the squalor in which this musical legend lives. The paint has long peeled off the mildewed gray walls of his concrete *rancho*. Behind an oblong sitting room, there's a tiny bedroom where a portrait of the Virgin Mary is lit by a single bulb, a kitchen the size of a suburban pantry. At least, this structure is permanent, which can't be said for the balanced heaps of tin and cardboard farther up the hill. It should look permanent: Sinval has been here for sixty-two years. No wonder the various cousins, friends and admirers who wander by refer to the Ant Hill as the Planalto do Sinval. Sinval's Plateau.

Besides, Sinval's front windows offer a view down through the chasm formed by green jungle flanks staggered into the distance, all the way to white housing towers and a patch of far-off Guanabara Bay. Somehow, his jolly helpmate, "Maria Teresa, my wife and best friend," a red-haired woman in a loose gingham dress, manages to produce from the kitchen an endless stream of tasty fish tidbits fried in garlic. Approving of more than the cooking, Sinval proclaims, "I will live with her until God wants."

To wash down the appetizers, I must, of course, sample what the old man claims to be Brazil's finest *pinga*, another slang term for *cachaça*, this one referring to the sound of the alcohol dripping down the still. "With a little honey," says Sinval, urging me to choke it down, "you can drink any poison!"

Of course, he considers the most deadly stuff to come from his native Minas Gerais. Sinval immigrated to Rio in his teens, a fledgling car mechanic who suddenly found that he had the stuff of song. Such talent was hardly surprising, considering that his father was a musician who formed a makeshift band from his thirteen children. But Sinval tells me, "When I wrote my first *serenato*, at age fifteen, it was like some spiritual presence spoke in my ear."

Mounted on walls as metallic as the hold of a ship are the rewards that this spirit earned: trophies, plaques, medals of honor and autographed photos of all the comely, tuxedoed legends of the twenties and thirties. The place of honor in Sinval's house is reserved for a publicity shot of Carmen Miranda, frozen with a headdress of pineapples and that merry South-American-way smile. "To Sinval," she has scrawled, "who gave me my best *sambas*." Never mind that Miranda and her "Banda de Lua" commercialized the *samba* in Brazil and abandoned it altogether once Miranda became Hollywood's generic dizzy *señorita*. In this house, at least, she is a living goddess.

"The poor woman! A fortune-teller told her she would die at twenty-six, only it was forty-six," says Sinval, stating the first of many facts freely mixed with fantasy. "When she went to work for MGM, she took me to America with her. I lived six months in a mansion in Beverly Hills. I never saw a city so big. It took a long time to go one block. And everyone cleaned the snow off their driveways!" I'm not sure how he could have seen snow in Beverly Hills. Other sources claim that he had been forced to leave her California mansion because of his race. "Later, I was sent around the country to entertain for *os heroes de Korea*. Everyone was so friendly, everyone invited me in. The color of my skin made no difference. Miss Claudette Colbert welcomed all the Negroes to Beverly Hills!" For Sinval, the U.S. is a golden land, unblemished by the problems of Brazil. "In America, you see, it's the blacks who don't want to talk to the whites. Here, it's the other way around. But what difference is there in color? With this visit, you are my blood brother. You can stay in my house whenever you like and you will find comfort unlike any in the world. I know it is a simple house but it is a pure house."

The composer's shack could be put in a child's storybook to illustrate the homily that no house can be poor when it is filled with friends—all of whom offer solicitous care of their urban village's medicine man. "Before, Rio used to be a family, with one for all, all for one," Sinval laments. "The forests touched the city. And even the animals had the right to live. But the city has become full of foreigners who must steal for a living." By foreigners, he probably means the poor from Brazil's Northeast. But he and the others of their generation have forcefully reminded me that Brazilian music isn't just about carnality, but gentility. "I was one of the founders of Imperio de Tijuca school," Silva goes on, without the slightest hint of braggadocio. "We called it Imperio after Princess Isabel, because she freed the slaves. Without her, I couldn't do anything. Today, they use the Carnival to express bad things. It's much too wild, with drinking and guns. I would call it the place of Lucifer."

For Sinval and the other founders, Carnival was a time of innocent, God-fearing fun. "Thank God, I am not one of those out on the street. It's a shame that so many old composers can't live better, because everyone stole the rights to their music.

Whereas I met a guy from the USA who wrote one Brazilian song and got enough royalties to support his family for a generation." Sinval hobbles over to a freestanding safe at the back of the room that looks like the kind Jesse James and his gang dragged out of banks in the Wild West. He has fetched a prized diamond ring presented to him by some Brazilian composers' association. Unfortunately, the old man's beaming face is so compelling that I forget to look down and drop the ring on the concrete floor. When I retrieve it and hand it back to his wife, it looks like the stone has been chipped. I feel awful, until I realize that real diamonds probably don't get damaged so easily. I feel better when Maria Teresa gives me a wink, then assures me, "None of these possessions are as valuable as a single person. Your presence here is a greater reward."

To make some small amends, I present them with a clipping of an article I'd already published on Brazilian music. Unfortunately, it's gotten dog-eared from sitting in my suitcase. "I'd rather have it like this than straight from the press," Sinval observes. "Now, this newspaper has the imprint of *calor humano.*" Human warmth: that's what Sinval's generation possesses in excess. "At least, with the Lord's help, I have been able to raise three daughters honestly, without cheating anyone or stealing anything. And those daughters have given me ten grandchildren. You know what we call them in Brazil? *Filhos açucarados.* The sugary sons, because they are so sweet."

It seems to me that every musician working in Brazil is but another sugary son of these first *sambistas*, heirs to a style of playing and of living so irreducibly graceful that it is referred to simply as *o tradição*—the tradition. Sinval surprises me by saying that, among his contemporary godchildren, he admires Milton Nascimento, hardly a traditionalist. Then I realize that Milton, too, is another black singer from Minas who doesn't mind letting his passions show.

With a beat-up guitar materializing out of the kitchen, Sinval offers me his lifetime of serenades. The old man's pluckings are jangly, off-key, his voice frail and quavering. He launches into tear-jerking ballads of love lost and found. But the sincerity in his voice fills all those who listen with an unshakable power. One particularly haunting tune is a tribute to the *tico-tico*, a bird in the forests of his native Minas. He has not heard it for over half a century. Yet he is still moved to celebrate this tiny bird. No wonder musicians are always invoking the power of love. It's not that they're all saints or hopeless romantics. It's just that their craft requires an open, defenseless regard for their subject. A song can't fake it. A song isn't kidding. What all of us go to music for is affirmation, not ambivalence.

"Adeus, Batucada!" As Sinval strains to reach the high notes of his eulogy composed for Miranda's funeral, a violent late-summer tempest moves over Rio. Within ten minutes, the slum's stunning vista of *centro*'s office towers, the Sambódromo, the sea and all the surrounding hills are swallowed by black clouds and rain. The cables which run off the electric pole in his front yard, illegal pirate lines to nearby shanties, sway to breaking. In one hour's deluge, Rio itself will come close to coming loose. Drainpipes overflow, streets turn to rivers, tunnels are closed. How fragile is this jerry-built wonder, clinging to jungle slopes by its fingernails! How vulnerable is this serenaded spot! For an hour or so, I'm stranded with Sinval and company up on his cramped perch. We, too, are about to be washed away.

But the composer keeps on *tocando*, plucking the strings while thunder booms over us, regular as a metronome. A single humble man groping for chords on his guitar, extolling sky and sea, venting the frustrations of heart and history—this remains Brazil's prime existential stance. By the time the storm quiets, I've heard Sinval's whole repertoire at least twice. The second time around, he's begun to blank out on the words. But it doesn't matter. For this one moment, at least, I see this Rio slum through the *sambista*'s eyes—and it truly is the most beautiful place on earth. The trick, of course, is appreciating a realm one never quite gets to.

"The secret of Brazilian music," Sinval tells me, "is writing love songs to a woman you'll never meet."

Music to Read By

REVIVENDO—Carmen Miranda (RCA)
SOUTH AMERICAN WAY—Carmen Miranda (MCA)

PLAY THE NOTE YOU KNOW

My last day in Brazil falls on the exact anniversary of the founding of Rio de Janeiro. "426 Years of the Cidade Maravilhosa!" proclaim the latest conversion tables posted in the taxis. If the cost of riding through Rio's marvelousness is rising another thirty *cruzeiros* per click, be thankful these cagey Cariocas still bother to consult the meter! After all, the marvelous city was built on miscalculation, a misreading right from the start. The river of January for which Rio was named turned out to be a bay. And the port disguised as a playground actually broke ground in March.

This March first, a birthday gift is being offered by the composer of that *bossa nova* classic, "Waters of March." Antonio Carlos Jobim will stage a free outdoor concert at Arporador Point, right where Ipanema's sweep meets Copacabana's curve meets the Atlantic's choppy aforementioned *aguas*. Since it's well known that this scion of bygone sophistication escapes his hometown's difficulties half the year in New York, Jobim is an oddly appropriate choice to serenade Rio. What's more apt is that my first guide to the mysteries of Brazilian music will now provide a tuneful summation, backup singers and all.

But first, I've got to make a last trek to the money changer. Farewell, shifty pal, familiar provider of the going rate! *Adeus!* Thanks to Collor Plan Two, the lines in the banks along Avenida Rio Branco stretch as long as they did under Collor Plan One. The newsstands are weighed down with front pages full of last night's murders, competing pictorials of X-rated Carnival action, scandal sheets bilingual and cunnilingual. At an art deco music store, where instruments are brought down from Brazil wood cabinets by a system of ropes and pulleys, I purchase a few gongs and shakers to break the silence back home. The fin-de-siècle cafés of the Rua Carioca—A Mais Carioca do Rio!—still serve doughy *pasteles* to a senile gentry. Desperate peddlers have unfolded sidewalk tables covered with a skimpy stock of black-market lipstick and bagged cashews. In the Largo Carioca, displaced Amazonian shamans hawk genuine snake oil, their feathered headgear the best promotion. One human sea lion bounces a soccer ball on his nose for hours on end. A sad-eyed Afro Houdini escapes before our every eyes from thick ropes wound tightly around his paunchy body. If only the escape from underdevelopment were so easy!

The anniversary is just another average day's frantic impersonation of commerce in Rio—until it is interrupted by the most modest of civic festivities. A small parade, unheralded and disorganized, winds its way through the side streets downtown. Victims of post-Lenten exhaustion, a portion of the *bateria* from the Portela *samba* school, kick off the procession with as much noise as they can kick up. A couple of vintage, open-air jalopies carry beauty queens in satin gowns and white gloves, but these schoolgirl volunteers must be the least beauteous they could have found in Rio. Some shameless few tag along, swept from the sidewalk by any excuse to *samba*, any opportunity for irreverence. At the very head of this state-sponsored debacle, a white-haired gent struts in a full Roman toga and black business shoes. He is Father Time in a land where time doesn't count. My last sample of the national flair for street theater, he bears a final bit of Brazilian protest, couched as always in bittersweet wit. The old man is tugging on a leash and dragging a stuffed cocker spaniel down the block. To his toga, he has pinned a placard which translates, "The more you study politicians, the more you admire dogs."

Such sentiments might be endorsed by the Cariocas who gather that night on Ipanema Beach—though the crowd isn't drawn from the *favelas*, the *samba* school rehearsals or the drug gangs. Are there any accurate statistics for what percentage of this country is sun tanned, sexy, and at ease? All three have got to be in the majority. Sometimes it appears that every Brazilian over fifty has been quarantined to the human anthill of the Serra Pelada gold mine, punished with perpetual labor for their loss of sexy *tesão*. At least forty thousand people have jammed into the end of the beach near the stage, most plopped cross-legged in the sand, some claiming standing room in the surf. Going by this concert-going bunch, you'd hardly guess that Brazil is in the Third World. Or that the city they have come to honor is in desperate decline, in search of tourists and a future, run by a police that murders children for pay. A municipality essentially bankrupt, stateless, lawless. I'm amazed that the Rio government has got it together to stage this free party.

"Let's insist that this city *be* marvelous!" Tom Jobim barks from his piano bench at the start of the show, sweeping back his gray mane and puffing on a Castroesque cigar. He doesn't dare claim that Rio is marvelous anymore. His music merely champions that miraculous subjectivity of passion which could turn any place into a song. Maybe that's why so many post-*bossa nova* boppers are still drawn by old man Jobim. But this is one of the least rowdy mobs I've had the pleasure to be trapped in. The only commotion comes when a hot electric wire is exposed beneath the audience, causing a merry game of hot foot, or hot *bunda*. The new generation around me still aspires to live in the style of these tuneful oldies: gently flowing, stylish yet casual, comfortable as broken-in espadrilles but also wise beyond their years.

"It's the end of all strain, it's the joy in your heart . . ." The composer has trotted out "Waters of March," as I knew he would on this date, putting as much emotion as he can into his spent voice. A chorus of four female friends and in-laws, barely professional themselves, back him up in soothingly husky tones. The women singers here always dare the deepest register, while male crooners lose no face if they waver in falsetto. Is this more of Brazil's basic bisexuality—or pansexuality—in notation form? All I know is that they make perfect tropical sirens, calling over the lapping of the waves. Jobim's backups beckon me to begin my life over again, to live it barefoot yet enlightened, in devotion to eternal elements. "It's a loss, it's a find, it's a hunch, it's a hope . . ."

I'm whispering in English while everyone else sings along in Portuguese. One last time, I witness a Brazilian audience asserting its democratic impulse to drown out all onstage autocrats. "I'm amazed at how you know all the words!" Jobim growls toward the masses in total sarcasm. He knows full well that his countrymen always know the lyrics to the worst drivel, let alone his oft-repeated classics. Here everyone can be a medium, each melody is part of the shared patrimony—especially melodies as replayed as these. The tune no longer belongs to one interpreter, even to the one who conceived it. As Carlinhos Brown said, the song already exists. It is merely sung through one individual. The beachcombers don't just hum "Chega de Saudade," the first hit of the *bossa nova* epoch, meaning, "Away with Longing!" They illustrate a collective state of nonlonging. Music like this can't be owned—or explained—any more than the waves.

Brazilians of all classes, colors and shapes share a common vocabulary of the nonlinear and the nonverbal. Whether artist or academic or healer or street sweeper, they all bandy about nouns like *alegria* and *folia* as though there really is some commonly accepted experience of these things. It's as though enlightenment and even mad spontaneous joy are simple ingredients in a bottle which merely have to be labeled properly and then poured out in standard doses whenever they're prescribed. Take two pinches of happiness and call me in the morning. Which is why there is so much sincerity when everyone joins in a rendition for Rio of

"Happy Birthday to You!" So banal a tune seems a squandering of these voices. When it's over, Jobim growls, "Bury my heart in the beach at Ipanema!" Who could blame him for such a wish?

I leave Brazil having acquired a good deal of *saudade*, that most commonly summoned of Brazilian emotions. This nostalgia for a life one has never quite led, this longing for all the sun and sustenance this land can bestow! Suddenly, I find myself getting misty-eyed for potent pungent *batidas* I could barely choke down, for beachside *barracas* where I snacked only at the risk of ptomaine. It doesn't matter that I've never quite found my spot at the party—or that I won't attain the proper *ginga* in my hips even if I work my backbone from now until I drop. While people quickly fade for me, places never do. I can get sentimental over almost any amalgam of geography and paving, most of all for those where I've never been—the imaginary destinations, the world that hasn't disillusioned me yet.

Is reality really the ultimate disappointment or an ongoing miracle? On this perpetual pendulum, I swing back and forth. If I ever came down on one side or the other, I would give up traveling. A new-age traveler, if there is such a thing, is just someone who uses parts of the world to piece himself or herself together. We see other cultures mainly as unrealized potentialities within ourselves. Is the part of me that has gone toward Brazil really hunting for some safe connection to the savage? Am I looking for the inner life made manifest or outwardness for its own resplendent sake? How many miles endured, how much heat rash and diarrhea, how many mango juices downed—*sem gelo*, without ice, please!—how many greasy grilled cheese *queijo quentes* gobbled, how many devouring alleys of poverty skirted, causing how much guilt and apprehension, how many waves without drowning, how many cold showers, cockroaches, cheating money changers, how many maps pored over to what end?

Will it really add a swing to my step knowing that a certain Carnival beat summons forth a certain African deity? Will all those hours on the bus, dying of thirst in the hellhole of Teresina, add anything to my enjoyment of a *bolero* by Chico Buarque? What do the cooings of Milton Nascimento have to do with the price of silver in Ouro Prêto? And what can the snores of the toothless hags heading back from Belo to Rio the day after Christmas have in common with the imaginary murmurs of that obscure object of aural desire, Our Lady of Ipanema? I can't say that the places Brazilian music has led me have been half as soothing or curative as the music itself. But they have been more rigorous and surprising. Seeing the conditions that the music transcends, the pain that it soothes, only makes me more impressed with the end product. After all, if the realms evoked by Brazilian singers really existed, then nobody would need the music.

"If you listen to my music, you will be saved!" The truth is in what Tom Jobim told me at the beginning—and in the eloquent attempts made by so many others for my sake over the subsequent months. "It is nature singing through us, our forests, our rivers," Hermeto Paschoal had said. It is the ultimate expression of Carnival's "freedom in the moment." Whatever "it" is, it is the beginning and middle and end of something that has no beginning or end. It is "the heartbeat of joy," as Joãozinho Trinta might put it. And if Brazil really is the beating heart of the world, that's because, in the words of the late Gonzaguinha, "Brazil is pure music."

Recalling all the remarkable musicians I've met, these custodians of joy who form Brazil's true elite, what's most remarkable is that not one ever expressed a hint of jealousy. They had nothing but adulation, even awe for their colleagues—"Say hello to Milton for me! Say *tchau* to Caetano!" instructed these spirits beyond worldly competition. And every last strummer revealed an unending reserve of hope when it came to their country. "Look, Brazil is something that comes right from your balls!" Moraes Moreira, Bahia's clown prince, had best embodied the brash Brazilian optimism, that impudent faith in the national myth of limitless horizons. "I think Brazil can be more than *um pais grande*, but *um grande pais*." Not just big, in other words, but great. "If our reality is sad, if people are hungry, then it's a tribute that we can keep singing and dancing. Stop the music and you'll see at once the tediousness of life. I'd rather have people singing and unconscious than highly conscious and miserable. The problems of humanity, war, and tyranny grow out of our neuroses. We wouldn't have a Hitler, a George Bush, a Saddam Hussein, if we weren't all little Hitlers, little tyrants. And when people sing and dance, that's when they're the least neurotic."

Music as mass therapeutic social engineering. That, in a nutshell, is the Brazilian answer for the evils of the world. And it appears to be working better than most other solutions. Just pick up an instrument and play the note you know. That's the quintessential Brazilian message I hear in Jobim's "One-Note Samba." Even if you're more than a trifle off-key, sing the world's praises. Learn to "love everything with our own true love," to paraphrase Caetano Veloso. Brazilian musicians are not afraid of beauty for beauty's sake, wit for wit's sake, topicality for topicality's sake, regionalism for regionalism's sake, dancing for dancing's sake. They are, in an exemplary way the whole world can hear, not afraid of life.

Just as some nations are meant to make cars, forge steel, build ships, grow rice, this one dedicates itself to encouraging and preserving the pleasure principle. There are always plenty of places left to manufacture dire conflicts and intractable disputes, lands where the slogan always reads *La Lutta Continua!* The fight goes on! There's no shortage of struggle on this planet. Only in Brazil, in Bahia to be exact, would they put out T-shirts bearing the admonition *A Festa Continua!* The party must go on! Somebody's got to keep the bacchanalia rolling so the rest of the world doesn't lose the hang of it. May Brazil long continue its haphazard research into the limits of effervescence, ass-shaking, childlike reverie! May its throaty singers long whisper sweet nothings in the ear of humanity! May someone somewhere remain "unafraid to be happy"!

For one moment at least, six bars and a chorus, the Brazil

before me is the Brazil made mythic by a Jobim encore. "Quiet nights of quiet stars, Quiet chords from my guitar . . ." Night has swept all incipient seediness from the bountiful sands, bestowed glamour and hidden the double-chins of the sagging row of once-gleaming hotels. Now the siphoned electric lights that cover the huge hillside mound of the Rocinha slum twinkle like the winking eyes of sexy, hovering angels. Wading into the floodlit surf, the usual inexhaustible supply of curvy mermaids show off their black curls and their black strophes of loincloth, mere slivers of shade between mounds of flesh. A clear sky shows the Southern Cross, the only cross Brazil deserves to bear. A splayed grid of stars nearly camouflages the turboprop flights from São Paulo coming in low for a landing over Guanabara Bay. Their red wing lights blink in double-takes of amazement. A vision of earthly paradise coalesces. The country of music is palpable all around me.

So I can go there whenever I want, I'm bringing back enough CDs and albums to get me nabbed as an unlicensed importer. If U.S. Customs questions me, I can show them that most of my contraband is personally inscribed to me with *um abraço*. Listen, I'll tell the man who stamps my passport, I've got a stash of *samba canção* here. There's high-grade *carimbó* and uncut *baião*, pure *forró* and first-class *frecote*. Those are my drugs of choice. Once I'm stuck on the freeway, officer, I need these sounds to transport me. Is there a law against that? I wish I could spin a few tunes for you now. You never heard such music.

Music to Read By

BRASIL—João Gilberto et al. (Warner Bros.)
RIO REVISITED—Antonio Carlos Jobim, Gal Costa (Verve)
THE ART OF ELIS REGINA—Elis Regina (Polygram)
AQUARELA DO BRASIL—Gal Costa (Philips)
DJAVAN—Djavan (Columbia)
PARA VIVER UM GRANDE AMOR—Chico Buarque and Others (CBS)
THE BRASIL PROJECT—Toots Thielemans and Others (BMG)
BRASILEIRO—Sergio Mendes with Carlinhos Brown (Electra)
BRASILIDADE—Sebastião Tapajós (Tropical Music)

INDEX

▲▲▲

ABOUT THE AUTHOR

John Krich's *Music in Every Room: Around the World in a Bad Mood* was nominated for the Quality Paperback Club's New Voices Award. His novel on the private life of Fidel Castro, *A Totally Free Man*, won a Special Citation, PEN/Ernest Hemingway Award. He is also the author of *El Beisbol: Travels Through the Pan-American Pastime; Bump City: Winners and Losers in Oakland; Chicago Is;* and *One Big Bed*. His travel and sports writing, reportage and fiction, have appeared in *Mother Jones, Vogue, Sports Illustrated*, the *Village Voice, Image, Commentary, California, The New York Times* and many others. He leaves his luggage in San Francisco.